DREAMING THE DARK

DREAMING THE DARK

Magic, Sex & Politics

New Edition

STARHAWK

Beacon Press   Boston

Beacon Press
25 Beacon Street
Boston, Massachusetts 02108

Beacon Press books
are published under the auspices of
the Unitarian Universalist Association of Congregations.

95 94 93 92 91 90 89   8 7 6 5 4 3 2

Library of Congress Cataloging-in-Publication Data
Starhawk.
  Dreaming the dark.
    1. Witchcraft. 2. Magic. 3. Control (Psychology)
  4. Sex—Religious aspects. 5. Religion and politics.
  6. Goddesses. I. Title.
  BF1566.S766 1988   299   88-47886
  ISBN 0-8070-1025-1

CONTENTS

Preface to the
New Edition

Six years have passed since *Dreaming the Dark* was first published, years that have seen both hope and despair intensified. When I wrote this book, I was newly taking into action ideas of power and consciousness. Now I look back from many years of experience in both resistance and renewal, in actions to stop policies of destruction and in experiments at building community and creating a culture of life.

Surprisingly, while I find much that I might add to the ideas here, I find little that I would change. My own commitment to the intertwining of magic, politics, and the erotic has only deepened. The community has grown stronger, tested both by action and by the trials of day-to-day living. The role of ritual, magic, and spirituality in my own life is, if possible, more constant and more integrated.

In rereading this book, the major theoretical shift I find I have taken has been away from object relations theory, all forms of Neo-Freudianism, and in fact, the whole bent of psychological theory that views our early childhood experiences as the determining factors in our future development. Of course what happens to us in childhood is important, but it must be seen in the context of a whole lifetime of experiences which either reinforce or help heal our traumas. Psychologists have constructed a myth — that somewhere there exists some state of health which is the norm, meaning that most people presumably are in that state, and those who are anxious, depressed, neurotic, distressed, or generally unhappy are deviant. Yet the same psychologists will tell us that almost everyone needs therapy, and that is true, because the "norm" is so rare as to be almost nonexistent, for we are all hurt by the culture we live in, with its hierarchies of domination and its undermining of our sense of inherent value.

To focus exclusively on our individual early childhood experiences is like observing a group of people who live on a toxic waste dump, who are diseased, and saying, "Let's treat their condition by examining how they were fed in infancy." We might very likely find that those who were malnourished as babies were more susceptible to illness than those who were well fed. But we would still be ignoring the fact that none of them were truly healthy, because they were living in a toxic environment.

We are all living in a toxic psychic and emotional environment (as well as a physical environment which becomes more polluted daily), because we live embedded in structures of power-over, which constantly attack our sense of self-worth and attempt to isolate and control us. (I have developed my own psychological theory more fully in *Truth or Dare: Encounters with Power, Authority and Mystery*.) In this book, I now find most satisfying the psychology that is based on the practices of magic, especially the analysis of Joy's trance in chapter 4. The least satisfying are the sections based on the theories I was taught in graduate school. But I invite the reader to keep an open mind, and judge for yourself.

There are some other changes I would make now. I would no longer make the blanket statement that Jews are people of color. Although I still understand the rationale for that position, I nevertheless would not, for example, attempt to join the people of color caucus at a conference by virtue of my Jewish heritage. Now I would say that Jews are in a unique position, sharing many experiences of discrimination, from stereotyping to genocide, and like other minorities (and some majorities, such as women) having to adapt to an alien dominant culture. But many Jews also share some of the privileges of the dominant culture, such as white-skin privilege. Over the years, especially as I have worked with women to build alliances across the barriers of race, class, and culture, my Jewish identity, as well as my Pagan one, has grown stronger. Perhaps, as we get older, we simply become more clearly who we are, even when we are several seemingly contradictory things. I am comfortable being both a Jew and a Pagan, celebrating Chanukah and the Winter Solstice.

The deterioration of the Middle East situation poses a very painful dilemma for those American Jews who are ranged on the side of liberation. We see Israel doing things we cannot condone, acting with brutality and callousness, and at the same time see the situation become ground for a new variety of anti-Semitism, where every Jew is somehow identified with the policies of the Israeli government, the large peace movement within Israel ignored, and the heritage of Jewish opposition to oppression discounted.

There are other places in the book where, were I writing today, I might be less absolute. The trancework I now do is much more fluid than that described here, often involves movement, dance, drumming, and storytelling, and I've dropped most of the laborious cautions as I came to believe their effect was the opposite of what was intended — that reassuring people that they would be safe actually implanted in their minds the idea that they were about to do something dangerous.

While I still favor consensus, I do believe that groups can decide to use other decision-making processes without losing their moral purity, and that consensus is not always the appropriate process. Consensus works when a group has the information it needs to make a decision. When the information is unknown — for example, when we don't know how the police might respond to a tactic — we often augment consensus with an oracle, usually the Tarot cards. When the issue is too trivial to warrant long discussion, I prefer to flip a coin.

When the issue is a matter of taste, such as what color to paint the living room, we usually decide by attrition — everyone who doesn't really care eventually gets sick of talking about it and leaves the decision to those who feel strongly.

But perhaps the greatest change that has taken place since this book was written is the emergence of the AIDS epidemic. Because of AIDS, we must exercise new caution in sexual expression. In a culture that fears and hates the erotic, the emergence of AIDS becomes a pretext for increased prejudice and persecution of those whose erotic desires and practices vary from what is prescribed. AIDS has revealed the frightening extent to which the dominant culture is willing to write off the lives and interests of those groups of people it considers of low value — gays, people of color, intravenous drug users. The disease has revealed a deeper sickness at the heart of our society, and uncovered our failure to love.

In a culture that valued the erotic, a disease that made us fearful and limited our expression of passion would be a top research priority (as would safe and effective birth control). But in a culture based on power-over, on systems of domination and punishment, a culture that fears the erotic because it moves always beyond the boundaries of control, AIDS can be seen as "proof" that the erotic is really bad, dirty, nasty, and dangerous as we have been taught. AIDS, of course, is passed on in many ways other than sexual contact. Yet all those diagnosed with the disease must live with the stigma that clings to it, and contend with the assumption, whether voiced or not, that they somehow deserve their diagnosis. While Fundamentalists openly make accusations of immorality, others place blame more subtly, disguising it as a critique of "lifestyle" or "addictive behavior," or a hundred other terms that ultimately are really saying, "You are bad — you deserve to die and I deserve to live."

But if the concept of immanence means anything at all, it is that we all deserve life in its fullest possible blossoming, that each of us is sacred. The Goddess, the universe, does not work on a punishment model. We only expect it to because we live so embedded in systems of punishment and reward that we cannot ask why without really meaning, "What have I done wrong? What am I being punished for?"

AIDS can also be a teacher. Those who are willing to face the mysteries embodied in the great processes of life and death, those who live with AIDS and those who open and touch and offer support to them, can find a new depth of connection and real intimacy. When we face the possibility of death, the simple moments of connection — looking into the eyes of a friend who understands what we say, sitting in a sunny window drinking tea, nestling into the strong arm of a lover, laughing together at a joke or tapping a foot to the rhythm of music, all the ordinary acts of life — become luminous and treasured, and we understand them to be the sacred gifts that they are. That is the true lesson of the mysteries and the real meaning of the immanence of the Goddess — that life itself has a value that is immeasurable.

AIDS also challenges us to confront the institutions and decision-makers that implement punishment, to demand that we shift our priorities to fund healing over killing, to speak openly about sex in all its varied forms, to educate and hope and love.

I began writing this book at the beginning of the Reagan years, when the political climate was swinging to the right, red-baiting was coming back into fashion, and the rhetoric of Armageddon was issuing from Washington. Many of us experienced not only political despair, but terror, convinced that nuclear war was imminent. Progressive movements seemed demoralized or nonexistent, and the activists of the sixties were fast becoming the yuppies of the eighties.

Those of us who took part in the actions described here certainly did not feel that we represented a mainstream trend in society. If anything, we saw ourselves as performing a holding action, maintaining certain values that had gone out of fashion, stubbornly refusing to give up our belief in the possibility of change and liberation.

Panic around the looming possibility of thermonuclear war did prove a strong motivating force, and in '82 and '83, shortly after *Dreaming the Dark* was published, thousands of people

turned out for actions and demonstrations, and a million people marched in Central Park.

Yet panic is not an effective long-term organizing strategy,
for it leads to burnout and discouragement. Time is needed
to change consciousness on a mass scale, to perform the work
of magic at the heart of political change. The fruits of organizing are never realized immediately. When we organize out
of panic, we are still caught in the story of Apocalypse, still
expecting time to come to an end, and within the confines of
that story we cannot possibly envision the actions needed to
heal and sustain the earth for the far future.

Dreaming the Dark is an attempt to tell a different story, to
reshape culture on the model of the circle, the ever-renewing
cycle. While only a small percentage of the people mobilized
in the early eighties remained active and directly involved,
those who did have deepened and developed the processes
and models presented here. I like to believe that this book
has been influential in helping people redefine power and
reshape its structures toward those of a community that can
sustain long-term struggle and creative vision.

Individual battles have been lost and won. The Diablo Canyon nuclear reactor was prevented from operating for many
years, but finally went on line in 1984. The actions, however,
had broader results — the public outcry and protest derailed
plans to build fifty more nuclear reactors in California, and
undermined the nuclear power industry.

The Euromissiles were deployed. But this year, when
Reagan found his popularity waning as the shady dealings
and illegal acts of the Iran-Contra affair came to light, he
negotiated with Gorbachev to remove them. Many of those
who participated in the actions of '82 and '83 will not recognize
this as our victory, yet we should claim it as such, as an
example of how sustained public outcry and resistance can
bring about a reversal in national policy, place limits on our
destructiveness, and change the agenda even of political leaders whose policies are the opposite of ours.

It has become fashionable in some New Age and even
feminist circles to disparage the importance of protest and

resistance, to claim that "what we resist persists." This may be true when we are speaking of our own emotions and desires, but it is nonsense when applied to the political realm, where what we don't resist persists unchecked.

Mounting resistance can be draining, but it can also be inspiring and empowering, provided that our acts of resistance tell a different story, a story of cycles of renewal and change, not apocalyptic destruction, a story in which each of us has value and all of our truths are important. We tell this story by the way we treat each other and those we oppose, with acknowledgment of the sacred life force in each individual.

Witches have a saying: "Where there's fear, there is power." When the structures we create to carry out actions of resistance tell stories of regeneration, fear, despair, and rage can be transformed into the sustained creative energy we need to renew the world. And this has, in fact, happened. In my own Bay Area community, the actions at Diablo and Livermore taught us how to use the tools of group process and decision-making we needed to begin living and working collectively.

The Goddess movement has also grown tremendously in past years. Ritual circles seem to spring up everywhere, quietly and organically. Some identify themselves as Witches or Pagan, others don't. I have taught ritual to nuns, priests, academics, therapists, activists, and thousands of people who fit none of these categories. Recently, within the Unitarian Church a covenant of Unitarian Universalist Pagans has been formed, and people from New York to South Bend, Indiana, are celebrating the seasonal cycles and the embodiment of the sacred in the earth.

Other related political and philosophical movements have sprung up. Scientists are giving new credibility to the Gaia Hypothesis, which marshals evidence for a new understanding of the earth as a living, self-regulating being. The ecofeminist movement draws connections between the oppression of women and the rape of nature, and names the connections between all systems of domination. Deep ecology challenges our anthropocentric view of the world, and speaks for the inherent value of all living beings.

I have watched this growth with great excitement and occasional alarm. At times, spokespeople for these related movements take positions or make public pronouncements in the name of Gaia that make my skin crawl — for example, the premise advanced by some deep ecologists that because the world is overpopulated, famine in Africa or the AIDS epidemic is acceptable or even desirable, part of Gaia's Greater Plan. Such positions miss the point.

The Goddess is not just an intellectual concept; She makes demands on us. At the Ecofeminist Conference in Southern California in March of 1987, Inez Talamantes, a Native American speaker, said, "If you have a vision of the goddess, if you dream of Her, you are obligated to work for Her for the rest of your life." When we really understand that the earth is alive, and know ourselves as part of that life, we are called to live our lives with integrity, to make our actions match our beliefs, to take responsibility for creating what we would have manifest, to do the work of healing. Integrity means that we cannot propose or accept a solution for someone else that we are unwilling to undergo ourselves. We expect to get back what we put out (three times over, in the Wiccan tradition). I propose this as a simple test of the ethical validity of any political or spiritual movement.

Also implicit in the understanding that the universe is alive is the realization that everything is interconnected, that the needs of the hungry child in the Sahel or the cancer patient or the tribes of the Amazon rain forest are aligned with my own true welfare, because we are not separate. So we are also called to compassion, to "feel with" others and act with others. Only a politics and a spirituality of compassion can possibly transform and heal the world, because without compassion we miss seeing the real interconnectedness of issues and cannot forge a vision or a strategy that can move us out of the stories of estrangement. And perhaps we should further test our movements by asking, "Are they rooted in compassion? Where is their heart?"

From compassion, we can generate community. To put it crudely, we didn't get into this mess alone, and we can't get out of it alone. We need sustained support, both to mount resistance and to enact our visions of renewal, support that itself embodies the deep value we recognize in each other. So, although the tools and principles discussed in this book help our individual growth and empowerment, they are not really aimed only at personal transformation. Their goal is to help us restructure our culture, creating the circles of support that we need, developing new ways to live and work and love.

Reclaiming, my own community, has grown. It has weathered many conflicts, but still meets, jokes, argues, and offers classes, summer programs, newsletters, and rituals. My affinity group, Matrix, is now also a coven. Raving Coven has scattered, as members' lives took them to different corners of the world, but I was taken in by the Wind Hags, who carry on strong.

Our community remains politically aware and active on issues ranging from military intervention to first-strike weapons to gay rights and feminist concerns. In 1984, I visited Nicaragua with Witness for Peace. The trip showed me that the possibility of revolution, of total social transformation, was not just a naive fantasy of the stoned sixties, that it can really happen. I was impressed with the deeply spiritual base of many of the Sandinistas I met. Although they drew their inspiration from Christianity, their vision of Christ seemed very close to my own conception of immanence. Liberation theology sees Christ as a sacred presence alive in the people, especially in the poor, and calls for justice to be enacted in this world.

My own understandings of interconnection have been enriched by the work I have done with WomanEarth Feminist Peace Institute on building alliances with women of color. My own priorities have shifted from opening to the new perspectives of those who come from a different race, class, or culture. I see more clearly how strongly all forms of domination are intertwined, and how impoverished we all are when we are cut off from receiving the rich gifts of vision that come from those who see from a different vantage point.

The deterioration of the environment has also grown more serious. I have come to believe (purely intuitively and with no hard evidence) that we will not end in a nuclear war, that we will, in fact, succeed in my lifetime in banning nuclear weapons. But for many generations to come we will be faced with the serious consequences of the toxic load on our air and water, the assaults on our immune systems from low-level radiation, the thinning of the ozone layer, the death of forests from acid rain and the wholesale cutting of trees, the loss of topsoil and species and germ plasm. To know the earth is alive is to ache to heal the wounds we daily inflict on her. Environmental issues will become more and more crucial in the coming years, but whether we can succeed in turning the tide of destruction depends on whether we can build a movement that truly includes the perspectives of a broad range of people.

As my own influence has grown (so that I paradoxically find myself in certain circles being treated as the authority on non-authoritarianism), my life has become more complex. I travel extensively and my schedule often leaves little time for the day-to-day organizing of actions and organizations. I much prefer success to failure, but I have become aware of the strange burdens a culture of estrangement places on creative people, for while most artists are ignored, discouraged, and unrewarded, those few who do achieve some recognition are often idolized and isolated from the very communities and experiences that inspire their work. This is a vicious circle I constantly struggle against, and I am fortunate in being surrounded by friends who are loving, challenging, and willing to manifest their own power-from-within. I live collectively, and still do much of my teaching, ritual work, and political work collectively, and we seem to muddle along in spite of the strains produced by my public acclaim.

I include the personal details of my life in my writing because they are the context that cannot be separated from the ideas presented in this book. I do try to live what I write, and I write about what I live — how else could I write? Besides, I am surrounded by people who keep me in line, with telling comments: "Starhawk, if you really believed what you wrote in *Dreaming the Dark*, you'd _____."

Writing personally has its hazards, because one's own life changes. About six months after *Dreaming the Dark* was published, I found myself in jail with about a hundred other women who had invaded and occupied the Vandenburg Airforce Base, where the MX missile was scheduled to be tested. We had been through a rather harrowing few days, and had been locked up in separate groups and held in college classrooms where we slept on cold floors. In spite of this we were continually taking stands for solidarity with people who had been isolated, which meant huddling in clumps together, refusing to move when we were asked to, going limp, and getting dragged away and thrown around. But finally we were booked and put in jail. Women and men were separated, and we women were held in a recreation room at the Lompoc Federal Prison, which seemed a haven of comfort with actual mattresses on the floor and edible food.

I had many friends in the group I hadn't seen for a long time, and in the morning we started to catch up on our lives, the current state of our relationships, our health, our emotions, and to gossip. I was talking to an old friend and mentioned that I had recently gotten divorced from my husband. She looked at me in shock, and burst into tears.

"I read what you wrote about him in your book, and I thought, at least there's somebody who has a really good relationship. And now you're breaking up — that means there's no hope at all!"

What I wrote about my husband, and about the joys of monogamy in chapter 8, was true when I wrote it. There were other truths, however, that I wasn't ready to face, or tell. Ed and I are still close friends, and in fact he walked in while I was working on this.

"How much should I tell the world about what our relationship was really like?" I ask.

"Tell all," he says. "I have no secrets."

I make a few suggestions, naming some of the more colorful incidents in our relationship.

"Not that!" he says. "What about the good times?"

"Do you remember any?" We both laugh, and then we start to remember them — walking in the park, taking the dogs to the beach, the times, not enough of them, when we camped or went away.

"And we never argued about money," he says. I look at him quizzically, and then we both laugh again. "We never had any to argue about."

The truth is, our relationship was stormy but rich, and someday I may write about it more fully. Now my life is rich in different ways.

Six years have passed, and the context has changed. I reread this book on airplanes, where I spend too much of my life, traveling to speak and teach ritual-making and magic. San Francisco, L.A., Minneapolis, New York, Boston. It goes with me to the Nevada Test Site, where I join a ten-day encampment from which we make forays onto the restricted zones where they conduct underground nuclear tests. I read it waiting in radio stations to be interviewed, with the blare of commercials in my ear, and early in the morning over a cup of tea in my sunny bed nestled into an east-facing window.

Late at night, at the close of May Day, Beltane, on a full-moon night in 1988, I begin this writing. I am sitting in the bay window of my collective house in San Francisco's Mission District, typing this into my computer terminal. The house is an old Victorian and my office is painted bright shades of orange and apricot and yellow, a color scheme few can tolerate but I adore. Nine of us live here, six women and three men. The texture of life is rich and full, sometimes like those fast-paced comedy films of the thirties in which hordes of improbable people dash in and out, dropping one-liners and eliciting bursts of laughter, sometimes days of intense conflict, confrontation, and truthtelling, sometimes a mad juggling act of commitments and relationships and responsibilities.

Right now, every emotion is deepened and heightened. It is the season of power, and we have been plunged into the mysteries of birth and death and the thin line between them. Our housemate, Phebe, has given birth to a premature child, Allison, and right now they are both in the hospital. Even as I write, Brook, the child's father, walks in, with hopeful news. Tomorrow Phebe should be out, and the baby has progressed so that she can actually be picked up and held. And although she cannot yet be fed, she is breathing and sucking a pacifier.

We visit her in the nursery. In this alien environment of tubes and needles and beeping monitors, she still struggles to open her eyes, contorting her face, raising her eyebrows first before the lids follow. We look into the milky gaze of her eyes, still focused on another place. Already, in her scant week of life outside the womb, this child has taught us to view every normal act of life, each breath, each motion, the ability to suck or to tolerate touch or to cry, as truly precious, a miracle. And so we cannot help but believe in the resilience of the powers of life. Fragile as her labored breaths, they are nevertheless strong as the grip of these unimaginably tiny fingers that reach and grasp and hang on tight to survival. We are the agents of those powers, and if we listen to them move, in our own breath, in our own hands, we will know what to reach for and how to hold to each other, and together we can shift the balance back toward life.

Acknowledgments

Writing this book has been more difficult than anything I have ever undertaken before. I have been sustained, encouraged, advised, criticized, babied, helped, and lovingly harassed in this undertaking by a number of groups and individuals, whom I would like to acknowledge:

My coven, Raving; sister covens Holy Terrors and Wind Hags; the Reclaiming Collective; and the Matrix Affinity Group are all part of what appears in these pages, as are the Social Change Trainers Core Group, the Abalone Alliance, The Livermore Action Group, and the Santa Rita Jailbirds.

The women's movement and the pagan community are the ground in which this book grew.

David Kubrin introduced me to the historical material I have used in this book, and he reviewed Appendix A "The Burning Times: Notes on a Crucial Period of History." Lauren Liebling inspired the title, and helped me shape the language in which the book is written, Kevyn Lutton stimulated my awareness of many political issues, especially those involving community. Bonnie Barnett transcribed the music and helped me to free my own voice. Liz Walker and Eric Bear introduced me to nonviolence training.

This is also my Master's Thesis in the Feminist Therapy Program at Antioch University West, and I wish to thank my advisers, Ani Mander and Susan Holbrook. Ideas expressed here were first formulated in courses taught by Barbara Blasdell, Gene Alexander, Lauree Moss, Tom Parsons, Terry Keeney, Susan Campbell and Toni Maher.

My editor, Marie Cantlon, has been a staunch friend as well as a great help in shaping the manuscript and clarifying the ideas presented. I have been very fortunate to be able to work with her and to have had the encouragement I have consistently received from everyone at Beacon Press.

Mary Watson, the copyeditor, fought her way valiantly and sensitively through a thicket of semicolons and, I hope, kept her sanity.

Rose May Dance not only accompanied me in many of the adventures recorded here, she typed the manuscript, a feat that tested even her highly developed psychic powers. She also held my hand at crucial moments. It is possible that this book could have been written without her — but it certainly wouldn't have been completed by its deadline.

Ed, my husband, keeps me fed and laughing. He helped on the research for the chapter, "Sex and Politics." Among his many talents is being a great dancer. Without him, life — and this book — would be a lot duller.

And of course there are many others not mentioned here by name. To all of you — thanks.

Prologue

❧⚬❧

Dreaming the Dark

This is a book about bringing together the spiritual and the political. Or rather, it is a work that attempts to move in the space where that split does not exist, where the stories of duality that our culture tells us no longer bind us to repeat the same old plots.

That space is dark and half-forgotten but within it lies a power that runs counter to the principle of domination upon which our society is based. In essence, this is a book about power. It talks about the differences between power-over and power-from-within, about the stories and thought-forms that convey power, about ethics based on power-from-within. Although it moves in the dark it is also about vision and about action — that is, about magic, the art of evoking power-from-within and using it to transform ourselves, our community, our culture, using it to resist the destruction that those who wield power-over are bringing upon the world.

This book begins in a conversation that unrolls like the dark ribbon of the road as we pass by orchards of almonds and fields of wild mustard. We are driving home from a women's conference — myself and my friends Lauren and Kerry. All weekend we have been hearing horror stories of rape, torture, footbinding, clitori-

dectomy, forced incarceration in mental hospitals, Witch burnings, mutilations.

We are questioning the value of telling the stories over and over
again. We know them. We know particularly the stories of the
Witches, because Lauren and I are Witches. That is, we practice
the Old Religion of the Goddess, although we practice it in
eternally new ways that change with every ritual, every moon.
And our Witchcraft is entwined with our politics.

The Old Religion — call it Witchcraft, Wicca, the Craft, or with
a slightly broader definition, Paganism or Neo-Paganism — is both
old and newly invented. Its roots go back to the pre-Judeo-Chris-
tian tribal religions of the West, and it is akin in spirit, form, and
practice to Native American and African religions. Its myths and
symbols draw from the woman-valuing, matristic,[1] Goddess-centered cultures that underlie the beginnings of civilization.[2] It is not
a religion with a dogma, a doctine, or a sacred book; it is a religion
of experience, of ritual, of practices that change consciousness and
awaken power-from-within. Beneath all, it is a religion of connection with the Goddess, who is immanent in nature, in human
beings, in relationships. Because the Goddess is *here*, She is eternally inspirational. And so Witchcraft is eternally reinvented,
changing, growing, alive.

Long after city dwellers had converted to Christianity, the
Witches[3] were the wise women and cunning men of the country
villages. They were the herbalists, the healers, the counselors in
times of trouble. Their seasonal celebrations established the bond
between individuals, the community as a whole, and the land and
its resources. That bond, that deep connection, was the source of
life — human, plant, animal, and spiritual. Without it, nothing
could grow. From the power within that relationship came the
ability to heal, to divine the future, to build, to create, to make
songs, to birth children, to build culture. The bond was erotic,
sensual, carnal, because the activities of the flesh were not separate from the spirit immanent in life.

The history of patriarchal civilization could be read as a cumu-
lative effort to break that bond, to drive a wedge between spirit
and flesh, culture and nature, man and woman. One of the major
battles in that long war of conquest was fought in the sixteenth

and seventeenth centuries, when the persecutions of the Witches shattered the peasants' connection with the land, drove women out of the work of healing, and imposed the mechanist view of the world as a dead machine. That rupture underlies the entwined oppressions of race, sex, class, and ecological destruction.

The Craft survived, however — secretly, silently, underground, in small groups called covens whose members were related by blood or deep trust. Its reemergence in this century is linked to a growing realization among many strata of people that the dead world of mechanism, the world of domination, cannot sustain our inner lives, nor our lives in community with each other, nor the life of the planet. The rebirth of earth religion is a part of a broad movement that challenges domination — that seeks to connect with the root, the heart, the source of life by changing our present relationships.

I am not, however, speaking for Witchcraft in this book, or for any other political or spiritual group. The view of the Craft I present is my own vision, and it is meant to be challenging, to present not only what is but what could be. Certainly, not all Witches share my political perspective, and few of those whose political perspective parallels mine are Witches. They are as likely to be Quakers, Buddhists, radical Catholics, or atheists. Although I belong to many (perhaps too many) groups — a coven, several different collectives, and an affinity group — all have been important in helping me formulate ideas, but I am not speaking for any group. I am sure members of every one of my circles will find something in this book with which they disagree.

Lauren and I are in the same coven. We have met together for three — four — five years, performed the rites, cast the circle, chanted, raised power, honored the Goddess immanent in ourselves and each other, shared visions, shared pain, fought and made up, cried and laughed. And now, driving together on the road in the dark, I tell her that when I write and speak about the Craft and the Goddess, I like to speak about the bond and the strength and the connection, not the horror — of what we do, not what was done to us. But I question myself: is this perhaps, just my way of trying to avoid pain?

"All of that," says Lauren, who is a poet as well as a Witch, "the torture stories and the rage come from the dark. But if you retell the horror without creating the dark anew, you feed it. You do not break the mold. We need to dream the dark as process, and dream the dark as change, to create the dark in a new image. Because the dark creates us."

Later, she writes to a friend:

"When we tell of the turning dark, the velvet dark, Hecate's birthgiving dark, the shadow listens to that also. And what we name feeds into the open imaginations that are listening. So their concept of what is narrowly called death can change."

The dark: all that we are afraid of, all that we don't want to see — fear, anger, sex, grief, death, the unknown.

The turning dark: change.

The velvet dark: skin soft in the night, the stroke of flesh on flesh, touch, joy, mortality.

Hecate's birth-giving dark: seeds are planted underground, the womb is dark, and life forms itself anew in hidden places.

The question of the dark has become a journey, as our conversation took place on a journey. How do we face the dark on the edge of annihilation? How do we find the dark within and transform it, own it as our own power? How do we dream it into a new image, dream it into actions that will change the world into a place where no more horror stories happen, where there are no more victims? Where the dark is kind and charged with a friendly power: the power of the unseen, the power that comes from within, the power of the immanent Goddess who lies coiled in the heart of every cell of every living thing, who is the spark of every nerve and the life of every breath.

For me, the journey began in a place of despair. During the writing of the early versions of this book's first chapter, I was haunted by visions of annihilation. Images of the city destroyed, of curling flesh, of the sudden flash in the sky — then nothing. I could not look at a friend, at my family, at children, without picturing them gone. Or worse, the long, slow deterioration of everything we love. Perhaps the value of the horror stories is that they bring despair to the surface, make us face it instead of feeling it as a drain on our lives so constant as to remain unnoticed.

Despair pushed me into an obsession with history, in particular, the crucial sixteenth and seventeenth centuries. I had to know how we got into our present predicament. Understanding that history helped me see more clearly the relationships among consciousness; power; and the reality — structures and institutions — that they shape. I compiled the material and wrote what is now Appendix A. It was later, pulling the threads of the book together, that I began to feel that history had an oblique rather than a central relationship to the question of the dark. (Nevertheless, if yours is the sort of mind that likes to start from the past and move forward, you may prefer to read Appendix A, "The Burning Times: Notes on a Crucial Period in History," first.) For me the question ceased to be: how did we get here? and became: where can we possibly go, and how?

So the journey became one of action. It was no longer enough for me to think about these issues, to talk and write about them. I needed to act on them in a more direct way than the cultural work of spinning Goddess circles and spawning community, more direct even than organizing marches or planning rituals for demonstrations, all of which I and members of my coven had been doing for many years.

In the summer of 1981, several of us from different groups within the Pagan community decided to take part in the blockade of the Diablo Canyon Nuclear Power Plant, which was constructed close to an earthquake fault in an ecologically sensitive area of the California Coast. Fifteen years of opposition, including two previous occupations of the plant grounds by members of the Abalone Alliance, had not deterred the Pacific Gas and Electric company from proceeding. Testing and operating licenses had been delayed for over a year during the freeze on licensing after the nuclear accident at Three Mile Island, but that summer Reagan was pushing hard for nuclear power and licensing was imminent.

The Abalone Alliance is organized into small, autonomous groups called affinity groups. Members of each affinity group decide together how they want to participate in each action, though all are unified by a commitment to nonviolence. Our group, called Matrix, particularly wanted to bring our knowledge of ritual and group energy to the blockade.

The blockade was called early in September, after the security clearance was granted, the last step before licensing. I spent nearly three weeks on blockade altogether, was arrested twice, and each time spent about four days in the women's jail.

The blockade became a crucial experience in my understanding not only of the theory, but also of the actual practice of political/ spiritual work based on the principle of power-from-within. Coming as it did between the writing of the first and second drafts of this book, it also furnishes a number of stories and examples.

Since then, my commitment to action has deepened, has become a matter of ongoing organizing, training, speaking, and participation in civil disobedience. There have been other actions, and I have been back to jail under other circumstances. Each experience teaches me something new, and some of those insights found their way into final revisions of this book. But although a book must end somewhere, the journey continues.

The Diablo blockade was an initiation: a journey through fear, a descent into the dark, and a return with knowledge and empowerment from within; a death and rebirth that began with a stripping process and promises something at the end.

For me, the journey that began in despair now reaches a place of hope and a sense of empowerment. That has been my experience writing this book. I hope your experience as you read it is one that evokes your own power.

Because alone no one can dream the dark into love. We need each other for that. We need all the power we can raise together.

These are not comforting times in which to make promises; the stakes are too high, we are playing with forms of death from which there may be no return, and all the endings are still uncertain.

We can only begin.

Take hands; for we are the circle of rebirth. If there is to be renewal, it begins with us. We can touch — through these words, these pages. We can know the dark, and dream it into a new image.

As life, friends. As source.

DREAMING THE DARK

Chapter One

❧ ⚬ ❧

Power-Over and
Power-From-Within

He says that he is not part of this world, that he was set on this world as a stranger.[1]

Circle One — three miles across: winds of 500 miles an hour; destruction of all buildings, including steel-reinforced office structures; most people in the area killed outright.[2]

Circle of hands . . . circle of arms around each other's bodies . . . circle of voices . . . circle of power.

Well my own daughter, Sherry, she's eleven, has deterioration of the bones in the middle ear. She just got a hearing aid and she already needs a stronger one.[3]

In the circle we chant each other's names. We place our hands on each other's bodies for comfort, for healing. We share our pain. "When do you feel powerless?" we ask each other. "And when do you feel a sense of your own power?"

Circle Two — six miles across: winds of 300 miles an hour; stone and concrete buildings destroyed; exposed people, if not killed, critically burned.[2]

"Giving birth to my baby — I felt power then . . ."

1

*"Planting my garden, or weaving . . ." "When I can speak
out honestly, and say what I really feel . . ." "Organizing —
putting out the flyers and seeing all the people come to the
march . . ." "Joining with other people to work together,
that's when I feel power . . ." "When I do what I'm afraid to
do . . ."*

*And she has a double row of bottom teeth and a sub-cleft
palate. She was born with a hole in her heart and an
enlarged liver. She has slight retardation too.*[3]

*On whose world is the sun going down,
Sisters and brothers, dare we claim it, dare we lose it again?*[4]
          Diane Di Prima
          Revolutionary Letter #70

As I write, the cats play on my desk, grooming themselves, bat-
ting my papers to the floor, or curling up to sleep, secure in the
familiar. Their minds do not encompass 500-mile-an-hour winds,
or the possibility that what is familiar can be transformed in a
flash to charred bone and flesh.

We cannot feel as secure. The newspapers describe what would
happen if the city were hit by a nuclear bomb; they tell of pesticides in well water, of a nuclear alert triggered by computer error,
of children damaged by chemical wastes.

It seems the sun is going down on everybody's world, that we
are about to lose what can never be reclaimed. Our acts of power
seem frail compared with the powers of destruction. There are too
many enemies, too many burial sites for chemical wastes, too
many weapons already in the stockpiles. There are too many job-
less, too many hopeless, too many rapists at large. Too many of
those who wield great powers are unconcerned. They do not feel
that they are a part of this world.

Circle Three — eight miles across: winds of 160 miles an
hour, destruction of brick and wood frame houses; exposed
people seriously burned.

Even the small acts that ordinarily bring us pleasure or comfort
become tinged at moments with horror. There are times when I
walk down the street, and smile at the man who sits on his front
stoop playing the radio, and the kids laying pennies on the street-

car tracks, and the woman whose dog plays with my dogs, but in between the blinks of my eyes they are gone. I see the flash, and then nothing is left — of these charmingly painted Victorian houses, of these ordinary people, or the features of the earth beneath these streets. Nothing — but ashes and a scorched, black void.

I know that I am not alone in being overwhelmed at times by hopelessness and despair. I hear the same fears from my friends, my family, from the clients who come to me for counseling. Everybody's personal pain is touched by this greater uncertainty: we are no longer confident of leaving a better world — of leaving a *living* world, to our children.

Yet the children must be fed, the dogs must still be walked, the work must go on, so we raise the barriers that defend us from unbearable pain, and in a state of numbness and denial we go on. The work may seem flat, but we carefully avoid questioning its meaning and its usefulness, even though we sense that something deep and sweet is missing from our lives, our families, our friend-ships; some sense of purpose, of power, is gone. And still the children grow up around us, no less beautiful than any other generation of children, and still when we poke a seed into the earth it continues to push forth roots and unfurl stem, leaf, flower, fruit. There are still moments when we see the processes of life continue to unfold, when we cannot help believing that life is moved by a power deeper than the power of the gun and the bomb; a power that might still prevail if we knew how to call it forth.

This book is about the calling forth of power, a power based on a principle very different from power-over, from domination. For power-over is, ultimately, the power of the gun and the bomb, the power of annihilation that backs up all the institutions of domination.

Yet the power we sense in a seed, in the growth of a child, the power we feel writing, weaving, working, creating, making choices, has nothing to do with threats of annihilation. It has more to do with the root meaning of the word power, from the (late popular) Latin, *podere* ("to be able"). It is the power that comes from within.

There are many names for power-from-within, none of them entirely satisfying. It can be called *spirit* — but that name implies that it is separate from matter, and that false split, as we shall see, is the foundation of the institutions of domination. It could be called *God* — but the God of patriarchal religions has been the ultimate source and repository of power-over. I have called it *immanence*, a term that is truthful but somewhat cold and intellectual. And I have called it *Goddess*, because the ancient images, symbols, and myths of the Goddess as birth-giver, weaver, earth and growing plant, wind and ocean, flame, web, moon and milk, all speak to me of the powers of connectedness, sustenance, healing, creating.

The word *Goddess* makes many people who would define themselves as "political" uneasy. It implies religion, secularism, and can be mistaken for the worship of an external being. "Goddess" also makes many people who would define themselves as "spiritual" or "religious" uneasy; it smacks of Paganism, of blood, darkness, and sexuality, of lower powers.

Yet power-from-within *is* the power of the low, the dark, the earth; the power that arises from our blood, and our lives, and our passionate desire for each other's living flesh. And the political issues of our time are also issues of spirit, conflicts between paradigms or underlying principles. If we are to survive the question becomes: how do we overthrow, not those presently in power, but the principle of power-over? How do we shape a society based on the principle of power-from-within?

A change in paradigms, in consciousness, always makes us uneasy. Whenever we feel the slightly fearful, slightly embarrassed sensation that words like *Goddess* produce, we can be sure that we are on the track of a deep change in the structure as well as the content of our thinking. To reshape the very principle of power upon which our culture is based, we must shake up all the old divisions. The comfortable separations no longer work. The questions are broader than the terms *religious* or *political* imply; they are questions of complex connections. For though we are told that such issues are separate: that rape is an issue separate from nuclear war, that a woman's struggle for equal pay is not related to a black teenager's struggle to find a job or to the struggle to prevent the export of a nuclear reactor to a site on a web of earthquake faults near active volcanoes in the Phillipines, all these realities are shaped by the consciousness that shapes our power relationships. Those relationships in turn shape our economic and social systems; our technology; our science; our religions; our views of women and men; our views of races and cultures that differ from our own; our sexuality; our Gods and our wars. They are presently shaping the destruction of the world.

I call this consciousness *estrangement*[5] because its essence is that we do not see ourselves as part of the world. We are strangers to nature, to other human beings, to parts of ourselves. We see the world as made up of separate, isolated, nonliving parts that have no inherent value. (They are not even dead — because death implies life.) Among things inherently separate and lifeless, the only power relationships possible are those of manipulation and domination.

Estrangement is the culmination of a long historical process. Its roots lie in the Bronze-Age shift from matrifocal, earth-centered cultures whose religions centered on the Goddess and Gods embodied in nature, to patriarchal urban cultures of conquest, whose Gods inspired and supported war. Yahweh of the Old Testament is a prime example, promising His Chosen People dominion over plant and animal life, and over other peoples whom they were encouraged to invade and conquer. Christianity deepened the split, establishing a duality between spirit and matter that identified flesh, nature, woman, and sexuality with the Devil and the forces of evil. God was envisioned as male — uncontaminated by the processes of birth, nurturing, growth, menstruation, and decay of the flesh. He was removed from this world to a transcendent realm of spirit somewhere else. Goodness and true value were removed from nature and the world as well. As Engels saw it, "Religion is essentially the emptying of man and nature of all content, the transferring of this content to the phantom of a distant God who then in his turn graciously allows something from his abundance to come to human beings and to nature."[6]

The removal of content, of value, serves as the basis for the exploitation of nature. Historian Lynn White states that when "the spirits *in* natural objects, which formerly had protected nature from man, evaporated" under the influence of Christianity, "man's effective monopoly on spirit in this world was confirmed, and the old inhibitions to the exploitation of nature crumbled."[7] No longer were the groves and forests sacred. The concept of a sacred grove, of a spirit embodied in nature, was considered idolatrous. But when nature is empty of spirit, forest and trees become merely timber,[8] something to be measured in board feet, valued only for its profitability, not for its being, its beauty, or even its part in the larger ecosystem.

The removal of content from human beings allows the formation of power relationships in which human beings are exploited. Inherent value, humanness, is reserved for certain classes, races, for the male sex; their power-over others is thus legitimized. Male imagery of God authenticates men as the carriers of humanness and legitimizes male rule. The whiteness of God, the identification of good with light and evil with dark, identifies whiteness as the carrier of humanness, and legitimizes the rule of whites over those with dark skin. Even when we no longer believe literally in a male, white God, the institutions of society embody his image in their structures. Women and people of color are not present in the top levels of the hierarchies that wield power-over. Our history, our experience, our presence can be erased, ignored, trivialized. The content of culture is assumed to be the history and the experience of white, upper-class males. The pain of all of us who are seen as *the other* — the poor and the working classes; lesbians and gay men; those who have physical disabilities; those who have been labeled mentally ill; the rainbow of different races, religions, and ethnic heritages; all women, but especially those who do not fit into culturally defined roles — is not just the pain of direct discrimination, it is the pain of being negated again and again. It is the pain of knowing that our concerns will not be addressed unless we bring them up ourselves, and that even then they will be seen as peripheral, not central, to culture, to art, to policy.

As we become separate, and are manipulated as objects, we lose our own sense of self-worth, our belief in our own content, and acquiesce in our own exploitation. When we women, for example, see men as embodying the *content* of the culture, and ourselves as not possessing inherent value, we submit to the rule of men and devote our energies and talents to furthering men's desires instead of our own. Historically, Christianity has reconciled workers, slaves, women, and people of color to the position of inferiors by denying value to the conditions of this life and assigning it to some future existence in heaven, where the meek and submissive will be rewarded.

Because we doubt our own content, we doubt the evidence of our senses and the lessons of our own experience. We see our own drives and desires as inherently chaotic and destructive, in need of repression and control, just as we see nature as a wild chaotic force, in need of order imposed by human beings.

In *The Death of Nature*, Carolyn Merchant documents the way the rise of modern science and the economic needs of preindustrial capitalism in the sixteenth and seventeenth centuries shifted the "normative image" of that world from that of a living organism to that of a dead machine.[9] That shift, accompanied and helped by the Witch persecutions, supported exploitation of nature on a scale previously unknown. (*See* Appendix A, "The Burning Times," for further elaboration.) The "machine image", the view of the world as composed of isolated, nonliving parts blindly moving on their own, grew out of a Christian context in which divinity and spirit had long been removed from matter. Modern science undermined belief in the last repository of spirit when it killed off God after he had sucked the life out of the world. Nothing is left now but the littered corpses, the hierarchical patterns of our institutions — the Church, the army, the government, the corporation — all embodying the principle of authoritarian power, all formed in the image of the patriarchal God with his subordinated troops of angels, engaged in perpetual war with the patriarchal Devil and his subordinate troops of demons.

No longer do we see ourselves as having even a dubious dignity as flawed images of God. Instead we imagine ourselves in the image of the machine as flawed computers with faulty childhood programming. We are left in the empty world described ad nauseam in twentieth-century art, literature, and music — from Sartre to the Sex Pistols.

In the empty world, we trust only what can be measured, counted, acquired. The organizing principle of society becomes what Marcuse termed *the performance principle,*[10] the stratification of society according to the economic performance of its members. Content is removed from work itself, which is organized not according to its usefulness or true value, but according to its ability to create profits. Those who actually produce goods or offer services are less well rewarded than those engaged in managing and counting this output, or stimulating false need. We are told in the business section of the morning paper that oil company Vice Presidents, for example, deny that their corporations are in the business of providing Americans with fuel and energy — rather, they are in the business of providing their investors with profits.

Science and technology, based on principles of isolation and domination of nature, grow crops and lumber by using pesticides and herbicides that also cause birth defects, nerve damage, and cancer when they infiltrate our food and water supplies. Claiming a high order of rationality, technologists build nuclear reactors producing wastes that remain dangerous for a quarter of a million years — and consign these wastes to storage containers that last from thirty to fifty years.

Estrangement permeates our educational system, with its separate and isolated disciplines. Estrangement determines our understanding of the human mind and the capabilities of consciousness, our psychology. Freud viewed human drives and libido as essentially dangerous, chaotic forces at odds with the "reality principle" of the ego. The behaviorists assure us that we are only what can be measured — only behavior and patterns of stimulus and response. Jung replaced a transcendent God with a set of transcendent archetypes, a slight improvement, but one that still leaves us caught in rigid, sex-role stereotypes.[11]

Sexuality, under the rule of the Father-God, is identified with his Opposition — with nature, woman, life, death, and decay —

the forces that threaten God's pristine abstraction and so are considered evil.[12] In the empty world of the machine, when religious
strictures fall away, sex becomes another arena of performance,
another commodity to be bought and sold. The erotic becomes
the pornographic; women are seen as objects empty of value
except when they can be used. The sexual arena becomes one of
domination, charged with rage, fear, and violence.

And so we live our lives feeling powerless and inauthentic —
feeling that the real people are somewhere else, that the characters
on the daytime soap operas or the conversations on the late-night
talk shows are more real than the people and the conversations in
our lives; believing that the movie stars, the celebrities, the rock
stars, the *People Magazine*-people live out the real truth and
drama of our times, while we exist as shadows, and our unique
lives, our losses, our passions, which cannot be counted out or
measured, which were not approved, or graded, or sold to us at a
discount, are not the true value of this world.

Estrangement permeates our society so strongly that to us it
seems to *be* consciousness itself. Even the language for other possibilities has disappeared or been deliberately twisted. Yet another
form of consciousness is possible. Indeed, it has existed from earliest times, underlies other cultures, and has survived even in the
West in hidden streams. This is the consciousness I call *immanence* — the awareness of the world and everything in it as alive,
dynamic, interdependent, interacting, and infused with moving
energies: a living being, a weaving dance.

The Goddess can be seen as the symbol, the normative image of
immanence. She represents the divine embodied in nature, in
human beings, in the flesh. The Goddess is not one image but
many — a constellation of forms and associations — earth, air,
fire, water, moon and star, sun, flower and seed, willow and
apple, black, red, white, Maiden, Mother, and Crone. She
includes the male in her aspects: He becomes child and Consort,
stag and bull, grain and reaper, light and dark. Yet the femaleness
of the Goddess is primary not to denigrate the male, but because it
represents bringing life into the world, valuing the world. The

Goddess, The Mother as symbol of that value, tells us that the world itself is the content of the world, its true value, its heart, and its soul.

Historically, cultures centered on the Goddess and Gods embodied in nature underlie all the later patriarchal cultures. Images of the Goddess are the first known images of worship, and are found in paleolithic sites. The beginnings of agriculture, weaving, pottery, writing, building, and city-dwelling — all the arts and sciences upon which later civilizations developed — began in cultures of the Goddess.

When patriarchy became the ruling force in Western culture, remnants of the religions and culture based on immanence were preserved by pagans [from the Latin word, *paganus* "rustic or country dweller"] in folk customs, in esoteric tradition, and in covens of Witches.[13] The cultures of Native Americans and tribal peoples in Africa, Asia, and Polynesia were also based on a world-view of immanence that saw spirit and transformative power embodied in the natural world.

Ironically, as estranged science and technology advance, they have begun to bring us back to a consciousness of immanence. Modern physics no longer speaks of separate, discrete atoms of dead matter, but of waves of energy, probabilities, patterns that change as they are observed; it recognizes what Shamans and Witches have always known: that matter and energy are not separate forces, but different forms of the same thing.

The image of the Goddess strikes at the roots of estrangement. True value is not found in some heaven, some abstract otherworld, but in female bodies and their offspring, female and male; in nature; and in the world. Nature is seen as having its own inherent order, of which human beings are a part. Human nature, needs, drives, and desires are not dangerous impulses in need of repression and control, but are themselves expressions of the order inherent in being. The evidence of our senses and our experience is evidence of the divine — the moving energy that unites all being.

For women, the symbol of the Goddess is profoundly liberating, restoring a sense of authority and power to the female body and all the life processes: birth, growth, lovemaking, aging, and death. In Western culture the association of women and nature has been used to devalue both. The imagery of the immanent Goddess imparts both to women and to nature the highest value. At the same time culture is no longer seen as something removed from and opposed to nature. Culture is an outgrowth of nature — a product of human beings who *are* part of the natural world. The Goddess of nature is also the muse, the inspiration of culture, and women are full participants in creating and furthering culture, art, literature, and science. The Goddess as mother embodies creativity as much as biological motherhood. She represents women's authority over our own life processes, our right to choose consciously how and when and what we will create.

The female image of divinity does not, however, provide a justification for the oppression of men. The female, who gives birth to the male, includes the male in a way that male divinities cannot include the female. The Goddess gives birth to a pantheon that is inclusive rather than exclusive. She is not a jealous God. She is often seen with a male aspect — child or consort. In Witchcraft, the male aspect is seen as the Horned God of animal life, feeling, and vital energy. Manifesting within human beings and nature, the Goddess and God restore content and value to human nature, drives, desires, and emotions.

Many people will prefer the concept of immanence without the symbol attached. I hope they will feel free to translate what follows in this book into terms or images that seem right to them. I prefer the symbol to the abstraction because it evokes sensual and emotional, not just intellectual, responses. However, I recognize that there is a danger in the use of any symbol — that people will forget the principles it represents. The Goddess could be taken as an object of external worship in a context no less hierarchical and oppressive than that of any religion of patriarchy. Let us be clear that when I say *Goddess* I am not talking about a being somewhere outside of this world, nor am I proposing a new belief system. I am talking about choosing an attitude: choosing to take this living world, the people and creatures on it, as the ultimate meaning and purpose of life, to see the world, the earth, and our lives as sacred.

To say something is sacred is to say that we respect, cherish, and value it for its own being. When the world is seen as being made up of living, dynamic, interconnected, inherently valuable beings, power can no longer be "seen as something people have — kings, czars, generals *hold* power as one holds a knife."[14] Immanent power, power-from-within, is not something we *have* but something we can do. We can choose to cooperate or to withdraw cooperation from any system. The power relationships and institutions of immanence must support and further the ability of individuals to shape the choices and decisions that affect them. And those choices must also recognize the interconnectedness of individuals in a community of beings and resources that all have inherent value.

It is challenging to try to envision a society based on that principle. The implications are radical and far-reaching, because all of our present society's institutions, from the most oppressive to the most benign, are based on the authority some individuals hold that allows them to control others.

A change this broad may at first appear threatening, utopian, or impossible. A society based on the principle of immanence would certainly not be utopian. It would be dynamic, alive with the drama of conflicting needs and choices, with a constant demand for new and creative solutions. Conflict, when it is not resolved with violence, spurs growth and keeps life interesting. Nor would the creation of such a society be impossible, although it would undoubtedly be difficult. It would mean choosing different priorities, envisioning new forms and new structures, and grappling with new problems.

All of us have vested interests in some aspects of our present society. The way we live provides many comforts and pleasures, along with the hurts, and even the hurts are familiar hurts that may seem preferable to the unknown. Change in society may mean some of us have to forgo the privileges of our status in hierarchical structures. But a society based on immanence would be one that values comfort and pleasure. Perhaps we would learn deeper pleasures, richer joys. Perhaps the comfort of knowing that the continuance of life is no longer threatened would be worth forgoing many things.

Much of this book is devoted to the work of envisioning immanence manifest in the structures of our individual selves and our communities. Much of it also tackles the question: how do we bring this about?

The answers I propose involve magic, which I define as *the art of changing consciousness at will*. According to that definition, magic encompasses political action, which is aimed at changing consciousness and thereby causing change.

Magic is another word that makes people uneasy, so I use it deliberately, because the words we are comfortable with, the words that sound acceptable, rational, scientific, and intellectually sound, are comfortable precisely because they are the language of estrangement.

Magic can be very prosaic. A leaflet, a lawsuit, a demonstration, or a strike can change consciousness. Magic can also be very esoteric, encompassing all the ancient techniques of deepening awareness, of psychic development, and of heightened intuition.

Those techniques, like any techniques, can be taught in hierarchical structures or misused in attempts to gain power-over. But their essence is inherently antihierarchical. As a means of gaining power-over, magic is not very effective — hence its association with self-deception, illusion, and charlatanry in our society. Magical techniques are effective for and based upon the calling forth of power-from-within, because magic is the psychology/technology of immanence, of the understanding that everything is connected.

When we practice magic we are always making connections, moving energy, identifying with other forms of being. Magic could be called the applied science that is based on an understanding of how energy makes patterns and patterns direct energy. To put it another way, at its heart is a paradox:

Consciousness shapes reality;
Reality shapes consciousness.

At this moment, my consciousness is shaped by many realities, from my class background to the caffeine in my bloodstream. I would be writing differently if I couldn't pay the rent this month, or if I were drinking peppermint tea instead of dark French roast.

Your consciousness is being shaped by the reality of these words that have the authority of the printed page. You would hear them differently if we were jogging in the park together — I in a torn sweatshirt, yelling at my dogs.

Yet the way our consciousnesses, yours — and mine too, as I write — are shaped by these words may cause us to act in new ways, to make different choices, to use our power-from-within in ways that are different from those we would use if we thought differently. And our actions, our choices, will shape the world around us in different ways.

Magic is art — that is, it has to do with forms, with structures, with images that can shift us out of the limitations imposed by our culture in a way that words alone cannot, with visions that hint at possibilities of fulfillment not offered by the empty world.

And magic is *will* — action, directed energy, choices made not once but many times, as this writing is an act of will as well as art, made up of hundreds of thousands of small decisions, of the choice, made over and over again to sit down at the typewriter and do it instead of the infinity of other things life offers. Those choices have led me to other choices, out of despair into action, risk, and hope.

And we have reason to hope. The forces of destruction seem great, but against them we have our power to choose, our human will and imagination, our courage, our passion, our willingness to act and to love. And we are not, in truth, strangers to this world.

We are part of the circle.

When we plant, when we weave, when we write, when we give birth, when we organize, when we heal, when we run through the park while the redwoods sweat mist, when we do what we're afraid to do, we are not separate. We are of the world and of each other, and the power within us is a great, if not an invincible power. Though we can be hurt, we can heal; though each one of us can be destroyed, within us is the power of renewal.

And there is still time to choose that power.

Chapter Two

❧ ☙

Thought-Forms: Magic as Language

I am struggling not to remove the idea from its context. Early in the morning I take my dogs down to the beach to run in the summer fog. The ocean whispers; all is soft, gray, and silver-blue. A line of birds skims the waves, winking out of sight as the crests hide it. The tide is running out. There are sand dollars at my feet and the fossils of sand dollars embedded in black rocks.

The thought-forms of immanence are embedded in *context*; they *are* context and content, as this fossil is now also rock.

Let me try again.

Let us imagine that we live in a culture where time is a cycle, where the sand dollar lies beside its fossil (as it does). Where everything is seen to return, as the birds return to sight with the movement of the waves. As I return to the beach, again and again.

Imagine that in that returning nothing stands outside; the bird is not separate from the wave but both are part of the same rhythm. Imagine that I know — not with my intellect but in my body, my heart — that I do not stand separate from the sand dollar or the fossil; that the slow forces that shaped the life of one and preserved the other under the deep pressure of settling mud for cycles upon cycles are the same forces that have formed my life; that when I hold the fossil in my hand I am looking into a mirror.

Or better, imagine that you are with me on that beach; that we are together (as we are); and that when we look into each other's faces, we see (as light is both particle and wave) ourselves mirrored and yet transformed by each other's unique, independent being; that we value the mystery of each other's being, which can never wholly be known, that we honor in each other the richness of our difference, honor that which we cannot predict in each other, that which makes us free.

And let us imagine that we are not alone, that we are together with our friends, our children, the people we love. And because we are aware of the world as returning, the forms of our thoughts flow in circles, spirals, webs; they weave and dance, honoring the links, the connections, the patterns, the changes, so that nothing can be removed from its context.

Even God.

Let us imagine that these children, at least, have never known a God who stands outside the world, that nothing in their minds is receptive to the principle of power-over. That as infants, they learned that the demands, the pleasures, and the innermost beings of their bodies were sacred because these children were honored by their parents; they were fed when hungry, suckled, held close to the bodies of both women and men.

Imagine that their mothers were not — by virtue of being mothers — expected to stay separate from the enterprise and activity of the world; that their fathers also cared for their infant bodies with all the tenderness we expect from women. Imagine that these children were never taught to separate flesh and spirit; never trained to view themselves, their bodies, their excretions with shame; that to their parents, even shit was something sacred, something to be returned in the cycles of returning.

When these children learn, they sit in circles; they move, they dance, they explore, they question, they teach other children what they themselves know. When they grow up to work, their work is not separate from their lives. Because they have no way to hold in their minds the absolute value of an abstract, they do not work for money as if it were a God. Because they themselves are not strangers in the world, they cannot hold the illusion that individual gain is possible at others' expense. They know — in their bodies, in their hearts — that what goes around comes around, that what is taken from the earth must be given back. Though they know that each one of them will die, they do not expect life to end. In their minds there is no Cosmic Referee to blow the whistle and yell "Game's over!" They cannot stand outside the world to own it, to profit from it. They cannot isolate themselves from the pain of other people; they are of the world, of each other.

The vision is not hard to construct. It comes clear on the beach, perhaps because this beach I return to is where I gather, together with my friends — the people I love — each year on the eve of the Winter Solstice. We meet to teach our bodies, our hearts, what we have come to recognize with our minds: that we do not stand separate from the cycles, from the seasons. So we chant, we hold each other, we light a fire. And as the sun descends to the water's edge to begin the longest night, we strip off our clothes and plunge into the cold waves. The water burns our skin to numbness, and we scream and yell and bellow, making deep, deep sounds as each wave hits, shocking us with our mortality, the vulnerability of our flesh. And as we let go, as we stop trying to hold out against the cold and the ocean's force, as we let ourselves feel and then feel again, deeper and deeper, there rises from under the shock and the cold a great exhilaration. We are alive! We sing it, chant it, shout it out; the moans change to sounds of power, the power that rises from within, from the springs of our lives that we greet as sacred.

The vision rises with that power, forms in the dark and appears in that moment when the splits are healed. Yes, say our bodies, our hearts, that is what could be. We could make a culture based on this power, this union. We feel so strong in the ocean, with our arms raised high to feel the wind on our skin, and the moonlight on the napes of our necks. We feel so close, as we emerge, hold each other, dry each other off. From that strength and that closeness, we could weave something healing.

Sometimes that vision is almost unbearable. It seems like a taunt, a mirage flung up to tease us as we march down the road to holocaust. And should we find within ourselves the hope and courage to work toward that vision, how do we bring it into focus when our own consciousness, our beliefs and plans, and the very ways we go about working are themselves molded by institutions of authority that are so much a part of us we that we cannot even see them?

Yet we can see. It is an underlying principle of magic that consciousness itself has structure, and that structure manifests in the forms of the physical world. Not the contents of our thoughts but the patterns by which they are connected are revealed everywhere around us.

This room in which I sit, for example, with its solid walls and concrete foundations, is a product of all the unspoken assumptions our culture makes about how we live. It is fixed, solid, filled with heavy furniture; a product of a world-view that sees things as fixed and solid. It is different from a house belonging to one of the Dogon people in Africa, where every space has a ritual, symbolic meaning as part of a mythic human body, and different from a tepee of the Plains Indians, built to be transported as part of the cycles of migration. This room is an object in a world of separated, isolated objects. The Dogon house and the tepee are sets of relationships in a world of interwoven processes.

Nothing is easier to see than consciousness once we recognize that it is embodied in the forms and structures we create. This point seems so obvious that it is almost embarrassing to present it. Yet I suspect that most of us have never quite looked at the world this way. We are easily confused by *content*, so the Communist Party and the Catholic Church seem very, very different to us. And yet their underlying structure, one of hierarchical tiers with each rising layer composed of fewer people who exercise power-over those below them, is very similar. Similar too, are the structures of the United States Government, of companies and corporations, of armies and universities, and of many groups that claim to be working toward a new consciousness, a revolution, or a new age.

Structure, not content, determines how energy will flow, where it will be directed, what new forms and structures it will create. Hierarchical structures, no matter what principles they espouse, will breed new hierarchical structures that embody power-over not power-from-within. A spiritual organization with a hierarchical structure can convey only the consciousness of estrangement, regardless of what teachings or deep inspirations are at its root. The structure itself reinforces the idea that some people are inherently more worthy than others. It doesn't matter what guru we follow. The fact that we are following anyone else will prevent us from coming to know the spirit, the power, within.

In the same way, political groups based on hierarchy and levels of authority inevitably breed new power-over structures. A revolution that challenges estrangement, that confronts the inherent violence of the few having power-over the many (or, for that matter, the many having power-over the few) cannot come through a structure that itself gives power to some over others.

We could say that culture is a set of stories we tell each other again and again. These stories have shapes. The shapes of the stories — not the characters, the setting, or the details — shape our expectations and our actions. It may be helpful to look at some of the stories that underlie modern Western culture, for only when we recognize them and see their implications, the structures they create in us, can we be free to change them.

Apocalypse. This is a story about time. It tells us that time is a thing, not a set of relationships, somewhat like a one-way street, that history is a story with a beginning, middle, and end, and that the end will be a big bang, a grand climax.

The main character in this story is a God who stands outside the world. The assumption is that after the bang, we too will get outside the world to something better. The story teaches estrangement. This world is only foreplay; this life is only a prelude.

Another version of this story could be called *Revolution.*

This story underlies the shape of most of our stories, our drama, our music, even our orgasms. It shapes the way we view death. And it creates a structure in our minds that allows certain absolutes to stand outside the world, where they take precedence over the values of the world, so that the state, which makes a law against murder, can manufacture weapons and go to war. So profit can be accorded a value that stands outside other values, can itself become a transcendent, absolute, final value.

Apocalypse often shapes the very way we work, driving ourselves to the utmost for a deadline or a crisis and then crashing, exhausted, feeling dead. It is hard, when expecting looming destruction, to pace ourselves. The crisis mentality keeps us from thinking, planning, working, and building for long-term change. It keeps us from being able to say, as my friend Alan Acacia is fond of saying, "I have a twenty-year commitment to the movement — so I can afford to take a rest."

It also keeps us expecting change to be swift, absolute, and clearly defined. We feel today that we are on the brink; and certainly we are in danger of making Apocalypse a self-fulfilling prophecy. Yet if we "win," if we succeed in changing consciousness and culture and preventing destruction, the change will not be immediate or sudden. It may well be a subtle shift, a different balance, a long-term change in relationships rather than a particular moment when we can say, "Here the change occurred."

The Good Guys/Girls Against the Bad Guys/Girls. This story is about values, and it too is a theme that shapes our culture. The Good Guys fight the Bad Guys: who will win? This story represents the thought-form we call dualism: all qualities can be broken down into pairs of opposites — one is good, idealized, and the other is bad, devalued. Psychologists call this thought process "splitting" — the inability to see people or things as wholes containing both desired and undesired elements.

In the split world, spirit wars with flesh, culture with nature, the sacred with the profane, the light with the dark. Men are identified with spirit, culture, the sacred, and are idealized; women are identified with flesh, nature, the profane, and are excluded from culture. Or woman is herself seen in split terms: virgin or whore, madonna or slut — not as a whole person in whom virtue and sexuality can both reside. Women's bodies and human sexuality can be redeemed only when they are controlled by men, or through the transcendent value of profit. So women become commodities, and sexuality becomes something to be marketed.

Light is idealized and dark is devalued in this story that permeates our culture. The war of dark and light is the metaphor that perpetuates racism. The metaphor itself derives from Indo-European mythology, and Merlin Stone argues that it originated as religious propaganda that justified the conquest of dark-skinned peoples by light-skinned Aryans.[1] The Indo-Europeans carried it to the East, where they conquered the darker Dravidian people of India. In the West, it filtered through Persian and Greek thought leaving its traces in the Old Testament. Finally it molded the imagery and symbolism of Christianity. It provided justification for the murder of women. (Witches met, after all, at night, and were charged with worshipping the Lord of Darkness.) It legitimized pogroms against dark-haired Jews, and gave a religious justification for the conquest and enslavement of Africans, Native Americans, and other dark-skinned people, whose color was seemingly, proof of being cursed by the God of light. The light/dark metaphor was the underlying theme of Nazi propaganda extolling the virtue of the pure, blond, Aryan race and warning against the threat of pollution by the dark Jews. We are taught the symbol system early: in how many fairy tales is the light-haired sister pure and good, while the dark-haired sister is jealous and evil?

The same splitting of light and dark buttresses the splitting of spirit (light) and body (dark), of male and female, of culture and nature. The split becomes the metaphor of hierarchy, of high (up, out, away from this world, this earth, out-of-body, spiritual, good) and low (base, beastly, bodily, earthy, animal, evil). It supports power-over.

Beware of organizations that proclaim their devotion to the light without embracing, bowing to the dark; for when they idealize half the world they must devalue the rest.

The Great Man Receives the Truth and Gives It to a Chosen Few. This story is about knowledge. Knowledge is given to a Great Man and passed by him to a select group, such as a Chosen People, a psychoanalytic society, or a cadre. Often the Great Man must suffer terribly to pay for receiving this knowledge. Sometimes he must merely defend it from those who would change or otherwise pollute the doctrine.

The Great Man, call him Moses, Jesus, Freud, Buddha, or Marx, writes a book, or his words are written down by others. His words now become the source of authority, of truth. All other knowledge is invalid unless it is based upon, or does homage to, the works of the Great Man.

This story legitimizes the authority of the select few who have received the one truth. It supports the illusion that truth is found outside, not within, and denies the authority of experience, the truth of the senses and the body, the truth that belongs to everyone and is different for everyone.

It also breeds the lie that there is only one truth, a lie that has destroyed more movements than the secret police. From that lie spring endless, fruitless, brutal debates over who is a true _____. (Fill in Christian, Marxist, feminist or another group of your choice.) The women's movement early saw through the story about the Great Man getting the truth — perhaps because Great Men are never women. (This is no accident, nor is it because women are less worthy of truth than men. It is because the Great Man story is always intertwined with dualism; women must be devalued in order for the Great Man to be so elevated.) Yet it took many years of painful struggle, of trashing and bitter debates, to see through the second level of the lie, to accept that there may be many feminisms, many truths, and that all may have important parts to play.

Making It/The Fall. Another name for this story might be *Saved/ Damned.* This is a story about success and failure. The older religious version has given way to the secular American version. At first, *Making It* and *The Fall* seem like two very different stories. In the first — a person of lowly birth is discovered (for some virtue or talent) and welcomed into the circles of the elect. In the second, a person who is a member of the elect, an inhabitant of the garden, owing to some weakness, some inherent evil or personal flaw, falls, and is cast down into the ranks of the ordinary.

But looking closer, we see the two are the same story in reverse. A person who lacks value gains it; a person who has value loses it. Both reinforce a consciousness and a power structure in which some people have value and others don't.

Often the two stories play together. A person makes it but then falls. Or a person falls and then is redeemed. Or one person makes it as her/his lover falls; as, in the movie "A Star Is Born," Judy Garland climbs to fame as her alcoholic husband slips from favor into suicidal despair.

What this story does is to keep us busy trying to make it, to push our way into the circles of the elect, looking for our personal salvation instead of challenging the consciousness that devalues what we already are. In this story, individual gain is the goal, and that purpose determines our values in the economic realm.

Those of us who don't make it are left with a sense of personal failure. Another name for this story could be *The Garden of Eden*, and yet another name is *The American Dream*. The story tells us that there is or was a perfect place, from which we have been cast out for our own sins, or to which we are denied entrance because of our own flaws and shortcomings. It supports "the individualist ethic in the American society which fixes responsibility for any failure to achieve the American dream on individual inadequacy. That same ethic . . . breeds a kind of isolation in American life that is common in all classes but more profoundly experienced in the working class, partly at least, because they have fewer outside resources."[2]

These are the stories of estrangement. You may think of others, but these four seem primary to me. They are the structures that shape our thoughts, our images, our actions. We have named them now, and it is a magical principle that knowing something's name gives us power — not over it, but *with* it. What we name must answer to us; we can shape it if not control it. Naming the stories, we can see how they shape us, and awareness is the first step toward change.

When we talk about stories, we are talking about language. Language shapes consciousness, and the use of language to shape consciousness is an important branch of magic.

Language both embodies and shapes our cultural thought-forms. "I am trying to write a noun-less novel," poet Meridel LeSeur said at a private reading. "Nouns are patriarchal. They separate us from things, naming the thing and making it an object. The American Indian languages have no nouns, only relationships. We won't get there for maybe a thousand years, but we can make a start." The language we use creates the context for whatever we say. A rose by any other name would not smell as sweet. If I call it a *Rosa rosaceae*, I have removed it from the context of gardens and moonlight, and placed it in an atmosphere of files, charts, test tubes, and botanical classifications. If you tell me I seem miserable, you do so in a different context than if you tell me I have an anaclitic depression stemming from deficiencies in gratification in the symbiotic subphase of development.

Language distributes power. The word *miserable* is a word I can use about myself; it gives me power to name, and so to own, my own feelings. Note that it is an adjective. It describes something I am doing (*feeling*). It is relational. The phrase *anaclitic depression* is a term used by professionals when speaking about persons other than themselves. It may be useful. It conveys, perhaps, a more precise diagnostic category, a fuller implied history, than *miserable*. But it is useful to professionals, not to me. It gives me no power to connect with my feeling because it turns my feeling into an object, a condition, something I *have* and so am distanced from, alienated from, as I am distanced from those who use the term about me.

There is a corollary to the principle that knowing something's name gives us power-with it. It is this: that the names we choose, the language that we use, also have power-with us, and shape us. Names embody thought-forms. They carry both the idea and the context. When we choose a false name, we place an idea in a false context and its shape changes, becoming, perhaps, something we do not intend. And because our language has itself been shaped by the culture of estrangement, whenever we choose the names that make things sound comfortable, acceptable, respectable, academically sound, scientific, we are almost always placing the thing we name back into the context of estrangement — removing its power and our own, alienating ourselves yet again. The names for the thought-forms of immanence, the names that carry power, often sound simple, childish, or threatening; sometimes they sound funny. They are uncomfortable words — take *Magic*, for example.

Or *Witch*.

The term *Witch*, people tell me over and over again, has negative connotations. It is a word that scares people, a word that shocks or elicits nervous, stupid laughter.

"If you're a Witch (heh, heh) turn me into a toad."

"Why be redundant?" I sometimes respond.

Yet I prefer the word *Witch* to prettier words, because the concept of a Witch goes against the grain of the culture of estrangement. It *should* rub us the wrong way. If it arouses fear or negative assumptions, then those thought-forms can be openly challenged and transformed, instead of molding us unseen from within our minds.

Language also conveys metaphors; these metaphors, the images we use, shape our thoughts and our actions. The thought-forms of estrangement become bound into our language as metaphors, and the metaphors reinforce the thought-forms, the constricting patterns in our minds.

So, for example, the counter-culture of the mid-to-late sixties — which was, in spite of its flaws, a movement based on the restoration of value to sexuality, sensuality, the body, feeling, nature, and joy in sensual life — became subsumed under (among other things) a search for spiritual enlightenment. And *enlightenment* (a noun) is a metaphor that skewers us firmly back into the story of duality; it negates the dark, the earth, the body, the dark cunt, the dark womb, the night. And so the same voices that, in the sixties, cried out for autonomy, spontaneity, and freedom, for a new culture based on nature, found themselves in the seventies extolling the virtues of silent meditation, of celibacy, of submission to a new set of male authority figures in more exotic drag. Others, who were not so caught up in the succession of cults, found themselves oppressed with a dreary sense of sameness, asking themselves, "Haven't I heard this before?" It was like hearing the same comedians retelling the same jokes, and they began to feel with a growing cynical despair, that nothing ever does really change.

Nothing *does* change, unless its form, its structure, its language also changes. To work magic, we begin by making new metaphors. Without negating the light, we reclaim the dark: the fertile earth where the hidden seed lies unfolding, the unseen power that rises within us, the dark of sacred human flesh, the depths of the ocean, the night — when our senses quicken; we reclaim all the lost parts of ourselves we have shoved down into the dark. Instead of *enlightenment*, we begin to speak of *deepening*, of *getting down* as well as *getting high*. We remember that in the old myths, the entrance to the realm of spirit was through the fairy mound, the cave, the crack, the fissure in the earth, the gate, the doorway, the vaginal passage. We call it *the underworld*, and we go within for our visions.

The magic that works is itself a language, a language of action, images, of *things* rather than abstracts. These things are seen not as objects but as consciousness-manifest. Magic speaks to the deep parts of ourselves that were formed before we knew abstractions.

While the language of words, of abstracts, of concepts, is shaped by culture and tends to move in the thought-forms of culture, the language of things, of images, can, if we open to it, take us deeper. The contexts of the images, the stories, have been twisted to tell the stories of the patriarchy, but if we let the *things* themselves, in all the richness and complexity of their existence, speak to us, we reverse the reversals,[3] or more — we dive below the cement-banked channels of consciousness and reach the underground rivers that are its source.

Take, for example, this cluster of *things:* a naked woman, a snake, a tree, an apple. Let us forget that they are the icons of The Fall, and consider, first, a real snake, perhaps the one that lives with me. I watch her slow movements, feel the strength in her long body, see her skin grow dull, her eyes cloud over until she looks lifeless — and I wake one morning to find her old skin crumpled like a discarded nylon stocking. She has slipped out, her scales iridescent, her eyes bright; she is hungry now, on the prowl, new again. And I could say that to me, the snake as a symbol now means, not The Fall, but renewal, resurrection. Yet that also would be false, because in the language of magic the symbol has no intellectually assigned meaning; it is a pointer that says, "Look. Pay attention to this *thing*." And in giving my attention to the living being of my snake, I learn — not just with my mind but with my senses, my experience — about renewal. Yet you might learn something else.

Perhaps the snake, with her slow cycles, her once-a-month meal, elimination, shedding, would tell you a new story about time — that time flows differently for her than for us, that time is not a thing but a relationship. Or perhaps she will tell you a story I cannot even imagine, because the richness, the mystery of her being is not exhausted by one story, or two stories, or a thousand insights. Revelation is continually happening.

Or I give my attention to the tree. I see the leafless winter sticks of its branches sprout green buds, leaves, blossoms; I see them swell into this fruit that I hold in my hand, this fruit that is itself a seed. And so for me the constellation of things becomes an experience of renewal, and I feel it in the flesh of my own woman's body, which seems so vulnerable, so mortal; yet I can know, with a sense deeper than words, how it renews itself. But for you the experience might be something else. Perhaps the woman and tree and fruit offer shade and nurturing and comfort. Perhaps, on another day, that is what they would offer to me.

The magic that works is a very concrete language. To change consciousness, to move out of the thought-forms of estrangement, we begin with what we can see and touch and hold, and we return to what we can see and touch and hold, knowing that what is concrete reveals what is intangible: the energy, the process that forms what can be seen, whether it is a snake, or a woman, or a tree. Things reveal, in their forms, in their movements, the processes that shaped them, as the rocks reveal in their roundness and their crevices the movement of water. That is what we mean by immanence.

Learning to work magic is mostly a process of learning to think-in-things, to experience concretely as well as to think abstractly. All of us begin life as young children thinking concretely, but this ability, instead of being developed and refined as we grow, is devalued in our culture in favor of abstract reasoning. Though abstractions have their uses, they separate us from the deeper levels of our feelings. Relearning the language of things requires that we reconnect with our emotions. Although it sounds almost ludicrously simple, it can be a long and difficult process.

"Ask for something you need from the group," we say to a circle of women, "something tangible — something we can give you."

"Inner strength," says one woman.

"Not tangible enough," we say. "We cannot see inner strength — we cannot hand it to you. We could rub your back, so that your body relaxes, so that your muscles feel our caring; we could bring you a cup of tea, offer you vitamins. But if you insist on inner strength, do a spell for it, make yourself a mojo bag. But then you must know these things: What color is it? What does it smell like? Is it a fragment of granite from the Sierras, or a pebble of California jade? When you collect the things that embody strength for you, when you put them together, when you open yourself to let each speak, you will know something about the sources of your strength."

The concrete reveals the unseen; the microcosm is shaped by the same forces that shape the macrocosm. As above, so below. And so the personal is political: the forces that shape our individual lives are the same forces that shape our collective life as a culture. Feminist consciousness-raising is a process based on sound magical principles. If we speak to each other as equals, not about abstract theories but about the concrete realities of our experience, we will see the common forces that have shaped our lives.

If we speak honestly. The magic that works is not the magic of lies, of illusions. Especially dangerous are the lies we tell ourselves, because they keep us separate, cut off from the power of what is.

What is (things, feelings, images) embodies energy, which physicists now tell us is not separate from matter. The magic that works is the conscious movement of energy causing change in accordance with will. Just as tangible things reveal the unseen energies that shaped them, the shapes and patterns that energy takes in its movement become manifest as things.

This is where our language begins to break down — or maybe where all language breaks down. Even if we were to speak of *ch'i* or *ki* or *mana*, or *the force* beloved by the *Star Wars* generation, perhaps any name, any noun, would be a lie, because energy cannot be separated. If we say that energy runs through things, we imply that energy is separate from the things that it runs through. Perhaps this is where thought itself breaks down. If we say that energy is motion, and follow the physicists in their pursuit of what is moving — we do not find any things, only patterns of probabilities. Magic reverses the processes of mechanist thinking, wherein we think in abstracts to control and manipulate objects. In magic, we think in things because they reveal underlying patterns, they tell us how energy is moving. We use things, images, and metaphors to shape the movements of energy, to change probabilities. So I will now speak in these metaphors, as if energy were a thing rather than moving relationships, until we evolve the nounless language that would let us speak more truly.

Shaping energy is surprisingly easy, almost instinctive. We move energy with our breath, our voices, with the movements of our bodies, and by making pictures in our minds. There are, however, a few basic principles.

The first is always to begin where you are, not where you think you should be. Even the states and the places we feel as negative, as painful, embody energy. Anger, rage, depression, cynicism, fear/resistance, are all sources of power when we use them as pointers rather than blocks.

Another principle could be phrased: start grounded; end grounded. To ground ourselves means to connect with the earth, with what *is*, to start where we are, to root ourselves. The earth is energy congealed; we could speak of it as a great storehouse of energy. When we move energy, when we raise power, we draw it up from the earth and let it drop to the earth. We never try to hold on to it, because energy always cycles and returns; as it moves in cycles, in waves, it rises and falls. It cannot move indefinitely in only one direction.

Like water, energy remains clear as long as it keeps moving. When it stops, it stagnates and dries up, leaving us with the scum as residue. And, like water, when energy sinks down through the earth it is filtered, purified. And when we draw it up again, it comes in its clearest state.

Energy binds groups together. We connect when we share energy through a common vision, a common task, through sharing in tangible forms, such as food, touch, song, and work.

But all of this remains abstract. Instead, let us think in things, and imagine ourselves meeting on the beach (or in your room) to do the magical work of changing thought-forms.

We take hands, and breathe together, making a circle.[4] We move our bodies; we bend and stretch and rock until our tight places relax and we can stand with our knees loose and feet planted firmly on the ground.

We breathe deep, from our bellies. In and out. Our bellies fill with air with each breath, blowing up like little balloons as we inhale, softly falling as we exhale. We draw the air in deeply until it fills every cell, until it blows through our bones and sinks through our feet.

We root ourselves. We imagine that our feet have roots that go deep into the center of the earth herself, and that we can draw up the power from those roots, as a tree draws water from the earth. And slowly, slowly, we can feel the energy rise through our feet, through our legs, through our thighs and hips. As it rises, it warms us, it relaxes us, so that we feel ourselves loose and glowing with it. And the energy rises through our genitals, and we feel them grow warm, we feel pleasure in them. It rises into our bellies; it glows in our bellies like the moon, like the sun. And our spines grow tall like the trunk of a tree as the energy rises. It fills our lungs and our hearts, and from our hearts it spreads out through our shoulders, down our arms, through our hands. From our hands the energy passes from each of us to the others. And it rises up through our throats, with our breath, through our heads and the centers of our foreheads, and it bursts out of the tops of our heads like branches that reach up into the sky and then sweep back down to touch the earth again, creating a circuit, making a circle. We can feel how the branches surround us and protect us.

And we feel the wind in our leaves, feel the sun, the moon, shine down on our leaves; and through our leaves we take in the light and draw it down through the twigs and branches into the trunk — and down, down to our roots, down into the earth. And we feel the light push our roots deeper, we feel them grow deeper into the earth.

And we feel how beneath the earth all our roots intertwine, how they draw power from the same source.

And we feel above our heads how our branches intertwine, how the same wind moves through them all, and the same light shines down on them all.

And we feel the energy pass from hand to hand, linking us in the circle. And we feel our breath mingle in the center of the circle and become one, so that as we breath together, in and out, we become one — one living, breathing organism.

We begin where we are. Each one of us chants our own name, and the circle sings it back to us. The sounds, the harmonies, are gifts. They call to our own awakening power.

We sing the names of those who have done this work of changing consciousness before us, and as we speak them, name them, something of their being enters the circle. "Harriet Tubman — woman of indomitable courage." "John Muir — man who was not afraid to love nature." "Isadora Duncan — who loved her body." "Emma Goldman — fiery spirit." The names continue.

When they die away, we look into the center of our circle. We envision all our images, all our energies running together, swirling and flowing, brewing like soup in a cauldron, until a new vision takes form, until we can see the *thing* that embodies the change we want to make.

When it comes clear, when we can each see it before our eyes, we breathe deeply again; we draw the power up; we let it flow with our breath, in our voices — as sound, a deep, wordless sound that makes the vision glow, that fills it with energy. The power builds and builds. It moves through us clearly; we feel our arms rise up with it, and we are there, in the vision. In ecstasy. Strong.

Then it falls. In silence, we drop down, press our hands, our bodies, against the earth, and let the power drain from us, back to its source, leaving us empty, relaxed, peaceful.

We ground it into our lives, into what is, when each of us envisions, and says one real, concrete thing we will do to realize the vision. Small or large, alone or together, it will be a step, a small change. We may write a letter, plant a garden, make compost out of garbage, write a book, organize a food co-op or a union — have an honest conversation with our parents. We sing each other's names again. We say, "You are the Goddess. You are God." And we mean it.

And so we open the circle, and we each go and do what we have said we will do.

And already the change is beginning.

Chapter Three

❧

The Ethics of Magic

About ten years ago, my friend Mary and I used to take her small son Bill out to a place in the countryside north of Los Angeles, where we could hike along a stream and walk under live oaks. The same area was popular with local teenagers, who left the stream littered with beer cans and garbage. Mary always brought some large trash bags with her. When we were leaving, the three of us would fill them with beer cans. Our efforts never seemed to make any appreciable difference, and once I asked Mary why we bothered at all.

"I know we can't clean it all up," she said, "but I believe in picking up the garbage that you find in your path."

The beer can principle, as I think of it, has served as an ethical guideline that allows me to keep my sanity in a society filled with exploitation, pollution, and destruction. It seems a good point of departure for discussing the ethics of magic. A common misconception about religions and cultures based on immanence is that they lack ethics or a conception of justice. For Western culture bases its ethics and its justice on the stories of estrangement. If we discard these, if we let unbridled nature reign, don't we risk social catastrophe?

It is hard to imagine catastrophes greater than those that the ethics of estrangement may be about to precipitate. Still, the world-view of immanence does carry with it a set of ethical imperatives, though they are based on principles very different from those of patriarchal culture.

The conception of justice in Western, patriarchal traditions is of a set of absolute laws that transcend the world, that are imposed on the world from outside. The laws, like the God who stands outside the world, are valued out of context, over and above the values of the world, of human feelings, needs, and desires. They are the laws of heaven, and must be followed whatever their consequences here on earth — because heaven, not earth, is what we value. So, although no Catholic of conscience would claim it is ethical to cause suffering to the poor, the Pope continues to ban birth control, even though its effect is to doom many of the poor to inescapable hunger and suffering.

The popular conception of justice, which shapes even the humanist institutions of the West, is built upon the stories of estrangement. After the Apocalypse comes the Day of Judgement, when the war of the Good Guys with the Bad Guys is ended and each is either Saved or Damned, Making it or Falling, depending on how well they have lived by the truth, the rules, entrusted to the Great Man. Such a story is an enormous support to all authority. It reinforces the ethic of power-over that teaches us that good people obey the rules. It places rules and authority in a realm beyond question, valued above reason or the evidence of the senses. It allows us to cause pain and suffering quite comfortably in defense of the rules. Perhaps fortunately, Western culture has never succeeded in living up (note the direction) to its own conception of justice. Heretics, rebels, and sinners have always tempered the rule of absolutes.

The immanent conception of justice is not based on rules or authority, but upon integrity, integrity of self and integrity of relationships.[1]

The world-view of immanence values each self as a manifestation of the Goddess, as a channel of power-from-within. People of integrity are those whose selves integrate both the positive and the negative, the dark and the light, the painful emotions as well as the pleasurable ones. They are people who are willing to look at their own shadows instead of flinching from them. They honor the shadow because they know that its very distortions reveal the shape of the ground underneath.

Integrity means consistency; we act in accordance with our thoughts, our images, our speeches; we keep our commitments. Power-over can be wielded without integrity, but power-from-within cannot. For power-from-within is the power to direct energy — and energy is directed by the images in our minds and speech, as well as by our actions. If these are consistent, energy flows freely in the direction we choose and we have power. If what we do is at odds with what we say or think, then energy gets blocked or mis-channeled. If I think and say that I hate pollution, and yet walk by and leave the beer cans lying at my feet, the energy of my feelings is dissipated. Instead of feeling my own power to do something, however small, about litter, I feel and become more powerless.

Directed energy causes change. To have integrity, we must recognize that our choices bring about consequences, and that we cannot escape responsibility for the consequences, not because they are imposed by some external authority, but because they are inherent in the choices themselves. If I leave the beer cans lying, and go away feeling powerless and depressed, my powerlessness is not a judgement imposed by an irate Goddess — it is an inherent aspect of the decision I made.

The ethics of integrity are choices based on internal consistency and inherent consequences. They are not based on absolutes imposed upon chaotic nature, but upon the ordering principles inherent in nature. Nor are they based on rules that can be taken out of context. They recognize that there are no *things* separate from context. The Pope, were he a representative of an immanent religion, could not ban birth control without acknowledging that he is also choosing the consequences of poverty, starvation, suffering that such a ban will bring. But of course, an immanent religion could not have a Pope who makes decisions that bind millions of others. In a religion of immanence, each individual is sacred. Each of us has our own direct line to truth; each of us is her/his own Pope, so nobody can be invested with authority over us. Only those who must bear the consequences of a decision have the right to make it. And those who make decisions must bear the consequences.

It is interesting to try to envision a large society based on this principle. At first, one is struck by how much less would get done. We could build no more freeways through neighborhoods if those whose houses would be destroyed could veto the project. We could build no more nuclear power plants or nuclear bombs, nor could we carry out any of the large-scale projects that involve forcing some people to accept conditions they don't want. We might no longer be able to carry out any projects that involve vast, sweeping changes in the land or in neighborhoods.

Instead, we would turn to changes that were small, organic, incremental, cooperative. We would have to transform our technology, our economy, our entire way of living. Instead of damming a wild river to provide electricity, we might need to construct a windmill for every house.

We would, however, be prevented from making vast mistakes — from bulldozing entire neighborhoods only to let the lots lie empty for years, from placing whole states in danger of irradiation, from waging war. Such an ethical principle could provide self-correcting feedback to culture, forcing us to evolve more slowly and more carefully. Indeed, cultures based on immanence have evolved very slowly, and have not developed Western culture's technological prowess. They adapt to land and climate rather than change radically the face of the earth.

Anyone who is uneasily contemplating the prospect of the wheels of production and/or progress grinding to a halt can, of course, relax. We are not, as a culture, about to switch to the ethics of immanence suddenly. We can, however, begin to apply these principles to our own lives, groups, and organizations.

What many of us discover, however, when we begin making decisions according to our internal integrity instead of externally imposed authority, is that what we have always called our conscience is really an internalized version of external authority, an inner self-hater that gets us to do what it believes is right by means of domination, threat, fear, and guilt — by telling us the stories of estrangement. "A good person picks up beer cans," the self-hater whispers. "If you don't, you're *bad*. You are breaking the rules. You will fall from the circle of the chosen, the elect. A terrible judgement will come upon you."

The next chapter will deal at length with the self-hater, but for now it is important to recognize that the ethics of immanence have nothing to do with guilt. They are based on pride, not guilt. I pick up beer cans not because I feel rotten when I don't, but because I feel empowered when I do. I can see that the stream-bed looks better and feel pride in having made that change, small though it may be.

The idea of an ethic based on the individual's sense of pride and integrity must make many people profoundly uneasy. Didn't Hitler believe in his own integrity? Aren't we throwing open the door to crime and vast selfishness?

Perhaps, if the individual self is seen out of context. But immanence is context, and so the individual self can never be seen as a separate, isolated object. It is a nexus of interwoven relationships, constantly being shaped by the relationships it shapes. Integrity also means integration — being an integral and inseparable part of the human and biological community.

In a community in which the sacred manifests through inner integrity rather than external authority, the integrity of every self is valued — yours as well as mine. No one's personal sense of righteousness — be that person a Pope or a Hitler — can justify her/his domination over others. I must recognize the sacredness of your will, as well as mine, and if they conflict, we must struggle toward a solution that both of us can freely accept. (More about that process in Chapter Six, "Building Community: Processes for Groups".) In such a community, good listeners might be valued more than loud talkers. Manipulation through fear, guilt, blame, or appeasement is unethical. Process becomes as important as content or product.

When personal integrity is valued, diversity also must be valued. No longer do we tell ourselves stories about the one truth, or the set of rules that everyone must follow. Immanence is polytheistic — it allows for many powers, many images of the divine. We do not try to coerce everyone into following the same trail along the stream; instead, we say that we each have our own path to find, our own trash to pick up. If we all walk the same track, then only a narrow strip gets cleared. If we spread out and go different ways, together we can cover a great deal more ground.

In ecological systems, the greater the diversity of a community, the greater is its resilience and adaptability in the face of change — and the greater is its chance for survival.

The ethics of immanence encourage diversity rather than sameness in human endeavors, and within the biological community. Diversity can even be used as a standard for judgement, leading us, perhaps, to favor a salt marsh over a subdivision, or a multitude of small businesses over the interests of a few large corporations.

Diversity fosters and is fostered by balance. As stated in Barry Commoner's fourth law of ecology: "There is no such thing as a free lunch. Because the global ecosystem is a connected whole, in which nothing can be gained or lost, and which is not subject to overall improvement, anything extracted from it by human effort must be replaced. Payment of this price cannot be avoided, it can only be delayed."[2]

Relationships of integrity are balanced: no one is attempting to get a free lunch at someone else's expense. Instead, the energy each puts out is roughly equal to the energy she or he gets back. No one does all the giving or all the taking. Giving and taking may swing up and down, but they swing around a fulcrum, a center. It is no more ethical always to give than it is always to take.

Life and death balance each other. They are not a good/bad duality. Life expands; death imposes limitations. When the two forces are in balance, a rich diversity of life-forms can coexist.

The ethics of immanence strongly value life — but not as an untempered absolute. For life, too, is relationship, interwoven in a dance with death, and death is the limiting factor that sustains the possibility of new life.

There is no external authority, no set of absolute truths, that can tell us precisely how to determine the meaning of our personal commitment to the dance. For some, preserving the dance of life/ death may mean neither eating meat nor using the products of domesticated animals. For others, it may mean refusing to register for the draft. For still others, it may mean keeping up the daily struggle to put food on the table and pay the rent.

Questions of life and death inevitably bring up the issue of abortion. For some women, a commitment to serve the life-force might make an abortion impossible. For others, an abortion might be the highly ethical choice not to bring forth a child that cannot, for whatever reason, be wholeheartedly loved and cared for. For a child is given life not just by its physical birth, but through relationships with loving, caring human beings. If those relationships cannot be assured, then the newborn is given only half a life, a precarious, starved existence.

But abortion is not truly an issue of right-to-life versus right-to-choice. To maintain the right of every egg and sperm to reproduce blindly is like maintaining the right of every cockroach and flea to populate the world endlessly. The question at stake is actually the right-to-coerce. Only our assumption that some people have the right to exercise power-over others allows us even to consider taking the choice away from the woman whose self and body and future are at stake.

For human life to be rich, joyful, loving, it must be the freely given gift of the Mother — through the human mother. To bear new life is a heavy responsibility, requiring a deep commitment, one that no one can force on another. To coerce a woman by force, or fear, or guilt, or law, or economic pressure to bear an unwanted child is immoral. It denies her right to exercise her own sacred will and conscience, robs her of her humanity, and dishonors the Goddess manifest in her being. It is the responsibility of an ethical society not to force every fetus conceived to be brought to term, but to provide support and resources so that every child born can be fed and sheltered, loved, nurtured, and protected.

Nor is death an absolute to be feared. Death, too, is part of the moving, changing process we call life, part of the cycle. For the stories of immanence do not end with a bang — or even a whimper — they are circular, they are stories about the way the moon wanes and becomes dark, only to wax again, about how the sun dies at the Winter Solstice and is reborn as the year is newly born. The Goddess is Crone and Reaper as well as Mother; the God is the grain that is cut down as well as the seed that is sown. But the harvest, the reaping of herbs — or of any rewards, returns, profits — must be practiced with respect for the balance of life and its continuation in the richest and most diverse forms. The animal herds are culled, not obliterated. When herbs are cut only a few are taken from each separate clump so that they may grow back in future years. Human communities must limit their numbers and their lifestyles to what the land can support without straining resources or displacing other species.

Death, in fact, becomes the source of power-from-within — for only when we acknowledge the ultimate limits both of our power and our responsibility can we be free to bring power forth. We can act freely only when we recognize that we are neither powerless nor omnipotent; that our active will, strong as it may be, is tempered by the activity of other wills, that our needs and desires must be balanced with those of others.

As life and death must be in balance, so must self and community. To act with integrity, we must see ourselves in context, as individuals and as members of a larger community (a society and culture that in turn are part of the biological/geological community of planet earth and the cosmos beyond).

To be a member of that community means both to be shaped by it and to have responsibility for shaping it — for preserving both its balances and the interplay of diversity and richness of life in its fullest expression. No one can live out the fullness of self when she or he is hungry or condemned to a life of poverty and discrimination. A woman cannot be fully herself when her roles are circumscribed, when she is not free to be strong and creative, to control her own body and her own sexuality, to be a leader and to be in touch with power-from-within. People cannot live fully when the color of their skin limits their freedom and opportunities, when their lives are overshadowed by the fear of war or the threat of ecological disaster. To live with integrity in an unjust society we must work for justice. To walk with integrity through a landscape strewn with beer cans, we must stop and pick them up.

Honoring the inherent value of self also means placing a high value on human needs and emotions. Our feelings — even our fears, our anger, our pain — are valued as part of our lives. We cannot be integrated without them. Integrity does not mean trying to get beyond anger or transcend negativity. It means that we stop trying to fit our feelings into the story about the Good Guys versus the Bad Guys; that we see them as carriers of power-from-within.

In the ethics of immanence, sexuality is also sacred, deeply valued, not just as the means of procreation, but as a power that infuses life with vitality and pleasure, as the numinous means of deep connection with others. Sexual integrity means honestly recognizing our own impulses and desires and honoring them, whether or not we choose to act on them. If we value integrity, we must also value diversity in sexual expression and orientation, recognizing that there is no one truth, or one way, that fits everyone.

Sexuality is sacred because through it we make a connection with another self — but it is misused and perverted when it becomes an arena of power-over, a means of treating another — or oneself — as an object. Sexuality, when valued, does not become an obsession. It is the ultimate movement of power-from-within whenever it is welcomed with honesty — in simple erotic passion, in the unfathomable mystery of falling in love, in the committed relationship of marriage, in periods of abstinence and chastity, in affectionate play between friends, or in its infinite other guises, which I will leave to the reader's imagination.

Coercion may be more subtle than physical rape or overt economic pressure. It includes psychological pressures that influence people to ignore their needs or repress their desires, political pressures to focus their sexual drives in so-called acceptable channels, and social pressures. By these standards, the attitudes promoted by most of the major religions are extremely coercive and unethical. When the ethics is based on integrity instead of authority, no one has the right to interfere with another's sexual choice. "All acts of love and pleasure are my rituals," is a statement Witches attribute to the Goddess. Sharing love and pleasure with each other is considered one of the best things human beings can do. A society based on the ethics of immanence would encourage all choices that allow that expression to be most honest, that would make us free to listen to our own deep desires.

Life, being sacred, demands our full participation. The ethical person engages in life and does not withdraw from it. Our ideal is not monastic seclusion or asceticism, but the fully human life lived in the world, involved in community. To be human is, by definition, to be imperfect. We accept our imperfections and are no longer forced to emulate the superhuman standards of the Great Man, a standard from which we must inevitably fall.

Honoring ourselves, our feelings, our human imperfections, allows us to start where we are, and let others start where they are. It means that we can allow ourselves to work like human beings, to stop and rest, to enjoy the stream and the fresh air and each other's company along the way. We do not have to work like automatons — and no one of us is responsible for doing it all. Cleaning up the stream is our collective, communal task.

For justice, inherent in the world and in the ecological balance of the biosphere, operates communally. The kid who throws the beer can may not be disturbed by its presence in the stream. The owner of the chemical company may not be the person who gives birth to a defective child. Nevertheless, their actions have consequences from which they can never wholly escape. And if we are not comforted by the story of a final Day of Judgement, when all scores will be settled, then it becomes an even greater collective responsibility, here and now, to change those practices that destroy the lives of individuals and the interplay of life-forms around us. No external authority — God, Goddess, angel, or convoy of visitors from another planet, will do this for us. *We* must create justice and preserve ecological and social balance. This is the prime concern, the bottom line, the nitty-gritty of the ethics of immanence.

But what makes kids throw cans in the stream? How do we confront what theologians insist on calling the problem of evil?

Evil is a concept that cannot be separated from the stories of duality. Power-over, violence, coercion, domination, hurtful as they are, are not evil in the sense of being part of a force in direct opposition to good. Instead, we can see them as mistakes, processes born of chance that spread because they served some purpose, structures that may now have outlived their usefulness.

The problem of evil is really a problem of randomness. Is the universe entirely controlled, directed, knowable — based on cause and effect — or is there an element of randomness? The new physics tells us that, indeed, there is a basic principle of uncertainty, of chance, at work in the innermost nature of things. Without randomness in a system, there could be nothing new. Or, we could say that because there is randomness at work new things develop, new relationships are formed; some of these further the diversity, the richness of the interplay of life-forms and create beauty — some do not. Power-from-within is also the power to say no, to bind, to cull, to limit, to stop.

To say no, to set a limit, is not necessarily to make a threat or to use power-over another. When 2000 people say no to the licensing of the Diablo Canyon Nuclear Power Plant by blockading and going to jail, they are setting a limit. When hundreds of thousands of Europeans march in the street to protest the presence of nuclear weapons in their countries, they are setting a limit to United States foreign policy.

Setting limits is something every parent must do; but good parents do not have to be authoritarian. You cannot beat children and make them stop throwing temper tantrums, but you can shut the door to the room and walk away, saying, "When you are done screaming, I want to hear what you have to say." The parent who beats the child sees her/him as an object to be controlled; the loving parent who sets limits sees that the temper tantrum expresses a moment in the relationship of child and parent. It is not something the child is doing alone, the parent plays a role in the child's tantrums, and when the parent changes her/his relationship the child's behavior too must change.

Nor is the nuclear plant an object; it too is one aspect of a complex system of relationships, that we can change by withdrawing our cooperation. And if we want to stop kids from throwing beer cans into the stream, we must somehow change our relationship to them, and, in so doing, change their relationship to the stream and, perhaps, to themselves.

Because every change we make is a change in a relationship in which we take part, we cannot cause change without changing ourselves. That is the origin of the magical dictum, "What you send returns to you three times over." In shaping any energy, we take the shape we create, we become the power that we call forth.

Immanent justice rests on the first principle of magic: all things are interconnected. All is relationship. Perhaps the ultimate ethic of immanence is to choose to make that relationship one of love; love of self and of others, erotic love, transforming love, affectionate love, delighted love for the myriad forms of life as it evolves and changes, for the redwood and the mayfly, for the blue whale and the snail darter, for wind and sun and the waxing and waning moon; caring love for the Cambodian child, the Haitian refugee, the farmer in El Salvador, the restless ghetto teenager; love for all the eternally self-creating world, love of the light and the mysterious darkness, and raging love against all that would diminish the unspeakable beauty of the world.

Love connects; love transforms. Loving the world, for what it is and our vision of what it could be, loving the world's creatures (including ourselves), caring for the stream, picking up the garbage at our feet, we can transform. We can reclaim our power to shape ourselves and the world around us.

Chapter Four

❦

Reclaiming Personal Power: Magic as Will

"Are you ready to hunt the shadow?" I ask Joy. She nods, and the blue-violet glow of her aura deepens, telling me she has slipped a shade further into the waking-dreaming state we call trance. She greets the four directions, casting the internal circle that becomes the temporary boundary protecting the self from merging with and getting lost among the shadows of the under-world.

She heads west, because it is the direction that feels *least* comfortable. The West is unbearably hot and dry. She is climbing a rocky hillside. "I should have started earlier," she cries. The climb is steep and there's a sharp fall-off to her right. "I'm dizzy." She claps her left hand over her eyes. "It's narrow — there's just space — nothing to support me."

She pulls herself along and stops, shaking. The fear is terrible. I stay with her, watching her breathing as she struggles to go on. A crack in the rock opens into a cave; she is pulling herself along, crawling on hands and knees. "I'm scared — I could get lost, get in and not be able to get out. I shouldn't be doing this by myself." She calls for a lost lover, for parts of herself that embody her power, but these cannot help her. Only a rope and a miner's lantern appear. The cave gives way to a small ledge on the side of the

45

cliff; she clings with her fingers, gasping and trembling, genuinely terrified. I put my hand on her belly, and tell her to breathe deeply, to remember the protective cape and spear she found in an earlier trance . . .

She affixes the rope to the ledge, and tries to let herself down. "I'm caught between the rocks!" she cries out. "The cliff that I'm squeezed against — it's alive! I see faces — monsters. They're laughing at me — mocking."

"What are they saying?"

"One says, 'So you're finally here — you think you can beat me but you can't' . . . I'm afraid the rope's going to break."

"Can you get the monster's name?" I ask, worried.

"It's awful!" Her hands are grasping the air, as if it were a rope, and her face is pulled down in distress. She writhes on the mat, breathing hard. "It's got big eyes — like an octopus — it's slimy — slippery — OH, NO! IT CAN'T BE! OH, NO! OH, NO!"

"Fight it, Joy!"

"I can't! It's stronger than I am!"

"Use your spear," I say, thinking, "Oh shit! I've let her get too far into this — and now I can't help her out."

"DON'T DROP ME!" she screams. "LET ME GO! DON'T DROP ME! LET ME GO!"

"Use your spear," I say, thinking, "She's talking about her parents."

"The monsters take and snap it in two! They're ripping up my cape. I'M BEING ABSORBED BY IT! THE MONSTER IS AB-SORBING ME! IF I DON'T LET IT, I'LL BE SQUEEZED TO DEATH!"

"Fight it, Joy," I urge.

The battle continues.

Reclaiming our personal power is a healing journey, but not an easy one. For the human psyche forms itself from the relationships one has with other people, things, and institutions. It is a mirror of culture. The relationships we have mostly known and the institutions of our culture are based on power-over. So our inner land-scapes are those of the stories of estrangement, and they are peopled by creatures that dominate or must be dominated. To free ourselves, to recover our power-from-within, the power to feel, to heal, to love, to create, to shape our futures, to change our social structures, we may have to do battle with our own thought-forms. We may have to change the inner territory as well as the outer, confront the forms of authority that we carry within. For we shape culture in our own image, just as it shapes us. If we are unwilling to confront ourselves, we risk reproducing the land-scape of domination in the very structures we create to challenge authority.

Change is frightening, but Witches have a saying, "Where there's fear, there's power." The culture of estrangement teaches men to deny fear — and women to let fear control them. Yet if we learn to feel our fear without letting it stop us, fear can become an ally, a sign to tell us that something we have encountered can be transformed. Often, our true strength is not in the things that represent what is familiar, comfortable, positive — but in our fears and even in our resistance to change. And so Joy will find her power, in the end, not in her image of her lover, or in her tools, but in the monsters and in the strength of their stranglehold.

Let us follow her journey meandering and digressing along the way, so that her battle can teach us some of the underlying princi-ples of the work of changing consciousness.

First note that Joy does not go alone. I am there — not to guide but to support her. Since I have been trained both as a Witch and as a psychotherapist, I know an array of techniques for getting people out of tight places. I don't intend to use them. My work is both simpler and infinitely more difficult; it is work that could be done by a friend, a lover, a coven member, a companion, but *must* be done by somebody — to be there for her and yet to let her have her own fears, her own journey, her own battle. I am there to stand for the human community, to hear and accept her fear, her grief, her monsters, her pain, her darkness, without taking them over or trying to cure them, so that what she encounters in herself will not isolate her, but will draw her closer to other human beings.

The solitary vision quest is romantic, but the cultures that send their adolescents out into the wilderness alone to discover their true names are very different from ours. A potential shaman raised in a tribal culture has a different psychic structure than that of a person raised in the culture of estrangement. In a tribe, the individual self mirrors the collective, the group mind; the solitary quest is a way of breaking free, of discovering one's unique, individuated self, so as to bring back something new to the group. But in our culture we are raised separately — to the point of pain. We are trained to compete from our earliest years, taught that drives and desires and bodies are objects to be controlled. What we encounter alone in the underworld, should we somehow manage to get there, are the ghosts and demons of our culture — the thought-forms of power-over. They can be enormously strong, they have all the force of Western culture behind them. They sustain their power with the constant mantra, the whisper in the ear that says, "You are separated, isolated, alone." There is no way that any one of us can defeat that whisper alone. No matter how strong we become, how many inner demons we conquer, how many insights we gain, how many spirit allies we acquire, we are ultimately confirming our own isolation unless our journey is grounded in a relationship with living, breathing, human beings.

And other living human beings can supply a perspective on our demons and our powers that we ourselves do not have, a perspective that can save our lives, or at least our sanity.

Let me illustrate with a personal story. Years ago, I made a meager living for a short while reading Tarot cards and palms at a succession of "Psychic Faires." These gatherings took place at hotels or bookstores, where twenty or thirty psychics of mixed breed, and various traditions, skills, and levels of integrity would perform fifteen-minute readings, often for hours or days on end. During slow times, we would entertain ourselves by reading for each other. One of the psychics who read for me told me that I was destined to be a great teacher and healer, but that it would be a "hard and lonely path," and people would not understand me. I took this with reservations — I have yet to meet the psychic (including myself) who will tell someone, "Face it, kid, your talents are mediocre at best — have you considered getting a regular job?" However, it disturbed me. I felt I must make a choice.

A few nights later I dreamt that I was on a train. The train passed through a desert and made many stops at towns the names of which all began "Rio _____." (*Rio* means "river" in Spanish.) A man and a woman were cleaning up ashtrays and cups in the smoking car. The woman told me to help. "Why should she help?" the man asked. "She doesn't even know if she's on the train or off the train." "It doesn't matter," the woman said. "She still has to do the work."

The next day, I decided to explore the dream further in trance. It was a sunny day, rare in San Francisco, so I went to Golden Gate Park, lay down under a tree, and relaxed — not very wise, since it was not a safe place. Without using a formal induction or much structure — also unwise — I let the dream take form again, until I was standing and talking to the man.

"What is this train, anyway?" I asked him.

"You know damn well," he replied.

"You mean this is magic — spiritual — Witchy work?"

"That's it."

I hesitated, because, on the one hand, I did know that I was already committed to doing it, or I wouldn't have gotten that far; on the other hand, the "hard and lonely path" did not attract me at all.

"Well," I finally said, "I'll go, but only on my own terms. I won't go without equal companions."

At that point, the man grinned. The woman suddenly appeared, grinning. It seemed that whole grandstands full of spirits had joined them. All shouted in unison, "Right, dummy! How could you ever do anything on any other terms but your own?"

I awoke with two further realizations. The first was that, while I was entranced, someone had come up quietly and stolen my purse.

The second was that I had come through a more dangerous test than I realized. Because if I had answered the man differently, if I had, perhaps, felt compelled to accept the burden of the hard and lonely path, those were the terms on which my further journey would have continued. And it would have been a false journey, as well as a hard and lonely one — based on self-inflation, leading not to growth but to a dreary playing-out and replaying of my own narcissism.

But there was a third realization I didn't come to, one that perhaps a living companion on that journey might have been able to point out — which was that in raising the question of equal companions, I showed that I really didn't feel equal. If I had, it would never have occurred to me that companions could be anything else. Although consciously I believed firmly in equality and collectivity, my unconscious identity was still that of the precocious child, the smartest kid in the class. Now I created situations in which I could remain one step above as the teacher, the focal point. Yet being central, keeping others peripheral, is a very lonely position.

Fortunately, I did not choose the hard and lonely path. The train, so to speak, that I am on contains many other passengers — real people, such as my friends, my students, my coveners, and my husband who are not afraid to challenge my assumptions, by saying, "Hey, you say there's equality here, but you have all the power!" Those challenges have been more frightening, more painful, and, at the same time, more truly transformative, than a thousand astral battles or cosmic train rides.

But they were transformative because I knew that my companions accepted me. They might not like that aspect of me that felt set-apart — but they did like *me*, and could accept me with my human flaws. I didn't have to hate my set-apart-self, which was, after all, not a unique piece of nastiness, but something fairly common among human beings, who would most all like to feel special, above others, not bound by the ordinary rules. And my set-apart-self also has positive aspects: it is creative; it makes me a writer; it allows me to speak in public, to teach.

It is a source of power for me.

Yet the power is creative because it is grounded in community. It is checked and challenged; the power of others whom I love and respect rubs against it. If it had pushed me further into isolation instead of pulling me into contact with others, it would have destroyed whatever true creativity was within me.

Let us return to Joy's story. Her journey is different from mine, because she has companionship. Her trance is also far more structured than mine was. And that is another important difference. I begin by telling her certain things: that she is going down into her place of power, the place that is the center of herself, where she can be in touch with the deepest parts of herself, where she will be safe and in control, where she can speak and move and yet remain in deep awareness, and where she will remember clearly everything that happens to her. I tell her that every time she needs to, or wants to, she can be back in her ordinary waking state of consciousness. The structure, the formal ritual of the induction, sets the trance state firmly apart from waking consciousness, makes it a separate territory that can be entered or left at will. These cautions do not differ from standard hypnotic techniques — except perhaps that I give the control to her, not to myself. I encourage her memory, not her forgetfulness, because the experience is hers and can only be fully integrated if it is remembered. Actually, Joy may not completely remember the trance, and I may not either, so I write it down. Like a dream, a trance fades quickly.

"Relax," I tell Joy, "and feel yourself rooted in the earth. Feel the energy enter into you, through your feet and the base of your spine. Breathe from your belly. Feel the breath move up through your body — to your spine, your belly, your heart — feel it radiate out from your heart, down your shoulders, down your arms, into your hands. Let it rise up past your throat, your head, your Third Eye, relaxing and soothing as it passes. Let it flow out the top of your head, like branches that sweep back down to touch the earth again, surrounding you, protecting you."

In a sense, all the images of Joy's trances could be seen as metaphors for movements of energy. But no modern English word quite conveys the meaning of *energy* in the sense I'm using it here. The Chinese *ch'i,* the Hindu *prana,* and the Hawaiian *mana* are clearer terms for the idea of an underlying vital energy that infuses, creates, and sustains the physical body; it moves in our emotions, feelings, and thoughts, and is the underlying fabric of the material world. Since energy is a concept central to magic, it is worthwhile digressing a bit longer to discuss it in some detail.

Energy is a freely moving fluid substance, and it also takes on patterns of varying stability that can be thought of as standing waves. Each human being is an energy pattern that many people can literally see and feel. I see the energy pattern as a treelike form, with roots in the energy-field of the earth, currents running up the body on both sides, at the front, back, and through the center — currents that are themselves hollow and can conduct energy downward as well. Energy vortices exist that correspond to the Hindu *chakras*. Branches extend down the arms and out through the hands. They also sweep up from the top of the head, down and around the body back to earth, creating the surrounding energy-field or aura, which is a protective yet permeable filter.

Although my description is metaphoric, vital energy is real and can be perceived, molded, directed, and changed. Western science is just beginning to acknowledge its existence, attempting to verify it with Kirlian photography, for example. Other cultures have always known it exists. It is the basis for Chinese acupuncture and Hindu yoga, as well as psychic healings, worldwide.

Emotional, psychological, and physical disturbances are also disturbances in the energy pattern, and vice versa. Each of the chakras is associated with particular emotions, body systems, and abilities. Although systems differ somewhat, the correlations I use are:

Base-of-the-spine: security, survival.

Sexual: sexuality.

Womb/belly: vitality (where vital energy is taken in, stored and radiated out to the body).

Solar Plexus: power (where power is sent out from the body; not counted as a chakra in some systems).

Heart: love, anger, emotional connections with others.

Throat: expression, communication.

Third Eye: psychic sight (in the center of the forehead).

Crown: in Eastern traditions — enlightenment; in daily life — energy intake and exhaust point (in the top of the skull).

Our personal energy field is never wholly separate from the earth's energy-field. We are each a ripple in the earth's aura. When we connect deeply with that greater source of energy, we can renew and replenish our own vitality constantly. Anything negative we encounter can pass through us into the earth, as lightning can be grounded. If we become partially disconnected, as we often do under stress, we become un-grounded in every sense. We are easily drained, fragmented, unable to concentrate or proceed deliberately, and emotionally ragged.

We begin all magical work by grounding, breathing from the belly (to open the lower *chakras*), and visualizing a connection, our roots in the earth (to draw energy from the earth so that we do not need to deplete our own). One of my tasks during Joy's trance will be to help her stay grounded throughout our work together by reminding her to breathe, by touching her when I myself am grounded.

When Joy has established an energy connection with the earth, I begin the trance induction. "You are sinking down, down, on a beautiful red cloud," I say, "and your whole body is red, as you go drifting and floating, down, down, rocking gently, on a beautiful orange cloud." I continue through the spectrum. I am grounded; I am breathing from my belly and my voice is low, relaxed, my words flowing in a smooth stream. We reach the blue cloud, the violet cloud. ". . . And your whole body is violet — and you go drifting and floating, rocking gently, and landing, very gently, very very softly, in the center of your own place of power."

We can each create a place of power in the *underworld*,[1] the underlying dimension of energy patterns beneath the physical world. Just as the light we see is only a small portion of the spectrum of radiation, we could say that the reality we generally experience is also only a small portion of the spectrum of possibility. Our minds and our senses cannot directly experience the deeper levels of reality anymore than our eyes can see radio waves; instead, we translate the deeper levels into images resembling those with which we are familiar, and through such images, we can shape the patterns of energy they represent.

The underworld has many levels. Those nearest the surface, the first we encounter, are personal, subjective, our own unconscious pattterns. Most of us never journey any deeper than the personal; until we are familiar with the subjective underworld, have cleared it of the worst of its demons, and can pass through its shadows in comfort, we cannot go deeper, into the communal, the cultural, the objective levels.

The place of power is our home-away-from-home in the personal underworld, our image of center, of strength, the place where we begin each journey and where we stop and re-center before returning to ordinary space and time. It is a place from which we can survey the landscape of the self.

To follow Joy's journey, or to make our own, we also need a framework for discussing the many aspects of what we call *self*. In the magical tradition I follow, we say that each of us is made up of three selves; Deep Self, Talking Self, and Younger Self. Deep Self is essence, the self that underlies personality, that goes beyond time or any one lifetime. It is the matrix from which the other selves are born — the Goddess manifesting. Although these are all metaphors, they are useful ways of thinking-in-things about who we are and how we develop.

From Deep Self, the matrix, Younger Self is born with our physical birth. Just as a baby sucks in milk, Younger Self grows and develops by sucking in energy, taking in love, from those who love and care for us. Younger Self reaches out to the world, grasps pieces of it, takes them in, and experiences them. It imitates actions, expressions, gestures; and, as it grows, the movements, energies, and sensations it mimics gradually form into images that are taken in and held, forming the internal landscape in which we live, and the creatures who people it.

Younger Self also feels hunger and satisfaction, pain and elation, terror of abandonment, and the security of love. Within the images and sensory memories of Younger Self are locked deep feelings and enormous energies. The landscape, the imagery, and the scenarios Younger Self creates become the patterns in which we live our lives, because they determine the patterns our energies take.

The roots of Talking Self also go deep into infancy, but Talking Self is not fully born until we grow comfortable with language. While Younger Self experiences and senses, Talking Self structures sensations, brings order, classifies, categorizes, and names. Language is our most powerful tool for structuring reality.

What is named becomes separated out. A name creates a boundary between the thing named and everything else. Talking Self's major task, when we are first learning speech, is to allow us to name ourselves, to separate our "I-ness" from "not-I". As infants, we share an energy-field with our mothers (or primary caretakers, if you prefer). The field expands, becomes more flexible; what we absorb from our mothers becomes (for most of us) less of an encompassing field and more of an internalized source of warmth, security, self-esteem. But not until we become language-users can we name that warmth, that esteem *me*, and grasp that mother exists separately from the image we have taken in of her — that she, in fact, lives around her own center, which she calls *me*. The boundaries and structures that Talking Self creates give us freedom to be individuals, to be separate from others. But they may also become constricting, overly narrow, or rigid.

Imagine Talking Self's domain as a house we live in, and Younger Self's domain as a garden that surrounds it completely. Beneath the garden are the caves and wells of Deep Self; outside it are the other realms of reality, the wilderness. There is no clear dividing line between Younger Self's garden and the wild until Talking Self builds a wall. Younger Self constantly brings in plants and animals. Some of them Talking Self may name and set out carefully in rows, others grow in any nook or cranny they can find. The garden of Younger Self may be pleasant and inviting, or overgrown with brambles and poison oak; it may contain nurturing plants or devouring monsters, the paths may be clear or impassable.

In order to walk out into the wild, we must first pass through the garden. Or, conversely, in order to examine any piece of the wild Younger Self brings in, in order to name it and set it on the shelves of our house, it must first be brought through the garden.

The clearer the paths are, the more familiar we are with their windings and turnings, the friendlier we are with the creatures that inhabit them, the clearer are our contacts with external reality — both physical and metaphysical.

So the place of power is the spot from which we can survey the garden, see what needs weeding or transplanting, explore the corners where shadows may be lurking.

When Joy reaches her place of power, I ask her to turn to each of the four directions and note what she can see and hear and feel and sense. In doing so, she casts a magic circle.

The magic circle, the four quarters and center, is another structured way we can think-in-things about the self. Each time we experience the circle, we experience our present inner condition, vividly, sensually. What we see in the circle tells us what to pay attention to.

In magic we often speak of *correspondences*. We say that the East corresponds with the element of air, with mind and breath. The South corresponds with fire, with energy and will. The West corresponds with water, with feelings and emotions. The North corresponds with earth, with the body, with silence, with material reality — including all its potentials and limitations.

Correspondences are simply clusters of experiences. If I experience the East, the rising sun, the dawning light, I know, in my body, my heart, about the awakening of ideas, the dawning of inspiration. If I feel the air, its swiftness, its changeability, its presence that is so real yet unseen, I know something about thought. And if I use the tool of the East, the Witch's knife, the *athame*, I see that it has a blade that can cut things apart, that can make separations, and that ability is a tool I need in order to think clearly.

The fire of the sun at noon can show me my own radiant energy, and when I hold the tool of the South, the wand, in my hand, and I experience it as once part of a living tree, I know the treelike pattern of my own subtle energy-form; I feel the way that energy can be channeled and expressed. The waves, the tides, the deep wells and still pools of the West show me the patterns of my own emotions; like water, they flow, they merge, they take the shape of whatever container appears, yet the tool of the West is the cup that contains the water. The earth of the North, if I dig in it, plant in it, experience the rounds of growth, decay, new growth, will teach me endlessly about renewal, and endings, birth and death; its tool is the pentacle, a new cluster of *things* that stands for my own body, its limbs and head, the five of my fingers, my toes, my senses.

The quarters balance each other; experiencing each one I can experience the need for its polar opposite. When I see and think in the East, using my knife to make divisions, I must also be able to feel, to flow, to merge, or I become cut apart. If I burst forth with expression, with passion, in the South, I must also be able to contain the fire, to ring it with stones from the North, or I risk burning down the forest. And if I allow myself, in the West, to merge, I need the power of the East to separate again. The earth, without the sun's fire, remains dead, silence without expression.

When we stand in the place of power and greet each direction in turn, we are doing two things. First, we are *casting the circle*; creating an internal boundary that makes us safe in dropping the structures with which we are familiar. The circle is itself a structure; it says to Talking Self, "Look, you who need so much order, within my boundaries you can forget your usual names, you can change categories. You will be faced with many new sensations and experiences, but don't panic. I'm here, standing guard — and only within my bounds do you take your holiday. When I am dissolved, then you can bring back the usual divisions, the ordinary boundaries. Until then, relax."

Ordinary consciousness is a marvelous thing; it allows us to live in the world, to think plan, create, work, and do. Practicing magic, we respect our ordinary boundaries: our goal is not to escape them, not to destroy the separations and divisions, but to slip in and out of them at will, with flexibility. For the boundaries, the separations, the names themselves are, no less than our experiences of oneness, manifestations of the Goddess, who is that-which-creates-structure.

The circle is also an energy pattern that contains whatever

power we raise so that power can be focused and concentrated. It protects us from intrusion, forming a barrier to any unwanted forces.

Casting the circle allows us to experience each direction as it is for us in the moment — to see where we are out of balance, what cluster of qualities needs work. So, for Joy, the East is warm and welcoming — a green garden and sunlit forest. The South is an ocean beach; it has been stormy in the past, but today it is calm. The West is a desert, bleak and uninviting. The North is another deep forest, green, cool, and comforting. The directions do not correspond, necessarily, with the traditional associations of elements because they reflect her internal geography. Her West, her emotional life, does not feel like an ocean, with its deep tides and burgeoning life. It feels, at the moment, like a desert, blasted with heat, lonely, empty, with no oasis in sight.

"Are you ready to hunt the shadow?" I ask when she has greeted each direction. Although we have agreed beforehand on the course of this journey, she is free to change it any time. Hunting shadows of the self can be dangerous; it means confronting and changing the most unknown and fearful of one's inner structures and energy patterns.

Joy's readiness for the transformation has come only after months of preparation. We have made several journeys into the dark together before, and we have spent many weeks talking about them, exploring the images and integrating a growing sense of her own power.

The shadow first appeared in an earlier trance. That day, Joy had gone to the South, which was stormy and turbulent. She had found a group of figures around a campfire; some could be seen clearly, one was a shadow. Later she had gone into a double garden; one side was full of flowers, the other, across a bridge, was a prison. In the prison was a bear, rattling its cage. Joy asked the bear what it would give her if she let it out. "Immortality, and the ability to growl," it replied.

The caged bear, in the language of things, expressed the way Joy felt and controlled her own energy — enormous power, potential danger, confined in structures that were too restrictive, that contained the danger but kept the power from being expressed, structures that were themselves being shaken. "Release the bear of the South, the power of your anger and your will, your animal nature — and you will reconnect with life. You will be able to growl, to express your power, to say no," was what the image said. For weeks, Joy had been working with the bear, experiencing its strength, growling literally as well as in her imagination — and making changes in relationships with real people outside herself, learning to say "no," to say, "This is what I feel." Now, armed with the bear's penetrating spear and protective cape, she felt ready to face the shadowy parts of herself that were still unseen.

For Joy, we could say, the process of change begins in the East; with a deliberate separating-out of her patterns of interaction, an induced dissociation, so that she can *see* them. Because she has a well-developed talking Self, seeing the patterns as *things* is useful. Joy understands herself already; she knows intellectually the roots of her problems, could name and discuss them and remain unable to change them. Experiencing the patterns as *things* forces her to dive below the categories her Talking Self creates, to free herself from her own tendency to rate, judge, rationalize, and attempt to control her own feelings in a way that imprisons them.

If Joy were different, if she, by nature or because of her experiences, thought-in-things so exclusively that she had trouble naming her feelings with words; if, indeed, she felt her feelings to be hallucinations, landscapes, voices, images; if her Talking Self were too weak to establish firm boundaries between what was inside her and what was outside, so that the bear in the cage seemed more real to her than I did, our work would be very different.

If Joy lived in terror that the bear might escape, overrun her, and cause destruction — to herself, to anyone she was close to, we might strive to place a more secure lock on the cage, or to construct a more pleasant, open, but still safe bear-pit. She might attempt to feed the bear cautiously between the bars. The work would have more to do with the North — with creating structure, strengthening her ability to contain her power before she can feel

safe to release it. We might have to enlist Younger Self's cooperation in building a Talking Self up from the bare foundations.
Instead of working in trance, we might work at naming the things
in different ways — as feelings, as past experiences, as aspects of
herself. Instead of learning to hold contradictory thoughts in mind
at the same time, we might work at accepting contradictory
feelings.

Or, let us imagine that Joy's Talking Self, faced with a garden
overrun with angry bears, had, under the stimulus of terror, gone
to work overtime and created an elaborate, mazelike structure, in
order to bind the energies that otherwise might seem uncontrol-
lable. In this structure, composed of fragments of the culture's
thought-forms hooked together, the caged bear might be Jesus,
and she, Joy, might have been chosen to hide him from his enemies. She might develop elaborate theories of the complex con-
spiracies his enemies had created; she might be convinced that she
was set apart for special persecution because of her secret; or she
might develop elaborate rituals to assure his safety. Our task
would again be different — to establish trust, to introduce
flexibility.

In each case, readiness is the key question, and the most difficult to answer. The tools of magic can be dangerous as well as
powerful: thinking-in-things can release energies that might better
be contained. Many people would insist that the tools should only
be given to people termed *professionals* — those who are trained
in diagnosis, who could label a hypothetical Joy "schizophrenic"
or a "paranoid psychotic," and, undoubtedly, prescribe the
proper drug to dampen her symptoms.

I disagree. Even if professionals, on the whole, had a high rate
of success with psychotic or borderline patients (and they don't),
even if psychiatric drugs were not addictive and dangerous (and
they are), even if mental hospitals were pleasant, healing places to
be, instead of prisons, even if mental health professionals were
not the lineal descendants of the witchburners, we cannot reclaim
our power, as individuals and as a community, unless we reclaim
our power to heal. Professionalism itself reinforces the thought-
forms of estrangement and alienation.[2] Whatever a therapist may

do for me — and a good therapist can indeed do a lot — it is still, ultimately, within a community of friends, lovers, family, co-workers, that I find intimacy and meaning. Community is the ultimate healer. And it is the community — the conditions and relationships within it — that causes unbearable pain to people, that ultimately needs to be healed.

Fortunately, there is one infallible test that tells us with whom it is safe for us to work magic. We can ask: "Do I genuinely like this person? Do I really want to be doing this now, at this moment?" If the answer to these questions is no, then we are not going to be helpful and our trancework may even be harmful. If we must change the questions in order to answer yes, asking: Do I feel obligated to this person? *Should* I like her or him? Will I hurt this person's feelings if I say no? Would I like this person if she/he changed? We are really feeling that we don't like the person as she/he is. Of course, the people most desperately in need of help are often the least likeable. However, we can freely offer practical or material help with fewer risks involved for both parties than when we misjudge our limitations in working magic.

I genuinely like Joy, and I trust her readiness and her judgement. She begins her journey in the West, and soon finds herself terrified, clinging to a cliff, afraid of falling. Her internal landscape expresses in *things* the quality of relationships she has experienced in her family and in the institutions of this culture.

Joy holds on to the cliff, she clings tightly, she is afraid to fall. The conflicts in her life center around the theme of holding on/ letting go — the fear of falling. Letting go of her lover, holding on to her mother, her fear of her parents' holding on too tightly to her, letting go of her father and mourning his death, holding on to wakefulness, falling asleep, holding on to control, to anger. Over and over, she is telling herself — she is living in herself — the story of The Fall.

Yet we know that the other side of that story is Making It. Joy was taught the story in her family, in the schools she went to, at the jobs where she worked, in the movies and the television programs she watched — for this is the story that characterizes

American life. We are led to believe that everybody can Make It, if they work hard enough. Yet in reality the rewards of the culture are reserved for an elite few, predestined for success by sex, class, and background. A sprinkling of others *do* Make It — just enough to perpetuate the myth that those who Fall by the wayside are victims of their own personal failings, not of the odds stacked against them. And even the elite must cling to what they have, for the abyss of failure yawns beneath their feet. One misstep, and over the edge they too can Fall. They can get a bad grade, or lose a job, a promotion, a lover, a gamble — lose whatever replaces for them the sense of inherent value this culture denies to their simple beings.

The cliffs Joy clings to become monsters. They jeer at her and mock her; try as she will, she cannot defeat them. One monster picks her up in its hand, begins to squeeze. She is faced with annihilation.

What are the monsters? At the time, I heard Joy's cry, "Don't drop me! Let me go!" as the cry of a child to its parents: "Let me separate, let me be myself without cutting me off." Yet the monsters are not her parents. They are more, even, than the embodiment of her relationship with her parents. The monsters are the appearance on Joy's landscape of a psychic structure common to all of us raised in this culture; the aspect of the self that jeers, sneers, humiliates, mocks, exults, "You think you can beat me but you can't." I call it the *self-hater*, after Doris Lessing, who describes it in *The Four-Gated City:*

> Then one of the voices detached itself and came close into her inner ear: it was loud, or it was soft; it was jaunty, or it was intimately jeering, but its abiding quality was an antagonism; a dislike of Martha; and Martha was crying out against it — she needed to apologize, to beg for forgiveness, she needed to please and to buy absolution, she was grovelling on the carpet, weeping, while the voice uttered accusations of hatred.[3]

To the schizophrenic heroine of Hannah Green's *I Never Promised You a Rose Garden*, the self-hater appears as an assembly of accusing, punishing voices she calls the "Collect", whose Censor has the duty of keeping her "worlds" apart, keeping her realities separate.[4] In the course of journeys we have taken in my coven to confront the self-hater, it has appeared as a monster, as a toad, as an ugly little creep, creeping about, as a wooden puppet with a clacking jaw. Although it takes on varied forms, it is always characterized by the mocking tone of its messages.

The self-hater is the inner representation of power-over. We have internalized it, not just from our parents, but from every institution in society with which we have contact. It is the structure in the psyche that perpetuates domination. It reminds us of our helplessness, our powerlessness. It blames the victim; it tells us we are bad when bad things happen to us, that we do not have the right to be, to feel, to do what we do. It is the inner gun that keeps us in an inner prison.

All of us, from infancy, have an inherent sense of helplessness, a vulnerability to situations in which we feel powerless.[5] As infants, as small children, we were helpless and entirely dependent for our comfort, for sustenance, for our very existence, on the care and good will of our mothers.[6] To an infant, abandonment, even temporarily, feels like death. But an infant or a tiny child has no word *death* — to name and contain what is in reality a feeling — a terror, boundless because it is nameless, a fear that goes bone-deep, that lies at our core, below words or even images, because we learned it before we knew words or perceived images. It is welded to that other feeling we knew in infancy: the primal, whole-bodied bliss, the comfort, the contentment of belly and blood when the milk flowed and we were loved and warm.

The terror becomes bound progressively as we grow older and develop strengths that help us cope with it. For most of us, the lucky ones, the so-called emotionally healthy ones, the fear that was originally conceived as, "I will die" becomes "Mommy will die;" then, "Mommy will stop loving me;" then, "Mommy will not approve of me." Yet the first fear is not gone, it is only covered over; perhaps it also binds our ability to experience its twin — primal joy in the body. Yet the covering is never entirely secure. Any separation, any rejection, sometimes any criticism, can threaten the delicate edifice of our sense of self-worth, can echo that primal terror.

The institutions of domination play on that terror. We are threatened with loss of approval, esteem, even livelihood if we fail in their schools or on their jobs. If we directly confront their authority, we must face the reality of their power to annihilate the power of the courts, the prisons, the guns. Every experience within an institution is a confrontation with the self-hater on its home ground.

The self-hater within is not just an internalized institution, however, nor is it an internalized person. It is a *thing* that embodies the relationship of domination; it makes us victim and persecutor both. The monster is not just the agent squeezing Joy to death; it is also her sense of helplessness, her conviction that she cannot win the battle. We dominate ourselves more thoroughly than institutions can.

For example, shortly after Reagan's election, I spoke at a university and suggested that we each write him a letter expressing our political stand, as an act of taking power. Many women were afraid. "I will get my name on a list," was a common worry. "It won't make any difference, anyway," was another. So although political repression has not yet progressed in this country to the point at which writing to one's president is a dangerous act, people repress themselves out of fear to a greater degree than any authority would dare. The self-hater is the voice that tells us we are each uniquely responsible for our pain and its solutions, that we are alone. And so, although each of us may, alone, have only a very small voice, we are willing, out of a sense of futility (a defense against fear) to throw away the voice that we do have, which might, combined with other voices, have become a loud roar, a bear's growl.

To reclaim our power, to change our internal landscape, we must confront the self-hater. As the Shaman descends into the place of death and dismemberment, we also must descend into fear, into terror, into despair itself. The confrontation must be more than intellectual. Joy does it as a trance journey, the culmination of many months of emotional work with her emotions and actions. Some people do it as a physical journey, a trip into the wilderness. Chapter 9, "Ritual as Bonding; Action as Ritual," talks about a political action as the confrontation. However the battle is fought, it is not fought once but many times, in many ways and in many dimensions.

Wielding fear, despair, and helplessness as its weapons, the self-hater takes its strategies from the stories of estrangement. Again and again, it tries to pull us into Good Guys/Bad Guys conflicts, by tricking us, over and over again, into defending the one truth entrusted to the Chosen Few, especially in movements that radically challenge the present authorities. Over our heads it holds the threat of Apocalypse, of The Fall, i.e., the threat of annihilation.

The first weapon we have in the battle is the knife of the East — our ability to name, to separate out the monsters and dissect them to find out what they are. But the knife is not enough to win the battle.

And so we turn to the quarter of the South, the direction of energy, fire, and will. Will is that quality found in the depths below despair, when we have looked at annihilation head-on, faced our grief and anguish, and then made the decision to act so as to cause change.[7] Will is the fighting spirit, that quality that says, "Yes, doom may be coming, but in that moment between the whistle and the flash, I will know that I have done my utmost to stop the holocaust, that I have worked to assure the survival of life."

When we think-in-things about will, we think of fire. Will is the energy of anger, aggression, of burning rage, released from the self-hater's grip and consciously directed. Its tool is the wand that channels energy, that transforms, that bridges heaven and earth, that turns ideas into realities. Fire also means *expression*. The finding of our will is tied to the expression of feelings, because expression frees bound energies. When we express our feelings, we assert our right to feel them, our right to be. Anger and rage especially fuel the self-hater when we cannot express them. We may fear that our own anger will evoke the annihilation that terrifies us — that it may cause the loss of someone we love, or cause that person to stop loving us. Yet we cannot own our power without owning our anger. For anger is energy — the deep, energy of the life-force that arises in response to threat. It gives us the strength to meet danger.

In Joy's battle, her anger, her own willingness to fight — to scream, yell, beat the pillows on the bed, make sounds, and use her voice — becomes the tool with which the monsters are defeated. Although ultimately we want to win the battle, we may first have to lose, have to let ourselves be dissolved and experience annihilation, if only to stop running in terror from it. We may, like Joy, be absorbed by our monsters.

Joy fights, but she's losing. I'm staying with her energy, watching the patterns change. Her aura glows as she breathes power up from the earth. She writhes on the bed, gasps and yells, and then suddenly she stops resisting.

"I'm being absorbed into the monster's arm," she whispers, "through its blood stream up into its brain. It's like a control room — there's somebody sitting at the panel. OH, NO! IT CAN'T BE! IT CAN'T BE!"

"What is it?"

"It's my Dad! He's at the controls. How can it be? It can't be."

"Her Dad," I think. "I thought it was her relationship with her mother. Can this be about her anger at him for dying — and her struggle to let him go?"

"He looks all green and decayed and sickly. There's four big puppets, they're dancing on strings and he's pulling the strings. They're mocking me."

"Can you get their names?" I ask. If she can get their names, she has power with them — this is one of the oldest magical principles, and a sound one. A name anchors an image to Talking Self, forces it into consciousness, makes it susceptible to conscious understanding.

"The first one — he has a terrible grin, and big teeth — his name is Joseph. Then there's one with awful eyes, Allen. He's trying to hit me."

"What are you going to do?"

"Stop it." She fights, this time with a sense of confidence that she lacked before. She has faced her terror and found out what it is; now she has nothing more to lose and so her power flows freely. This time she wins. But there are more monsters.

"There's one with a yellow scarf around her neck. She's trying to strangle me with it. Her name is Mary." Again, she fights and overcomes another monster. "The last one is just a skeleton too, he's attacking me."

The fight begins again. Joy uses her magical tools, knife and wand, breathes fire up from the earth, and scorches the skeletons. The control room is ablaze.

"I pour water to cool it," she says; "now I'm in control."

Joy's knife — her ability to understand — is not enough to free herself. She wins the battle when she brings in her wand, her energy, her choice to fight. The control room goes up in flames that scorch but transform.

The monster, in part, is animated by her father; it is the image in which she can experience the quality of his energy. When she is absorbed by the monster, her independent, self-naming, self-defining part gives in to the aspect of her that feels like a child, that is willing to take the child's position of helplessness, dependency. But when she reaches for her wand, her will, her consciously directed energy, she takes her own power as an adult, as one who decides and directs her own destiny.

But the monster is more than a parental figure. When Joy and I discussed the trance, the puppets at first seemed a mystery. But as we probed the meaning of their names, they took on associations with Christianity — in particular, the feeling of her early religious upbringing, the sense that she could make some irrevocable, damning mistake, could Fall into sin, be cast into Hell. The Fall, for her, was a story that strangled, that paralyzed her energy.

Her energy is freed by fire, by expression of anger, but she does not get stuck in the South; she moves to the West, cools the room with water, with love, nurturing, merging, integration.

The cup of the West is also a tool we can use to transform the self-hater and ourselves. For having cut ourselves apart with the knife of the East, and burned in the fires of the South, we must cool ourselves, reintegrate, merge again in new ways, or we remain burned out and dismembered.

Although Joy's journey began in the East, other people might need to begin in the West by connecting, by forming a strong bond with someone. The struggle with the self-hater, instead of being a fiery battle, might be a long, slow, effort to form a relationship, to challenge isolation.

In magic nothing is completely destroyed; it is only transformed. Although we treat the self-hater as if it were a being apart, it is not. It is part of ourselves, and so we cannot get rid of it, because it contains our energy, our power. If we split it off, we lose that source of power — or see it reflected back in menacing forms from others, who become the monsters we fear.

So Joy, having defeated the shadows, the puppets, the monster, takes control. She becomes herself the animating spirit of the monster, which is no longer a monster. Having faced her helplessness, her fear of annihilation, her fear/wish to be passive, dependent, a child — she is now able to take the position of the adult, no longer cowering or clinging, no longer jerked by the strings of authority to perform according to someone else's wishes. And, having taken the position of control, she is able safely to let go of control, to Fall.

"I'm looking out the eyes of the monster," she says. She has merged with the monster — but it has been transformed. Earlier, she was terrified of falling. Now, she says, "I want to fall. I want to find out what happens when it's dark. I cut the cord, and I give myself a push."

She has cut the umbilical cord, let go of her wish to hold on to the past, let go of its fears and unfulfilled promises, and she falls into the unknown future.

"I hurtled through space and I became a red rocket, a comet, a star. I could see all these other stars, and I enjoyed being a part of it."

The dark has been transformed; it is no longer fearful. Now it holds brightness. And in what was the monster, a beautiful woman who radiates light and power stands at the controls.

The woman assures her that the control room can be a safe place now — that the lights on the panel can give her information and warn her of danger.

"Is she you?" I ask.

"No. My image of the Goddess."

Joy falls. She moves into her deepest fear — and the story that kept her constricted, afraid, now becomes the imagery of her liberation. She lets go. She dissolves. She leaps into the dark — into her very fear of dissolving — and recovers, instead, an ease, a comfort, a sense of being at home in the body, a sense of rightness in her being.

The body, the material world, belongs to the fourth quarter of the circle, to the North. The body, through which we take pleasure and experience reality, is itself finite, limited in time and space in a way that emotions, energies, and sensations are not. Transformation of our inner landscape may transform our bodies and cure physical ailments as well as emotional pain. Facing our terror of annihilation, reintegrating our split, warring parts, frees us to cherish the passionate unrepressed "animal/poetic"[8] body — and by extension to cherish nature and all of life.

Finally, earth represents the physical world, so-called real life. The transformation of the self-hater must be *grounded*. This means given material reality, in the form of changes in Joy's life, work, and relationships. Reclaiming our personal power means reclaiming our ability to engage reality, not retreat from it.

The woman in the control room of Joy's transformed monster, whom she calls her own image of the Goddess, represents a new type of control in Joy's life, a power based on a different relationship. The esoteric term for the *thing* that embodies power-with, not power-over, is The Guardian of the Threshold. The Guardian sets limits and defines boundaries, that is why she (or he) lives on the threshold, the gateway, the place of passage.

Power is only useful when it can be contained as well as expressed. Earth symbolizes containment, limits, and silence. When we feel confident that our anger, our aggression, can be contained, we can feel free to express them in a way that harms no one. The Guardian embodies our power to choose when to express something and what to express, when and what to keep silent — not out of guilt, but from a sense of honor and self-esteem. Containing emotions and energies is not the same as suppressing them. A ring of stones contains the fire (but does not smother it with dirt) so that the flames can warm us without burning down the forest.

To have free will, to make choices, is to be able to say no as well as yes. If the self-hater is simply banished, and not transformed into the Guardian, no real change takes place. I, for example, have been a mild workaholic most of my life, driven by a fairly strong self-hater. After years of magical work and therapy, my self-hater gave up. I found myself with enormous energy, and proceeded to take on even more work and projects because they all looked so exciting that I simply couldn't say no. I am still working on getting to know the Guardian better (which is why my discussion of the Guardian, you will notice, is shorter and vaguer than my discussion of the self-hater). My Guardian is slowly teaching me to recognize and listen to the warning signals from Younger Self that say, "Take it easy. Slow down." I need to do things more slowly and deliberately, to take naps, to eat better, to let the machine answer the phone — not to feel so set-apart, and thus share responsibility, and power, more widely with others.

For Joy, the Guardian represented a new relationship with self-discipline. She could say no to television and yes to working on creative projects without having to beat herself. She could take pleasure in her abilities.

For someone else, the Guardian might represent the ability to set limits in relationships, to connect without being overwhelmed, to assert her/his own thoughts and feelings without needing to attack. For yet another person, the Guardian might mean the ability to say no to drugs or alcohol.

The Guardian is an aspect of the deep self. It is a conscience based not upon guilt but upon integrity; as such, it allows us to call forth power-from-within, to control and choose our actions — not to control our feelings. And the Guardian is a healer.

For just as our inner landscapes mirror our culture, so this culture mirrors our internal structures. The culture of power-over creates pain. The lives of those who fall victim to its outward oppressions are filled with pain; and the inner lives of both oppressor and victims are hurtful and bleeding.

Transforming the inner landscape is only a first step. Unless we change the structures of the culture, we will mirror them again and again; we will be caught in a constant battle to avoid being molded again into an image of domination. Reclaiming personal power gives us the courage to demand a change in the basis of society's power. Facing our dread of annihilation allows us to face, unflinching, the real possibility of global annihilation, to face our own despair and rage at the pain inflicted by our culture, and to make that pain become active resistance to destruction; to create with that pain a vision of a new culture based on another source of power, to work for that vision, to risk ourselves in its service, even when the work seems hopeless or overwhelming. Refusing the domination of the self-hater, we break free of its imposed isolation — free to connect with others, to join our power, our wills, together. Bringing to birth the Guardian, we become Guardians — of ourselves, of each other, of the community of life.

Chapter Five

❧ ☙

Goddesses and Gods:
The Landscape of Culture

Magic has often been thought of as the art of making dreams come true; the art of realizing visions. Yet before we can bring to birth the vision of an integrated culture, we have to *see* it. We have to see new images in the mind's eye, venture forth into a changed landscape, tell new stories. But the stories of estrangement have shaped our minds; how do we break free of them unless a new vision is already there to help us?

The images, the stories of immanence, do abound — in our own cultural past, in myths and religions of many present-day cultures. So our vision-seeking lands us inevitably in the realm of religion, however unwilling we are to go there, because what we term *religion* is the soil of culture, in which the belief systems, the stories, the thought-forms upon which all other institutions are based are consciously or unconsciously grown.

When we turn to the religions of immanence, whether we call them Witchcraft or Paganism or polytheism or spirituality, whether we draw on sources from Celtic, Greek, Native American, Eastern, or African mythology, we encounter paradox. We encounter the God/dess: the all, the interwoven fabric of being, the dance, the weaver — we say — and the web of connection, the pattern, the spiral. "She," we call her. But She is before sex; She whose name cannot be spoken because She is the circle — before it is broken by a name that separates-out.

Yet the Goddess has many names: Isis, Ceridwen, Astarte, Miriam, Oshun, White Buffalo Woman, Kuan Yin, Diana, Amaterasu, Ishtar, Changing Woman, Yemaya . . . And She has many aspects: Maiden, Mother, Crone, moon, earth, tree, star, flame, Goddess of the cauldron, Goddess of the hearth, Healer, spider, Lady of the Wild Things. And the God who is Her male aspect, or, we could say, the other pole of that once-unbroken unity, also has many names: Pan, Dionysos, Osiris, Dumuzi, Baal, Lugh, Coyote, Alegba . . . And He too has many aspects: child, dancer, father, sower of seeds, Horned God, Hunter, Dying God, Healer, Green Man, sun, tree, standing stone.

Since Jung, most thinkers who explore mythology have looked at the Goddesses and Gods as *archetypes* that represent underlying structures of the human psyche. Archetypes are then organized into dualities — they tell us how to divide the world and its powers, how to divide our nature, into masculine and feminine, in spite of the fact that historically the aspects of Goddess and Gods overlap and are interchanged.[1] She may be sun and He may be moon; She may be sky and He may be earth; both have roles to play in the drama of birth, growth, and death.

The concept of archetypes is itself a symptom of estrangement, derived from the Platonic notion that the world itself was not the real, but only a shadow, an imitation of perfect preexisting forms. To a Witch the world itself is what is real. The Goddess, the Gods, are not mere psychological entities, existing in the psyche as if the psyche were a cave removed from the world; they too are real — that is, they are ways of thinking-in-things about real forces, real experiences.

"Would you like to have a vision of the Goddess?" I ask groups when I speak in public. When they nod, I tell them to turn and look at the person sitting next to them. The immanent Goddess is not abstract.

The images, the symbols, the aspects, are doorways, not definitions. There is no underlying feminine nature or masculine nature — there is the reality of what we experience, in our differing bodies, in the differing impact that culture has on each sex. Yet what we can envision, we can experience; and what we experience, name, make conscious can be integrated. The symbols tell us, "Look at this. Experience this thing; become this thing; open a channel so that the power can flow through you." And though the symbols, the images, do not exist outside of us who perceive them, the forces, the powers-from-within, are real. But when we speak of these powers, we mean power in the sense of *to be able*. The Goddess, the Gods, are our potential.

So I speak of the Goddess as weaver, as spider, and I begin to pay attention to the spiders who build their webs in my corners. I experience the web as a rhythm of strands and spaces. I see that there are points of connection and openings, and that this interplay of stuff and space gives the whole web a tension that is taut, yet elastic; that springs. I meditate on the web and it is the feel of that tautness that I take in, that I savor until I know it, can call it forth at will. I search in my own life for those points of connection, for those spaces — in words, in relationships — and knowing the *feel* of the web gives me the power to be able to feel for that same tautness in the knots and the spaces of my life.

And because the spider, the web, are real and contain all the richness of reality, they may give me other powers on other days. As I see the spider draw threads from her own body, I can learn to draw cords of energy from my body, to weave these into new forms; to draw words from my head, my hands — to weave on this page.

The imagery of the Goddess, of the God, can become doorways leading out of patriarchal cultures, channels for the powers we need to transform ourselves, our visions, and our stories.

The imagery of the Goddess points to the power of the mother in our lives. Symbols of the Goddess and the God can help us to be able to integrate that power, to make it conscious and available instead of denying it and fleeing from it.

As infants, we share an energy-field with our mothers. At first we know no sense of difference, only a shifting ground of as yet undifferentiated feelings/sensations: warmth, coldness, pleasure, satiation, the smell and taste of sweet milk, pain, gnawing hunger, aching frustration, rage, love. Slowly we come to consciousness, helpless and dependent; slowly, as we master our limbs, our voices, our senses, we develop the awareness of an I-ness that separates-out from the engulfing field.

Yet that field, *mother*, remains for a long, long time the ground against which we see ourselves. We become separate, congeal into our own being, but she remains amorphous, omnipresent. Her presence evokes the ancient feelings, the deep longing for infant bliss — to be held, to be rocked, to be taken care of, as we lie passive. At the same time it evokes that ancient terror, the ground under our feet may disappear for good as it does in those moments when we cry and are not soothed, when we hunger and are not fed. And it evokes rage against our own helplessness, against our own powerlessness, against her overwhelming power to give or to withhold comfort.

As we grow, as we learn to walk and talk, to play, to handle objects and tools and toys, we develop a new source of pleasure in the feeling of mastery, of control, that strengthens the sense of I-ness. We become slowly conscious of more than self and ground; conscious that the world is peopled with I-nesses. These others are different from us, and different from the mother-ground, and as we grow we find that, more and more, we can make connections independently of mother, we stand out more distinctly to ourselves, we move a step further from engulfment; we assuage that terror of being sucked back into helplessness, the terror that is so strong because it is partly a desire for that early bliss.

Here culture steps in to make the experience of the girl-child very different from that of the boy-child. For as the girl struggles to emerge from the mother-ground, to find others whom she can imitate and become like, to become a person truly distinct from her mother, culture reminds her of her essential sameness — she is the same gender. In our culture, gender is the basic division, the primary duality.

In a thousand subtle ways, culture discourages the girl-child from pleasure in mastery and rewards her dependence. As she looks at the world of adults, she sees, over and over again, that the world of mastery, the rewards of effort, belong to men. But the seductive promise patriarchal culture makes to her is this: you will be taken care of; you can recapture that luscious passivity, that sensual dependence, and as for your terror of helplessness, your fear of slipping back, of being swallowed by the ground, why, you yourself will become the ground, a better ground, a more fertile ground. You yourself will grow into the magical, powerful mother. You will be the earth herself. Although men play at being masters, it will be you who supports them. So the girl, in patriarchal culture, does not have to differentiate herself fully. She never has to learn to see her mother, not as the ground, but as another I. She can remain fluid, indistinct, flowing around another, enfolding or engulfing, taking the position of ground rather than self-being, perceiving others' feelings rather than knowing her own, adapting to others' needs and desires. She becomes the support that gets walked on.

For the boy, patriarchal culture has another message: you are different, you are distinct from the mother-ground. You are a different gender. And what is more, you are superior. The world of mastery, of control, the pleasure that arises from your own distinctness — all this belongs to creatures like yourself.

But the price is high. Patriarchal culture's promise to the boy is that he can build a self around the core of his difference from the mother-ground — a self whose deepest pleasures come not from the soft enfoldment of the body with flesh, the soul with caring, but from mastery, competence, control — untainted with dependence and terror of abandonment. "And at the same time," culture whispers, "you can *own* a source of those good, nurturing feelings, a mother-creature of your very own."

So the boy trades terror for terror, and dependency for dependency. For competence and mastery can fail. In building his sense of self around his difference from his mother, the boy is asked to cut the ground from beneath his feet, because in the push and pull of longing/fear, desire/terror in his connection to his mother, is the source of *feeling* that goes far deeper than the pleasures of performance. Fleeing the threat of death, he will cut off the source of life. Never will the boy develop his own source of the magic mother-stuff, his own source of self-nurturing. He will be dependent on the woman he possesses, as the small boy was on his mother. He will desire her and be terrified of her. And always there will be the gulf he can never afford to bridge — because the core of his identity is based on his difference.

Nature, the world itself, will come to feel to him like the mother — alluring, threatening, desirable, dangerous in a way that it is not to women. Again and again, over and over, he will need to assert his fragile mastery, his control, his power-over others. He will take his revenge on the body of the earth.

Our culture is shaped by the images and the realities of that revenge. The icons of pornography, the reality of our technology that destroys and pollutes, the reality of rape, of institutionalized violence against women, of violence in all the institutions of domination, all these reflect that revenge.

The split between culture and nature determines the character of work itself. It is no coincidence that so-called industrial discipline began to be imposed on labor in the late sixteenth and seventeenth centuries when the workplace began to be split from the home, when women were gradually driven out of many types of productive work, and when the revenge against nature was played out in the Witchburnings. In a mechanistic society, whether capitalist or communist, our underlying conception of work is that mothering, nurturing, *feeling* should be excluded.

The time structure of work and the lack of childcare facilities make it difficult for someone who is entrusted with the primary care of a small child to work a full-time job; these problems also make it impossible for the majority of men who are full-time workers to share equally in childcare, even if they wish to do so. We assume that personal concerns should not intrude upon work, that neither a child's illness nor a broken love affair should impair a worker's efficiency. It is the rare workplace where coworkers can genuinely offer each other comfort and emotional support; most often, they are in competition with each other. The work itself that we do often demands that we stifle feeling, ignore our bodies' demands, deny boredom and exhaustion.

Mastery and control, not feeling or nurturing, determine one's place in the work hierarchy. Jobs with high status are those in which the worker controls things or people. The work of nurturing — childcare, teaching, nursing — does not win society's rewards. Those whose work involves control are better paid, and access to money allows them greater control in all areas of life.

Dinnerstein, Chodorow, and other theorists have suggested that bringing men into childcare on a basis equal with that of women might heal our cultural split. Yet, at present, that is an option available only to a privileged few whose jobs allow great flexibility. Implicit in this idea is a much more radical demand; in order for men to share in rearing children on more than a token basis, we would need to restructure the nature of work, i.e., our entire economic and social structure.

Let us imagine, for a moment, a different type of restructuring; we bring the care of children into the work world. They would no longer be isolated in childcare centers, but part of our daily activity, as they are in a tribal village: (In the fantasy that follows, I have deliberately not changed the conventional distribution of power by gender, only childcare arrangements).

> You arrive at the corporation for your meeting. The receptionist who greets you is nursing her two-month-old baby. Its crib lies beside the typewriter. She directs you down a corridor where two seven-year-olds on skateboards careen past you. The meeting takes place in a conference room with large glass doors overlooking the playground, which is equipped with slides, swings, games. One member of the committee is appointed recorder (to take notes); another is appointed to handle any crises that might arise among the children. In general, the children play well together — the older children keep an eye on the younger and intervene in any dangerous pursuits. At the end of the meeting, you set up another appointment with the Chief Executive Officer. "Friday afternoon is my time with the kids," he says, checking his appointment book. "Why don't you meet me at the zoo — we can talk this over at the monkey cage."

In such a world, productivity might fall — or it might be measured on a different scale, one that takes into account the quality of relationships in people's lives, in which the bottom line is no longer profit, but the needs of people and the well-being of the next generation. The decisions taken, hand-in-hand with one's child while observing the elephants and tigers, might be fewer, but more grounded in humanity, than those taken hand-in-hand with the third martini over an elegant, childless lunch. They might also be more protective of life.

It is unlikely that such a scenario will ever take place. Before receptionists are encouraged to nurse their babies in corporate halls, we will have to do away with the hierarchy of executives and receptionists, with the corporate structure itself, which is maintained by the split that separates work and nurturing. For only our denial of feeling keeps us willing to submit to the authority of power-over.

We are in a double-bind. We struggle to end culture's revenge against nature, to take a new position. Yet we ourselves are mother-raised, and we carry within us the deep ambivalence, the unspoken wish for revenge that leads us to acquiesce, that leads us, even in our own struggles, to separate mastery from nurturing, to isolate our feelings, our children, our deepest terrors and desires.

So we turn to the imagery of the Goddess for healing, because the images of the Goddess say to us, "Remember. Re-member the power of the mother — re-own the ground upon which you stand, the longing and the terror — make it yours with consciousness that pushes deeper than the triumphs and failures of your own personal mother, that allows you to know in yourself the movements of the great powers of life and death, of nurturing and limitation, of which your own infancy, your own mother, was only one expression."

We can name that ground, that nurturing power, *Gaea*, and the name separates Her from our infant/body memory of Her power, lets us experience Gaea as separate from Mommie, distinct. Because She becomes distinct from Mommie, we can develop our own relationship with Her. When we have our own connection to the ground, we no longer need Mommie to be the ground; we can separate, let her become a distinct I-ness in our eyes, a distinct self.

For a man, the personal relationship with Gaea is a way out of the cultural trap, because a man who embraces his own connection with the Goddess experiences the power of nurturing within himself, independent of his tie to a living woman. Just as, once the ground has been named, a woman can no longer remain completely merged with it, so, too, a man, once the ground has been named as a living reality, can no longer remain so comfortably split from it. Gaea makes the power of the mother a conscious force, something with which we must come to terms.

That coming to terms, the making of connection, we call *invoking*. When we invoke the Goddess we awaken Her imagery, Her symbols, in our own minds; we hold them there, let them draw forth the power (the ability to do) that they contain. They take root in Younger Self until they become new patterns of subtle energy within us that manifest as action. I might invoke Gaea with a poem, a song or a chant:

The earth, the water, the fire, the air,
Returns, returns, returns, returns.

Within a ritual or celebration:[2]

"Sink down," a voice says. "Feel your knees getting weak, and your body heavy. Let yourself sink to earth. Touch your hands, your arms, your face to the earth. Rest there. And as you rest, you begin to dissolve. Your skin, your bones, your eyes, your very breath drops away. You are formless, resting in the earth, rocking in the dark breast of the mother. Everything you knew, everything you were, all the little worries you carried in your mind, the things that seemed so important — they are gone now. Let them go. You are nothing — a space in the dark.

"But now, in that nothingness, that space, you begin to feel a spark. Something pushing upward. A heat. A power — the power of earth. Something flows through you again — you hear a beat, a rhythm. It is your heartbeat. You take a breath. Slowly, slowly, you begin to rise"

Powers of the earth
Powers taking form
Rising to rebirth
Rising to be born

We rise as the chant builds. We return to form, singing, breathing, swaying, dancing with each other in the circle.

She changes everything she touches
And everything She touches, changes

We sing, joyfully. We are whole again, separate, ourselves. We are changed.

But most important, the Goddess is invoked in our awareness of our lived experience. So, I plant my garden, and I know Gaea in my hands and under my fingernails, I know Her as the seeds push up, the leaves unfold, the fruits swell and ripen. And because I have named this power, awakened to it, chanted for it, placed its images in my psyche, my experience of it is deepened and enriched.

That experience encompasses death, as well as nurturing. The lettuce seedlings sprout thickly — I have to pull many of them out, and it saddens me to destroy the shoots, waving so bravely, so new. I dig into the earth and find a nest of earwigs, or uncover brooding snails, which I smash. The garden is full of things that have to be killed so that other things can grow — and some of what I want to grow gets eaten down to the stem before it has a chance.

Annihilation is present in the midst of life; it is not separate from life, as the presence of terror was not separate from our first experience of love. Yet in naming the death-force as one of Gaea's aspects, calling it Hecate, Kali, Anna, the Crone, I become both less merged with it and less removed from it. The Crone, too, becomes a source of power — to end, to limit, to destroy. As I invoke that power, as I savor it in my experience, it too becomes less alien — not so much an outside force that overpowers me but more my own.

Hecate is called the Goddess of crossroads, i.e., choices. I must choose which of the lettuces to pull, which to leave. I wield the terrible power that I, as an infant, attributed to my own mother: the power to annihilate. I can, I must, choose that power again and again; for every choice I take annihilates some other possibility.

Invoking that power instead of fleeing it, I develop a sense of mastery that is not based on denial of feeling. It is the mastery of art, which is based on feeling — the erotic interplay of the strands and the spaces, that tells me what to spin, what to cut; the limit set by the Guardian that strengthens; the frame that makes the picture stand out.

To choose is also to begin. The Mother, and the Crone, are almost always seen with a third aspect: the Maiden, who is birth, the renewal that comes from the choice. To invoke the Maiden is to invoke the power of the self emerging from the ground.

The many faces, the qualities of the Maiden become pointers, saying, "Experience this — and make its power your own."

The Maiden is Athena, patroness of art and culture — not the patriarchal Athena, born from Zeus's brow, but the ancient, primal virgin, complete unto herself, whose power is to create herself, to create the works of art and culture that differentiate self from nature — not out of revenge, but as a way of being at one with nature in creating beauty. Athena is also the warrior; She can fight, She protects Her own. For in order to be selves we must be able to fight, to protect our boundaries and our creations.

The Maiden is also Artemis, Lady of the Wild Things. To invoke Her is to awaken the wildness of self, the feelings that will not be tamed, and the integrity of self that upholds our right to feel, to be different, to be the people we are and to walk the path that we do. That freedom comes with being Virgin, as Artemis, too, is Virgin, complete within ourselves, having our own independent relationship with the Mother and the Crone, the forces of life and death. Artemis lives in the forest, in the wild. She is not bound by city walls, and through Her we can invoke our own power to escape the walls and strictures of culture, the rule of the self-hater, so that we are bound not by rules and authorities, but by our own experience of balance, by the consequences of our actions.

Artemis is the Bear Goddess — and we remember what the bear promised Joy: immortality and the ability to growl. We can see Joy's freeing of the bear as her willingness to unleash the power of Artemis, the wild self, to make it her own instead of caging it. In return, the bear restored to Joy her wild feelings, her growl, her ability to protect herself — Hand-in-hand with immortality comes freedom, not from the cycle of birth and death but freedom from the child's relationship to birth and death, the relationship of fear and helplessness. For the power of the Maiden, of the self, is that of renewal, of beginning.

And so the Maiden is Kore-who-becomes-Persephone, She who descends into the underworld, into death, and rises again, eternally renewed. Kore is kin to Isis, Inanna, Astarte. The story of the rape of Kore is a late addition, an historical reference perhaps to the destruction of the early Goddess Culture,[3] or a patriarchal attempt to subvert the power of the myth. The myth itself is a story strung together around the original experience, which was a ritual, the celebration of the Thesmophoria, in ancient Greece. The ritual was one of descent and rising. On the first day pigs, cakes of dough, and pine branches were cast into the sacred cracks of the earth, and on the third day, the day called *Kalligeneia* (Fair-born), the previous year's decayed grain was drawn up again, to be mixed with the new seed-corn. The ancient Kore shows us the power of life and death united; teaches us the secret that renewal cannot be separated from decay, that it is death that makes life fertile.

The phone rings, as I sit here writing of Kore. A friend's neighbor has disappeared. Two days ago she left for work — and hasn't been seen since. He calls to ask me to do a ritual for her.

I stop writing, and invoke Kore — not only the early Kore, but the later Goddess, the Kore who is a survivor, who rises from rape, who offers hope and the promise of renewal even in the underworld. We need Her too, in a city where every day women are raped, beaten, murdered in the parks and on the streets. We can know Her power in ourselves, in our friends who have survived rape, and beatings, and the damage inflicted by this culture. We can find Her in women who enter the domain of the dark, who work within the regions of pain to transform them. I think of the daughter of one of my teachers, who after being raped worked to establish a rape crisis center. I think of a seventy-four-year-old woman who counsels dying patients.

We need the rage of Kore's mother, the rage that will not submit, that rises out of despair, that brings results. Demeter, who called the first sitdown strike in history, who invented passive resistance, who said, "Nothing will grow until my daughter is returned" — whose demands must be met. Demeter — who always refuses to ignore the horror of Her loss and continue with business-as-usual; Demeter — our own power to grieve and yet make that grief a force that compels change, that brings about renewal.

For the Goddess, who is immanent, reveals herself in living women, and so She changes. Today Demeter reveals herself to me in Helen Caldicott; now She is present in my own rage at the planned licensing of the Diablo Canyon Nuclear Power Plant's reactor, on a site close to an earthquake fault. I go to a meeting to help plan the blockade, and Demeter appears as a man, who, together with his teenaged daughter, plans to risk arrest by blockading the road to the plant. For Demeter's power, the rage that heals, is not sex-specific. Her image, Her presence, can unlock that power in any one of us who opens to it.

So we return to the God. The God is a problematic figure today; His many names, His many aspects seem somehow less satisfying, less transforming to many people than do images of the Goddess. It is difficult for many of us to respond in new ways to male images, when all our lives we have been asked to respond in male frameworks. The old myths — even those of the Craft — often seem too firmly heterosexual, based in a vanished world in which everybody comes neatly coupled, two by two, like animals in the Ark. It is too easy to see the Goddess and God "dividing the work of divinity by sex roles" as a student of mine once complained.

Yet the symbols of the God can have great transformative power, a power that reaches below words, beyond reason, that shatters the constrictions culture places on men and women. But this power does not come from the god as a role model — someone to be imitated. The faces of the God point to experiences, they too say, "Look at this. Feel this. Know this within yourself and name its power so you can draw it forth." The God, like the Goddess, can become one of "the symbols of another reality-principle." He can be the "image of joy and fulfillment; the voice which does not command but sings; the gesture which offers and receives; the deed which is peace and ends the labor of conquest; the liberation from time which unites man with god, man with nature."[4]

Just as naming the nurturing-mother-force lets us, at the same time, separate from it and reconnect independently with it, so giving a name and a face to maleness lets us, both men and women, establish a connection that is independent of the false roles and destructive stereotypes of masculinity — independent even of identification with the men in our lives who themselves have been shaped and molded by the false expectations.

By *maleness*, I do not mean any of the qualities that have been arbitrarily assigned to men as if they didn't apply to women. I do *not* mean such things as aggression, assertion, activity, yang-ness, rationality, and logos. I mean only the power of being at home — strong, potent, and awake to feeling in a male body.

Many women today would argue that they do not need any connection with maleness, regardless of the way it is transformed or defined. For some, that may be true. For other women and men, maleness has been so tainted by the male roles our culture offers that it cannot be approached cleanly.

It is the culture, rather than any specific individual, that needs transformative images of maleness. Some would even argue with that statement, defining maleness, men themselves, as the problem, maintaining that men are flawed at a deep, perhaps genetic level. But that analysis is too simple, another Good Guys/Bad Guys story, trapped in a dualistic thought-form. It ignores the conditions that make men and women what we are — and ignores the way those conditions vary in their pain in different classes and races.

Images of the God should not be seen as dualistically assigning powers according to gender. Instead, they are a way of thinking-in-things about questions of sameness and difference. In a culture in which gender is the primary division, we need images of both genders to enable us to come into all of our powers.

As small children, we spend an enormous amount of energy working out questions of sameness and difference. Who are we like? Who are we unlike? Thus we gradually come to have a sense of who we are, to shape ourselves. It is simplistic to think that little girls identify with Mommie exclusively, and little boys with Daddy (always assuming there is a daddy on the scene). We each make a complex nexus of interwoven identifications and dis-avowals. I am: a girl (like Mommie), thin (like Daddy), brown-eyed (like Mommie), and who loves salami (like Daddy), and good at art (different from both). In that complex, difficult work of differentiating, of forming a self and pulling away from the ground of mother's being, we use whatever other important people are around us. Often (in patriarchal culture), for girls as well as boys, that separate self, the part of us that feels free and autonomous, out of the realm of mother's control, comes to be identified with maleness. This may hold true even for women who consciously — emotionally, sexually, and politically — commit themselves to an identification with women.

This might change, of course, if our childcare arrangements changed so that men as well as women became associated with the fears and pleasures of infancy, but only if all the elements of our culture that again and again reinforce the identification of self as male and the *other* as female also changed.

The male self, in a culture in which men rarely care for young children, comes to seem pristine, clean, uncontaminated by the dark mixture of desire and fear that the power of the mother evokes. In a culture in which mastery is the realm of men, the male self comes to be identified with all that represents competence, control, adventure, spirit, light, transcendence of the body's dark demands. Yet that so-called freedom is actually denial — of the body, of feeling, of vulnerability and mortality.

Denial is reinforced because our political and economic system depends on it. The structure of work, we have seen, is based on that denial. War — another activity reserved for men, also requires men to deny fear, to deny the natural instinct to run like hell from danger. That denial makes possible the closing off, the numbing, that lets men commit atrocities, torture, murder, rape. A man, identifying selfhood with himself, can easily see anyone who is different as the other — as not fully human, as ground to his swaggering figure.

The images of God that may prove liberating are those that point firmly back to the feeling-body, to sex, to the power of mortality. It is not any individual person or group that needs those images; it is the culture as a whole that needs to reconnect maleness with earth, with flesh. Otherwise, we are not forced, as a culture, to come to terms with earth, with flesh; the figure of the pristine, transcendent male is always there to take the load off, to promise escape into some better place. He is also always there to offer the false promise that the self can entirely free itself from ground, that mastery and control can win entirely over the deep forces of life and death, that nature can be tamed.

Alan Acacia, friend and my co-teacher in a class on Magic for Men, spoke of the need for images of Father Earth. At first I found the phrase jarring, almost offensive. It seemed the power of the father had raged on too long without being revived now, within the Goddess religion. But as I thought about it, as I allowed myself to experience the Earth-God — I realized that this image is indeed prevalent in the mythology of earth religion. Father Earth is the Green Man of the Craft, the God who is pictured crowned with leaves and twined with vines, the spirit of vegetation, growing things, the forest. The image says, "Experience this: you are rooted in earth, know the force that twines upward — how it is to flower, to swell into fruit, to ripen in the sun, to drop leaves, to ferment, to be intoxicating. Know the cycle, over and over; you are not apart from it. It is the source of your life."

The God is an animal: stag, goat, bull, boar. He is the Horned Shaman in the prehistoric cave, He carries the bird wand, He smiles through owl eyes. His image says, "Remember — that mastery is not all; remember the deeper part of yourself, still untamed, whose strength is that of instinct; remember that you bleed, smell, feel — that you can be in your body with animal grace, that there is an elegance, a control not imposed by the mind on nature, one that rises from the body, that arises from being in the world, in the moment, as if we belonged, just as an animal belongs where it is."

The God is the Hunter. I think about the hunter as Ed and I are camped in the wilderness by a lake high in the Sierras. The water is so clear we can see the trout pass by as we look down from the white granite rocks where we sit. In the evenings, the trout rise to feed. They, too, are hunters. As I watch the one we have adopted as our trout, watch it glide smoothly back and forth near the rock, and then leap, in a flash, grabbing a whirling insect as it hits the water's surface, I realize that being a hunter is a state of consciousness, a relaxed alertness, a readiness to move in an instant, to take without hesitating. It moves in an instant because something in the trout's mind is shaped like an insect; something in the hunter's mind must reproduce the prey, must know it so well that the hunter becomes the prey. And while hunting is not a male quality (Artemis is a Hunter, too), perhaps the Hunter is telling us that this consciousness is a doorway men can use to attain what women do more easily. They can develop the ability to merge, to let another being in as part of oneself, to flow around that being, to become ground as well as self.

The Hunter becomes the agent of mortality; he wields the terrible power of annihilation, and yet the part of him that becomes the prey gives way to that death. So something else is given life. And the powers of life and death are united in Him as well as in Her; they are not exclusively the powers of women, and so they cannot be contained by controlling women. They are the powers that underlie all of life.

The God is phallic. He is the maypole, the hermstone, the penis — the dying and reviving God. Pan is all — desire and terror — panic. But the God is more than just physical fertility. As phallus, He says, "Experience this — pleasure. Know, in your own body, how it peaks and fades, and give way to it, not as the pleasure of performance, of mastery, but as the deeper pleasure of the enfolded body, the deep desire you can know again when you no longer deny the dark." The penis, when it is no longer the instrument of control, becomes the emblem of vulnerability, of feeling. As such, it is freeing to men — because the penis-as-weapon is a dead, wooden instrument that brings no true pleasure.

The God, too, descends into the underworld. The image of the God who grows and dies with the year says, "Look — experience the seasons, the endless round of birth, death, and renewal." What He sacrifices is the male potential to remove himself from the realm of birth and death, as the Goddess who descends sacrifices Her potential to remain the ground of birth and death, instead of the self who suffers death.

In estranged culture, the image that links the male with mortality is, of course, Christ crucified. The iconography of Christianity is hardly different — as many have pointed out — from that of the ancient Virgin Goddess and her sacred child, who dies only to be reborn into immortality. Perhaps that similarity explains some of the power of Christianity — its hold on the heart and the mind. For the image of the tortured male body on the cross confronts our unconscious hope that maleness itself can remove us from the sphere of mortality, from death and pain. But instead of forcing us through that confrontation to a deeper connection with our own mortal flesh and life, Christianity cheats us with the false promise of an otherworldly resurrection. Whatever potential for integration the Christ-figure may promise, it has too often been lost in the hierarchies of the church and chapel, in the authority of dogma, in the thought-forms and stories of estrangement.

Because the Gods reveal themselves in living women and men, they change. The myths change. Perhaps they revert back to their original forms. Perhaps they take us to places we have never been.

So we see that Kore descends, not because She is carried off, but because She herself knows that it is time to leave Her mother, to explore beyond the domain of sunlit earth that Her mother rules. She searches for the crack, and when She finds the chasm that leads downward, She enters — fearful, yet moving ahead, bearing Her torch to light the way.

Demeter mourns, She searches, She rages. Kore walks, deliberately, of Her own free will, into the dark. Does She go to offer comfort to the twittering ghosts of hell? Or to gain knowledge deeper than the surfaces of things? Or does She enter the dark to change it — to dream it into the new forms She holds in Her mind?

And the God descends. Beautiful Boy, He is named Adonis, Osiris, Dionysos. The women mourn: the Goddess mourns, their tears stain the ground; His blood runs in red carpets of flowers. Kore is the poppy; He is the anemone. He chooses to go down because, like Icarus, He has flown and found that His attempt to escape earth brought only another sort of destruction. Now He wants to know His body, His bones from the inside; He feels life stirring in Him, rising up from below, and He wants to know its source, to abandon Himself, to be one with that source. For that, He is willing to sacrifice.

So they descend, each winding their own way down through their own path, maze. The labyrinth.

And so they meet, at center, in the womb of the dark, the heart of earth. Their meeting is a shock; they are shattered. For He sees that She is not the encompassing earth but a self, like His own, moving through the labyrinth. And she sees that He is no shining immortal; He has grown bulls' horns on His way down, He is animal. They are forced to look into each other's eyes.

They feed on the fruit of the dead, the pomegranate. Fruit of Persephone, fruit that bleeds, that stains their hands and their fingers. This fruit is crowned with a flower like an open cunt; peel it back and find the clitoris. Or it is a ball filled with seeds. The seeds are red and also white like the moon. Like flesh. Like the poppy, the anemone. They are sweet; they stain the lips. They are red crystals, embedded in a matrix.

They are clear as water. Tears. Seeds.

The fruit of life.

Like all seeds, their instinct is to rise, to push their way upward.

As Goddess and God feel that power move in their bellies and their limbs, so we feel it arise inside us, as our own power to call them forth, to bring up the mysteries of the dark and renew the light. We invoke them, we become them: He who goes down and arises, She who changes everything She touches.

But we have eaten of the fruit of Persephone, and we are changed. We can never again be wholly severed from the dark, the earth, the flesh. Within us, Persephone dwells, not as queen, but as friend — of the underworld. Within dwells the Dark God, not as demon, abductor, overlord, but as comforter who consoles us with the promise of renewal. They are the open-eyed dreamers, and what they dream into being in the underworld are the visions that rise to restore the earth. Our visions. Our power.

Chapter Six

❧

Building Community:
Processes for Groups

We are all longing to go home to some place we have never
been — a place, half-remembered, and half-envisioned we can
only catch glimpses of from time to time. Community. Somewhere, there are people to whom we can speak with passion without having the words catch in our throats. Somewhere a circle of
hands will open to receive us, eyes will light up as we enter, voices
will celebrate with us whenever we come into our own power.
Community means strength that joins our strength to do the work
that needs to be done. Arms to hold us when we falter. A circle of
healing. A circle of friends. Someplace where we can be free.

Glimpses. A circle of friends sits on the lawn of a white farm-
house in the Midwest. There is a red barn, and a weeping willow,
and a fire in a cauldron at night. We sing and raise power and
speak with passion to each other. "This is the richest soil in the
world," someone says, and suddenly I feel sure that we could still
do it; in spite of everything, we could still make a way to live that
would be worthy of the richness of this land. America destroys so
much — the cultures that were here before white America arrived,
the buffalo, the forests, the wilderness — and yet the land is rich
enough and vast enough to let us build anew. Here, beside this

92

cornfield, in America's heart, I can see that the community I envision is not so different from that which has existed before. A circle of tepees on the plains, the gathering of neighbors to raise a barn — these are not so different from the promise the land whispered to my immigrant grandparents fleeing servitude in the Russian army, the promise inscribed on the Statue of Liberty, the words we hear ringing again and again in all the documents we learned about in school that were said to be America's foundation. Liberty. Justice. Equality. Freedom. In a dimension just the other side of our eyelids exists an America that keeps those promises, and sometimes when we blink too slowly we think we are there. Home.

In that America everything speaks with passion: the fields, the mountains, the trees, the birds, the children. Everything shines from inside out and everything has a dark, secret core where power lies. All things give away to each other, as the Indians say the animals and plants give away in death so that their deaths feed life. The America of the give-away has hands overflowing with abundance to fill every empty belly, a generous heart that doesn't ask for returns, and a wild spirit that will try anything once. That America takes in strays, and her people know how to stick together. They know how to laugh and they know how to love.

When we open our eyes with the imprint of that America still stuck to the lids and look around us, the America we see appears unbearable. In this America we say to the child, "This won't hurt," and then apply the electric current. In this America we hold fast to every last crumb and lock things up tight until we ourselves are locked up in pain from our clenched fists and our clenched jaws. We are lonely, in this America — we are terrified as we see America putting its machinery into gear for a war that will kill us all. Mostly, we feel powerless. We feel there is nothing we can do.

Community. It is not enough to confront our self-haters, to change our inner psychic structures, to spin new myths and new stories. As long as we feel powerless in the political and social arenas, we cannot be free. We cannot make the decisions that most affect us. And if we identify the immanent Goddess with reality, then our spiritual practice must confront reality. The territory of the quest moves beyond the individual self, out of the wilderness into the streets, to the nuclear power plants, the weapons labs, and the jails. It moves to places where the drama, the clash, is played out, where the battle of our times is being fought.

Action is ritual, myth, vision, quest. For most of us are not living in the wilderness, able to discover in the heart of wilderness the shapes of fear that form our inner limitations and break through them to power. The shapes in our minds that limit our power-from-within are mirrors of the prison, the gun, the guard. To reclaim our power, we must move into the territory of the real threats with which our culture controls us. Like Inanna, Persephone, Osiris, Dumuzi — like all the Goddesses and Gods who descend and return — we too can enter the kingdom of that which we fear most, although for us it may take the form of a weapons lab or a county jail. We can dissolve the shadow of the inner bomb when we openly confront the makers of the real bomb. Within that kingdom, when we join in community, in solidarity, we too can find sources of strength and renewal — the true magic that dissolves fear.

And so we move toward each other, if only because the battle is too large for any one of us to fight alone. In community, we call forth power in a dimension that moves beyond the interests of the personal self, for power-from-within cannot exist in a vacuum. Power-from-within is more than a feeling, more than a flash of individual enlightenment or insight; it involves our sense of connection with others, our knowledge of the impact we have on others. Power-from-within is the power of the give-away, that comes from our willingness to spend ourselves, to be there for others at the price of risk and effort.

In this America we are taught to put self-interest first, to compete, to better ourselves as individuals. And so we are controlled by promises and threats — controlled at a level so deep that we are rarely conscious of it. At times a vision, an experience, may open our eyes.

Going to jail for a political action is an experience that can teach us more about consciousness than a hundred growth seminars. For in jail we experience the controls of our culture directly. We see their naked operation, unclothed by the usual niceties. Power-over is a vise, a clamp that holds us with our own hopes and fears. For there are always privileges to be won if we behave, and there is always someplace worse they can put us, something they can do to us or take away from us, if we refuse to be controlled. So we are caught. In jail we cannot escape knowledge of this control: the system itself has devised a thousand minor rituals, a thousand petty rules to drive the lesson home again and again.

So the purpose of cuffing our hands behind our backs is not to prevent us from attacking the police; it is to acquaint us with the extent of our helplessness. The purpose of the airless, windowless holding tanks, with their open toilets that can only be flushed from outside by the guards is to make us aware, when we are taken to a more decent place, that we can always be returned to a place that is worse. The purpose of stripping us to search us, of having us bend over, spread our cheeks, and cough is not really to discover if we have contraband stuck up our assholes, it is to teach us that humiliation is the favorite weapon the system has devised against the self.

We come out of jail angry, on fire with rage that does not retreat, because as we look around us, day by day, we see the same vise in operation. Everywhere we are surrounded with the pretty pictures of rewards to be won. They are plastered across the billboards and the magazines, they cavort on television. Yet it is not really the image of the car, the dress, the hot tub, the gold chain that we respond to, although these offer pleasure — it is the sense of status, the acknowledgment of our worth, they represent.

And on the other hand, the prison, the mental hospital, stand as the representations of the worse place — where they can take us if we resist control. Yet it is not that most of us live in constant fear of being carted off to jail, but rather that the jail is a symbol of the thousand petty rituals of punishment we face in our jobs, our homes, on the streets. There are endless ways — from the boss's reprimand to the headwaiter's sneer to the look on the grocery clerk's face when we pull out our food stamps, for the culture to confirm our lack of worth.

Immanence means that each of us has inherent worth — yet we cannot feel self-worth because we believe it as a theological doctrine. We feel it when we connect with another person, when we can comfort someone in distress, ease someone's pain, do work that means something to us. We feel our own worth when we help shape the choices that affect us.

To call forth power-from-within, to free ourselves, we must be willing to move beyond self-interest, to cease grabbing for the carrot and flinching from the stick. We must be willing to give away.

In community, we have power to heal each other and to help each other, power that goes beyond the individual self.

Here is a story: a woman is raped. This is not unusual: women are raped every day. This woman, however, is part of a strong and supportive women's community. She believes she knows who the man is; but she cannot marshal enough evidence to prosecute a case. Perhaps she has a few doubts, herself, about sending someone to prison, where he may very well be raped, and will certainly not be reformed. Whether or not we agree with her doubts, she feels them.

She turns to her community. A group of women goes with her to the place where the rapist works. They wait until he leaves the building, and they surround him.

The women have no force at their disposal. They cannot call on the guns and prisons of the state. They simply confront the man with his act and his responsibility. They appear to him as a living community to say, "What you have done is intolerable to us."

The man is ashamed, embarrassed, defensive. He is forced to look his victim in the face, to see her in a new context. Does he change? We cannot know. But in that community, he causes no further problems.

Here is another story: a young man has been in and out of mental hospitals most of his life. He is diagnosed as schizophrenic. His sister is part of a supportive community of political people belonging to many collectives and cooperative households. After discussion with her friends, she invites him to come and live near her. He moves into another cooperative household. At first he barely leaves his room. Gradually, with encouragement, he ventures out. Friends find him a job in a community business. He is not treated as a sick person — he is treated as a whole person. After a year, he finds another job on his own. He falls in love. He moves in with his lover. He no longer *is* a sick person.

Another woman has what is called a psychotic break. She checks into a mental hospital at a respected university. In the hospital they tell her she needs to get angry, to express herself. After the third day on which her assigned psychiatrist has rushed through the ward without responding to her questions, she kicks a chair in frustration. They lock her in a small room. She and her lover decide the hospital is making her sicker. She checks out.

She cannot stay alone because what is called her illness expresses itself as terror. She belongs to a feminist consciousness-raising group. The six other women in the group take turns being with her. None of them is a therapist and none knows what to do with someone who is in a state of terror — except to be there. It takes six of them, because one woman alone would have been drained and overwhelmed. After a few days the terror begins to subside. The woman is able to fight the inner demons, to regain a sense of control. She is never hospitalized again.

In community, we discover what we are truly worth as we help each other through the losses and the crises, as we work together to heal the damages inflicted by this culture. Within community, we can identify the vise of self-interest and resist its control. We can be free.

Community counters estrangement — it reconnects us with others, and with the natural community that surrounds and sustains us. Historically, the institutions of domination have established themselves by destroying community — from the enclosure movement and the witchburnings in Europe, to the colonization of Africa, Asia, South America, and Polynesia. This pattern continues with the destruction of Native American communities, traditions, and ways of life in the Black Hills and in the Southwest. If we see our work as re-inspiriting the world, then we must be intimately concerned with preserving and creating community. We must challenge the principle of domination by resisting the destruction of communities that remain, and by creating communities based on the principle of power-from-within, power that is inherent in every being.

There is a belief sometimes mouthed by members of so-called new-age spiritual groups that when you resist something, you give it energy, you create it. This is a simplistic misconception that comes from a misunderstanding of how energy works. It confuses resistance with denial. When we deny something, we create it — or at least, we create conditions in which it can grow and flourish, precisely because there is no resistance. In Nazi Germany, it was not the resistance to fascism that allowed the spread of Anti-Semitism and led to the death camps, it was the widespread denial, the refusal to admit that such things could happen. It is not resistance to the possibility of nuclear holocaust that will bring it about, it is denial.

Resistance causes conflict. In America as it is today we are taught to fear conflict. Women, especially, learn to be peace-makers, to back down when confronted, and to avoid challenging others. It isn't nice to say no.

We confuse conflict with violence, yet the two are not synonymous. Violence is not anger; not shouting; not a feeling, a mood, or any specific action. I define *violence* as the imposition of power-over. The manager who imposes a speed-up on the line may be inflicting violence, even though she/he is soft-spoken and smiling. The Diné woman who points her rifle at the government offical who is trying to force her off her land is resisting violence.

Whenever we try to cause change, we can expect conflict. If there is no resistance to a change, nothing is truly changing. Instead of fearing conflict, we can learn to welcome the freeing of energy it represents. When we pit our energy against an oppressive system, it must meet our power with its own. Its energies, its resources, are diverted from their destructive work.

There is a certain element of daring involved in resistance — at times it feels like pulling the tail of a monster at a feast to disturb it. The forces we must face may seem, at times, overwhelming, yet a colony of ants can disrupt a picnic of giants.

To do so, however, we must attend the giants' picnic instead of our own. Or so it seems. Resistance demands our time and our energy. Yet, if we do not resist blindly by mirroring what we are fighting, resistance itself can become a creative task. The very threats we face spur us to bond together in new forms, to see what controls us and to invent the means to free ourselves.

Magic is the art of turning negatives into positives, of spinning straw into gold. In the act of resistance we can spin the gold of our vision, can join together in ways that embody new stories, new forms, new structures, based on immanence.

Community is built from groups. The result of any creative work that requires more than our individual energies ultimately depends on how well we can work with others in groups. That realization is disconcerting, for groups can be maddeningly frustrating as easily as they can be supportive and empowering. There are, however, processes we can use in groups that help them to develop and work so that they increase and augment each individual's energy.

To empower individuals, groups must be small enough so that within them we can each have time to speak, to be heard, to know each other personally. The time we give to a person and the depth of attention we pay to her/his words and feelings are measures of the worth we accord her/him. We enact the theology of immanence, the belief that we are each inherently valuable, by creating groups in which each person is given time and attention — given respect.

If we think of a group or a circle as a living entity, we can imagine that, like a person, it has a Talking Self, a Younger Self, and a Deep Self. It also has a structure that is determined by the responsibilities of each person and the relationships among individuals in the group.

The Deep Self of a group is the underlying spirit, the sense of connection and common purpose, the bond. That bond is created and strengthened by sharing energy — working together, sharing food, touching each other, making rituals, singing, chanting, nurturing, laughing.

The concept of a group-mind (and even that of a group bond) is a delicate subject to put forth in an age of cults. But the bond we are talking about is never one that requires people to stop thinking independently, to lose their individuality. On the contrary, a small group that functions by means of the principle of immanence — one that accords each person respect for her/his views, ideas, and feelings — strengthens the individual's sense of self.

The Talking Self of a group is the thinking self, the group's ideas, policies, philosophies, and conversations. Younger Self is the feeling self, one which is often ignored in meetings. It is also the group's sense of humor, of play. A sound group must incorporate and work with all these levels.

Talking is what most groups do with most of their time. Unfortunately, nothing can be accomplished without talking about it beforehand, during the event, and afterward. Hence, groups have meetings.

Some meetings are better than others, but no meeting is as much fun as a walk on the beach, a dinner with friends, or a cozy evening with one's lover. Meetings are work, and people almost always prefer to be doing something else. People will, however, attend meetings if they feel that the work is worth doing, and that their contributions are important.

In most hierarchical groups, at any given time in a meeting, a very few people will be doing all the talking. The others will be silent — sometimes impressed, more often bored, doodling, writing letters to absent friends, or thinking about what to eat for dinner. The few talkers end up making the decisions and formulating the plans; the others abdicate or feel subtly discounted. When groups work in this fashion, they reinforce the thought-forms of estrangement. Members get the idea that some people are valuable and others are not. And very often in groups — even radical and progressive groups — the people who do most of the talking and receive most of the group's time and attention are those considered more valuable by society as a whole. It is not that the men, or the middle-class people, or the white people, or the highly educated people consciously conspire to keep others silent — it is that they have been subtly conditioned since childhood to believe that their opinions, and those of people like themselves, are valuable. Women, working class people, people of color, and people without formal education, are conditioned to think of their opinions and feelings as valueless. They are taught to listen to an inner voice that murmurs, "You shouldn't say that. You only think that because something is wrong with you. Everybody else knows more about things than you do."

Feminists who became conscious of the difficulty many women have in speaking up have developed a process that helps overcome the problem. We go around the circle, and each person is given time to speak without interruption. No one has to fight to hold the floor, or to assure that she will have a chance to talk. And even those who think their opinions have little value sometimes are surprised to discover how much they have to say when the meeting's structure allots them time in which to speak.

The Native Americans do *rounds* in the sweat lodge, passing a rattle from one person to another. Whoever holds the rattle may speak, chant, call the elements, pray, or sing, as she/he feels inspired. The group-thinking and group-feeling processes that encourage shared power and circular structure are based on rounds.

When we do rounds, the quality of our listening is as important as the quality of our talking. If we maintain that everybody's concerns and views have inherent value, we are obligated to listen to what each person is saying.

At the same time, when we speak we must become aware of whether or not other people are actually listening. Instead of repeating ourselves over and over because we sense that we are not being heard, we can learn to comment on the level of attention, to ask if people are bored, to shut up if necessary. Inflicting boredom on others is a form of violence.[1]

ACTIVE LISTENING EXERCISE

This exercise can help us become aware of how well we are (or are not) listening to others. It also helps us learn what we feel when we *are* being listened to, so that we can notice when we start losing our audience.

Divide into pairs, and choose a group timekeeper. Pick a topic related to the group's purpose. (See Appendix B, "Tools for Groups," for a list of suggestions.)

Each speaker talks on the topic for two minutes without interruption. (Times can be extended if you wish, but it is useful to practice with the two-minute limit in order to discover how much can be said in a short time.)

The other partner listens both for content and for feeling. At the end of the period, she/he briefly restates what she/he heard, without adding judgements (even approving judgements). In this culture, we are all trained to seek approval. One purpose of this exercise is to discover how good we feel when we are heard — whether or not we are praised. For power-from-within is the ability to base our actions on our own values and sense of rightness — whether or not others approve.

Switch roles. Then tell each other what you liked or didn't like about your partner's response, and how you felt doing the exercise. Share responses in the group as a whole.

This exercise is useful in a group in which people feel disconnected from each other, because most of us connect more easily with one person than with a group. It can be done several times, changing topics and partners to create new lines of connection. It is also useful when groups are in conflict and no one is listening to anyone else, or when a group is in a situation that evokes strong and frightening feelings.

The quality of a group's Talking Self can be judged by the quality of the language members use. Language that works in groups is the same language that works magic; it is simple, strong, concrete, direct, evocative of images and sensations. We cannot come into our power unless we can speak with passion. The clearer we are in our language, the clearer we are about our feelings.

Cliches and buzzwords mask our feelings, even from ourselves, by providing prepackaging for our experiences. When we hear ourselves using jargon, we are avoiding original thinking and avoiding being open about our feelings. When we say, for example, "That really pushed my buttons," we are using a stock phrase so that we don't have to say, "You hurt me. I feel angry. I'm scared." Whenever members of a group decide to "give each other strokes," I question whether they honestly like each other.

CONSCIOUSNESS-RAISING ROUNDS

The group picks a subject, such as success, our mothers, or sex. We go around the circle. Each person is given time to speak. Time may be allotted for questions, clarifications, or responses. We speak from personal experience. When the circle has been completed, we have an open discussion about the common threads and the differences among us. From that discussion, we may develop an analysis.

This is the basic process from which much feminist analysis developed. We empower ourselves by seeking the truth in our experience, by making our own truths, not those of the Great Man, the basis for our theories.

A similar process is called *Quaker Dialogue*. Each member of the circle speaks about a common problem, and how she or he resolved it. We do not comment on each other's statements or discuss them — but we learn from each other's solutions.

BRAINSTORMING

This is a process for group thinking and/or problem-solving. When an issue or problem arises, we express it in the group. Members are encouraged to think up creative solutions, ranging from the wild and improbable to the practical. The ideas are written down (preferably on a large sheet of paper so everyone can see them). They are not discussed or criticized. The purpose of brainstorming is not to refine one solution, but to see how broad a range of ideas we can formulate. Criticism and a focus on practicalities, at this stage, only dampen our creativity.

A brainstorm may or may not take place in a round, but even in a free-form discussion, group members should be sure that everyone in the group is encouraged to speak, and that a few members do not dominate the process.

After the brainstorm is over, we can pick up a few of the proposed solutions, refine them, and decide on a course of action.

FEELING-SHARING ROUNDS

It is the fourth day of peanut butter and processed cheese in the gymnasium used for the women's jail at the Diablo blockade. Spirits are high, but most of us have not been arraigned yet, and we are expecting to spend the rest of the weekend here, where you cannot close a door and escape, even for a moment, from everybody's high spirits. We begin to hear grumbling around the edges — a sound of brewing discontent. About fifteen of us gather in a circle in the yard. One after another we speak, without being interrupted, without being questioned, or answered, or given advice.

"Everyone's always talking about this wonderful unity we have — and I feel lonely. Terribly alone. My affinity group doesn't get together and there's all this superficial contact — everybody hugging and all that, but nobody I can really talk to."

"I came here out of despair. I really couldn't afford to take the time but I just couldn't stand reading the headlines every day and feeling like there was nothing I could do. So here I am — and it felt so good to be out here, to be doing something, anything — even if it was just being a body, sitting in front of that damn plant. But then, when you see the forces they've got, the power — there's so many of them and they've got all the weapons and the courts and the laws. All they have to do is sweep us up like so much litter. And I don't know, I don't feel full of love and peace and all of that garbage — I'm angry! I'm really fucking angry. I want to hit someone or kill somebody. But I *don't* want to."

"I had to leave my kids to come down here — and that's okay, that's why I'm here, because of my kids. But Jessica's only three and I'm worried about her, and I just want to go home! I want my own bed. I want my own toothbrush! I want to be able to close the door and have some quiet and I can't stand people walking on my mattress."

And as each woman says what she feels, the rest of us murmur in agreement, "MMMMMMN. Yes, I feel that too. And that. And that. And some part of me — even that." Until it begins to seem that we are all aspects of each other, or of some larger self, each of us expressing one facet of the whole. And the whole is rich; it is infinitely richer than silence, it is deeper than a cheer, a bright song, a group hug. We begin to feel that we know each other, that we are connected, no longer alone.

In feeling-sharing rounds, we go around the circle, and each person speaks about whatever feelings she/he previously thought were unacceptable. Each person may ask for response, or she/he may prefer not to. People are also encouraged to express any fears they might have about having exposed their feelings.

The Younger Self of a group is the feeling Self. A group bond is an emotional bond, and, of course, we connect by sharing affection, joy, pleasure, laughter, and trust. But our negative feelings — anger, guilt, shame, sadness, loneliness, and despair — are potentially even more powerful sources of connection. These are the feelings we tend to hug secretly to our chests, as the self-hater whispers in our ears, "You are the only person sick enough or nasty enough to feel like that." To Younger Self, the conflict, when we feel emotions that are not nice, can become one of life or death: Do I, feeling like this, deserve to be connected to the human community? Do I deserve to exist?) To be loved? Younger Self is trained by the culture to believe that everything it feels is wrong. We are raised to compete with others from the moment we can speak, and yet taught that good people aren't competitive. We are raised in a climate of violence, in which force is the national answer to every question, yet taught that anger and aggression are nasty. We are trained to feel that we are worthless unless others give us approval.

Yet Younger Self does feel angry, competitive, jealous, bitchy, dependent, weak, scared, and lonely. Often Younger Self believes it is the only one who feels these things, that everyone else is altruistic, kind, even-tempered, generous, brave, honest, and thrifty. Younger Self may fear that its feelings are so negative and so nasty that devastation would occur if they were released.

The more we remain silent about our negative feelings, the more separate and alienated we feel, and the more the unexpressed feelings become sources of group conflict. But when we feel that our anger, our pain, can be accepted and shared, we feel that our right to be the people we are is accepted at the deepest level.

Younger Self sniffs the air of a group very cautiously before it decides it is safe to show its true face. Unfortunately, most of the ways we habitually respond to feelings convince Younger Self that they are not acceptable. Nobody likes to see someone else in pain, yet when we try to cheer people up, to make them feel better, to solve their problems — or when we argue about the content of the feeling — we are telling Younger Self: No, it is not all right to feel what you're feeling.

Groups get into trouble when members begin to take over each other's problems, to give advice. Giving people new information can be empowering; giving advice makes people dependent, implies that they are not smart enough to assess the information for themselves. If we tell Joan to fold up her mattress during the day so that it will not get stepped on, we have told her nothing she couldn't figure out for herself. And we have deflected the conversation from the full range of her emotional experience, negated her feelings, instead of accepting them.

There are many techniques for working with feelings in groups. We can begin each meeting of the circle with a *weather report* — giving each member a short time to talk about her or his emotional weather. We can stop periodically in the midst of discussions to breathe, to relax, to ask each person to state in one or two words what she or he is feeling. We can pay careful attention to the style of our communications, avoiding blaming, placating, computing, or distracting.[2] We can state our criticisms as *I messages* such as, "I feel hurt when you do that," instead of voicing attacks such as, "You're a creep!"

Frankly, all of the techniques above may be helpful, but none of them guarantees a circle's emotional bonding. In fact, they may work against it. In any group in which a great deal of value is placed on correctness — be it social, religious, political, or psychological — Younger Self tends to dive under the bedclothes. True feelings are not necessarily correct and when we express them honestly, they may not come out in forms that merit the growth-movement's seal of approval. Younger Self prefers an atmosphere of irreverence, teasing, gossip, and, occasionally, open conflict to a hushed respect for propriety of any sort.

The truth is, you can't fool Younger Self. Talking Self may respond to the content of another's messages — Younger Self will respond to the emotion behind them. It doesn't matter how carefully you phrase your statements as I-messages — if you are feeling contempt for someone, that person's Younger Self will feel it. It doesn't matter how often you say, "I hear you." Younger Self knows whether or not you are really listening.

To convince Younger Self that its feelings are accepted, we need to listen honestly, and to feel our own responses honestly. For emotions never exist in a vacuum. A circle has a group heart, just as it has a group mind. Anyone who is feeling pain, rage, or fear is in touch with an important aspect of the group reality, that each person must, on some level, be sensing. If we cannot allow ourselves to draw forth our own painful feelings, if we try to shove them away or deny them, then we cannot accept them in another person.

SELF-CRITICISM WITH RESPONSE

This process is variously called Criticism/Self-Criticism or (by the Movement for a New Society) Evaluation/Self-Evaluation. It was developed by the Chinese Communists and has been widely adapted. I prefer to do it in the following manner:

The group decides on one or a number of questions. (See Appendix B, "Tools for Groups," for suggestions.) An example is: How much time do I take up in the group, as compared with others? The groups does a round, with each person evaluating herself or himself on the question. After each person speaks, the group responds, telling her/him how accurate they feel the evaluation was, and perhaps augmenting it. The purpose is to discover what, if anything, the person needs to change, and how the group can be helpful.

I once kept a quote from Gertrude Stein pinned up on my wall. It said something like, "No artist needs criticism, only honest appreciation. If he needs criticism, he is no artist."

In context, what she meant was that an artist must learn to be her/his own critic, not dependent on the judgement of others. A self-criticism session asks us to evaluate what our standards are and whether or not we meet them, instead of listening to other people tell us how we fail to meet their standards. In some groups, criticism/self-criticism is done by focusing a session on a general evaluation of one individual. I prefer the process described above because I believe that neither strengths nor weaknesses within a group are solely individual — they are qualities of the group as a system. So if Jane takes up far too much of each meeting talking, the problem is not that Jane talks too much — it is equally that Laura never says anything, that Tom goes to sleep instead of telling Jane that he is bored, or that the group needs stronger facilitation. Also, encouraging people to criticize themselves reinforces their sense of self-worth — their attitude that they are indeed capable of knowing what to do and whether or not they are doing it.

GROUP BONDING EXERCISE

(This works best in units of from four to eight people.) Sit comfortably in a circle. Ground, and center, and breathe together. If you like, do the Tree of Life. (See the description on page 30.)

Go around the circle clockwise. Each person says her or his name, and the group repeats it.

The name can be spoken or sung. The group may speak it once or three times, and may sing it back to the person.

Now everyone closes their eyes. Again, go around the circle. Each person says her/his name, and the group repeats it. As we repeat each name, we visualize that person.

Again, go around the circle. Each person says her/his name. This time, with our eyes still closed, we let ourselves picture that person's energy. We may sense a quality or an image, and as it comes to us we say it out loud:

"Rose."

"Warm."

"Turquoise and red."

"A colorful tropical bird."

We take time for each person until images have stopped coming and silence falls. (We are practicing our sensitivity to the ebb and flow of group energy.)

After we have gone around the circle, we focus on the center — breathing together, and visualizing all the images, and qualities, and energies of each of us flowing into the center. Gradually, an image or scene will begin to be created by the group energy. We describe it to each other, as aspects surface in our minds, until we are all clearly in the same place.

"I see a jungle."

"I see bright-colored birds flying."

"I see a mountain — a volcano."

"Yes, the jungle lies on its slopes."

"And I see a cave."

"In the side of the mountain."

"And we can follow it down to the fire."

We can continue with the group vision as long as we like. It may become an elaborate mutual journey. We may find a group symbol or an image of power. We may discover a task.

When we are done, we breathe together again, and return ourselves to ordinary space and time, grounding whatever energy we have raised. Then we can talk about the vision and discuss its meanings.

In Reclaiming, we find that when we teach groups this technique, many people come away from the first exploration feeling annoyed or angry, feeling that the images are shallow and stereotyped. When we ask people what they were seeing that they did not say, often we get answers such as:

"I was seeing bones and blood — but everyone else was seeing flowers, so I didn't want to spoil their trance. But now I feel alienated."

"You're kidding — *I* was seeing bones and blood. But since nobody else was, I didn't want to say."

As we continue around the circle, we discover that nobody was really *in* the pretty scene the group created. Rather, all were seeing much darker and usually more powerful images, but they were withholding them from the group. The discovery of how much we all withhold is disconcerting, and the trance exercise becomes a model of group process in ordinary situations.

If we repeat the exercise, with each person committed to expressing even negative images, we will discover a much deeper level of group power and bonding.

CONSENSUS DECISION MAKING

The process of decision making that embodies the principle of power-from-within is called consensus. Consensus was used by the Quakers (whose doctrine of the "inner light" reflects a Christian conception of immanence), but the process has been used informally among tribal groups for centuries, especially in Native American cultures.

Jerry Mander, in an article on the forced relocation of the Hopi and Navaho peoples in the Big Mountain area of Arizona, quotes Oliver La Farge, the Bureau of Indian Affairs Hopi Agent, on Hopi consensus:

> It is alien to the Hopis to settle matters out of hand by majority vote. Such a vote leaves a dissatisfied minority, which makes them very uneasy. Their natural way of doing it is to discuss it among themselves at great length, and group by group, until public opinion as a whole has settled overwhelmingly in one direction.[3]

Consensus is not the same as voting. Nor does it merely mean unanimity. Groups sometimes think they are using consensus but revert to voting when they cannot reach unanimity. They are not truly using consensus, however, because the process is based on a principle that makes it entirely different from voting.

When we vote, we are still in the framework of duality. "Here are two alternatives," we are saying, "choose one over the other. The choice most people make is the one we will act upon — whether the others like it or not." The majority wields power-over the minority.

The principle of immanence, however, gives no one authority to wield power-over others. With consensus, we tell a new story.

We say that everybody's voice is worth hearing, that all concerns are valid. If one proposal makes a few people — even one person — deeply unhappy, there is a valid reason for that unhappiness, and if we ignore it, we are likely to make a mistake. Instead of spending the group's energy trying to force or manipulate people into agreeing to something they don't want, we can drop either or both alternatives and look for a new solution, a more creative option that can satisfy all concerns. We can afford to do this because the universe is not truly divided into either/or choices. It is rich with infinite possibilities.

The consensus process works best with a facilitator who calls on people and keeps the meeting focused. (See Chapter Seven, "Circles and Webs: Group Structures," for more notes on facilitation.) One person puts forth a proposal. In a small group not pressured by time, the group may do a round on the proposal. More often, the facilitator asks if anyone wishes to speak about it, either to speak for it or to voice questions or concerns.

The concept of *concerns* is important. Negative reactions are not expressed as hard-and-fast positions. Instead of saying, "I am categorically against it," we say "I am concerned about it," and we give the reason. Voicing concerns leaves room for the proposal to be modified to meet those concerns.

For example, someone might say, "Kathy wants to join the group; I propose that we accept her."

Someone else might reply, "I like Kathy, but I'm concerned that the group is growing too big."

There are many ways that the proposal could be modified: we could decide to admit Kathy, and no one else after her; we could ask Kathy to wait until someone else dropped out of the group; or we could decide to help Kathy form a group of her own.

If a person feels that her/his concerns cannot be met and the rest of the group is enthusiastic about the proposal, that person can "stand aside." For example, a member might propose that the group study and discuss a certain book. Perhaps one member has no enthusiasm for the project, or is already overwhelmed with things to read from work or school. She/he could decide not to participate, and let the rest of the group go ahead.

If one person has strong objections to a proposal, especially ethical objections, she/he can *block* the proposal. *Blocks* are used rarely and carefully. I can think of only a few instances (out of hundreds of meetings I have seen in which the consensus process was used) when anyone has blocked a proposal. Yet the ability to block a proposal gives each individual ultimate power to influence the decisions that affect her/him. If one person feels strongly enough about an issue to block it, she/he is probably aware of important factors the rest of the group should consider more carefully.

People may raise objections to a proposal, as well as concerns. When feelings run strongly against a proposal, it may be dropped instead of modified.

Consensus takes time. It works most efficiently in small groups; when a group is too large, it becomes impossible to hear everybody. Time spent reaching consensus is well spent, however, because proposals that are wholeheartedly agreed to by a group are carried out wholeheartedly. Voting may seem quicker (although not always — groups can spend long periods attempting to cajole one faction to change its position) but often an unhappy minority undermines a project pushed by the majority, or simply fails to carry it out.

No group, however, can decide by consensus whether to be shot or hung. The consensus process is not effective for choosing the lesser of two evils, for deciding between bad alternatives. It does not work in a dualistic framework.

For example, in the women's jail during the third or fourth day of the Diablo blockade, when about three hundred of us were crowded into a cold gymnasium sleeping on pads crammed wall-to-wall on the concrete floor, we were given a choice by the guards: forty more women were arriving; we could have them in our room, making the crowding worse, or they could be isolated from us in a separate, and even colder room.

Instead of breaking down into affinity groups, we began to debate the question all together — always a mistake. Consensus works badly in large groups at the best of times. We were given fifteen minutes to make the decision. The pressure of time is another factor that makes consensus more difficult.

Feelings ran deep. Many women felt strongly that they could not stand to be crowded further. Others felt equally strongly that the new women should not be isolated. The tension caused by days of poor food and physical discomfort began to show.

Even so, the consensus process worked as consensus works: we came up with two creative solutions. The first was that the new women should go into the other room, but that free passage should be allowed between the rooms. This was vetoed by the guards. The second solution was that women from our group should go into the other room, and the new women should come into our room. This, also, the guards would not allow. So the fifteen minutes passed, and we came to no consensus. The guards made their own decision, and we women felt we had failed each other.

Yet in reality we did not fail, we were manipulated. Even though we could see at the time that we were being set up to be divided, we didn't see how to stop the process. Looking back, however, we could have recognized, when our solutions were turned down, that we were not actually being given the chance to make a decision that would suit us. We could, at that point, have refused to cooperate any longer with the illusion that was being perpetrated. Our withdrawal would have made the reality of the situation clearer — that the guards, not us, were responsible for the conditions we were forced to endure.

When consensus does work, however, everyone feels both a personal sense of triumph and a sense of closeness to the group. The process requires maturity, and flexibility, along with willingness to give way for the good of the group, to listen rather than hold forth, to invent rather than insist. Oddly, as people practice consensus, they become more mature, more flexible, more willing to listen and to give away. Consensus calls forth the best that is in us, and so empowers us to work together in community.

Chapter Seven

❧

Circles and Webs: Group Structures

In the circle, we all face each other. No one is exalted; no one's face is hidden. No one is above — no one is below. We are all equal in the circle, the womb, the breast, the eye, the cunt, the sun, the moon — the forms of immanence.

All groups have structures — open and hidden. Just as individuals have bones and flesh, and also a subtle energy-body in a treelike pattern formed by currents of power, so too a group has an outer form and an inner form.

We can change consciousness, we can transform our inner landscape, tell new stories, dream visions in new thought-forms. But to change culture we need to bond in new ways, to change the structures of our organizations and communities. "Function follows form," we could say (reversing the Bauhaus dictum). For as we have seen, structure determines how energy will flow.

The structures of estrangement are hierarchies. Their form is the ladder. In schools, in corporations, in government bureaucracies, in social agencies and professions, we are expected to climb from rung to rung. The function of a ladder is to be climbed. The rungs keep those above separate from those below. Upon each rung, we wield power over those below, and must bow to the authority of those above. The higher rungs are populated by fewer and fewer people, so a small number always exercises power over a much larger mass.

The structures of immanence are circular: clans, tribes, covens, collectives, support groups, affinity groups, consciousness-raising groups. In a circle, each person's face can be seen, each person's voice can be heard and valued. All points on a circle are equidistant from its center: that is its definition, and its function — to distribute energy equally.

Creating and working in circular structures, however, is an enormous challenge. We are familiar with ladders; we understand them even when we dislike them; they make us comfortable because we know what to expect. Circles are unfamiliar territory, new ground. The experiences we have within them can be healing or heartbreaking, wonderful or extremely frustrating, intimate or alienating, more intense than any other relationships except family ties.

Changing the structure of a group can be a powerful way of changing the relationships among people within it. Every group has both an open and a hidden structure. To a large extent, especially in nonhierarchical groups, structure can be thought of as patterns of communication that determine how information flows. Information is power — it enables us to do what we otherwise could not do. In a hierarchical group, only a small number of people have access to information and they make decisions. In a nonhierarchical structure, everybody makes decisions and so all must have access to information. Most nonhierarchical groups do not pay enough attention to the ways in which information spreads among group members. Systems to spread information — newsletters, flyers, telephone trees, meetings, and (most of all) conversation — are the life blood of any group. Groups thrive when people within a community have many informal meetings, go to the same parties, run into each other on the street, meet for coffee, and generally enjoy each other's society, because a network of friendships creates a grapevine that is the only truly efficient way to spread information. People often ignore leaflets, but everybody listens to gossip.

The formal roles people take on in a group are its bones, the underpinnings of its outer structure. To assure that power is shared within a group, formal roles should rotate among members. People can practice a role, such as facilitator, in a relatively safe setting — a meeting of a small group in an unstressful situation. Virtuoso facilitators can reserve their talents for moments of great need — for example, legal meetings in jail that take place shortly before arraignments. Good facilitators should also rotate, however, so that they, too, learn a variety of skills. A good, though of course flexible, rule-of-thumb is: never perform the same job twice in succession.

Groups function best when their formal structures are clearly defined and understood. Following is a description of six of the formal roles often performed in a variety of nonhierarchical groups, ranging from collectives to covens. (I personally dislike most of the names for these roles, but haven't invented any better ones.)

THE FACILITATOR

The facilitator observes the *content* of talk in a meeting. She/he keeps the meeting focused and moving. Commonly, when people are discussing one proposal, they will drift off the subject and begin talking about something else. The facilitator reminds them of what the subject is, and if necessary sets aside a future time to discuss the related issues that surface. From time to time, the facilitator may give a brief "state-of-the-meeting" report, saying, "This is what we are talking about. . . . These are the positions and concerns. . . . This is what we have already decided that is relevant." Making reports and restating proposals is especially necessary in long, tense, exhausting meetings during which people have a tendency to forget what they are doing.

The facilitator calls on people. When several people raise their hands to speak, she/he can give them numbers and let them speak in turn. When people are assured that they will be called on, their anxiety levels are lessened, and they can more easily listen to others.

The facilitator should maintain neutrality on the issue being discussed. If she/he has a strong position, or wishes to speak to the issue, another facilitator can be chosen.

VIBESWATCHER

A vibeswatcher (used in the Abalone Alliance) watches the process of a meeting. In particular, she/he remains aware of levels of tension and anxiety. She/he may interrupt the meeting periodically to suggest that people breathe, that feelings be acknowledged, that personal attacks be stopped. In large or tense meetings, a vibeswatcher can be appointed. In smaller meetings, every person present can take on some of this responsibility.

PRIESTESS/PRIEST

In a ritual, the priestess or priest watches the energy of the group. She/he keeps it moving, starts and stops phases of the ritual as the energy changes, *channels* the energy by opening her/his own body to let it flow through. The priestess/priest develops a dual consciousness, an ability to be ecstatic in the moment and, at the same time, to keep a practical eye on what everybody else is doing, whether the cauldron is burning too high, and whether the children are getting trampled underfoot. Especially in large rituals in which many people are unfamiliar with magic, the Priestess/Priest must assure that the energy starts grounded, stays grounded (in the sense of maintaining connection with the earth) and is returned to the earth at the end. It is helpful to have more than one person acting as priestess/priest within a ritual.

PEACEKEEPERS

Peacekeepers (used in the Abalone Alliance) function not only during meetings, but whenever the group is active. They help keep order and deal with crises. At demonstrations, marches, and blockades, they may function as monitors who are trained to defuse potential violence from outside the group or from within it.

Peacekeepers do not have arcane or professional skills. They may have practice in calming and centering themselves, in active listening, in establishing communication with hard-to-reach people. They may encircle a violent person and walk her/him out of the area, or sing to drown the voice of a verbally abusive person. Their value is not so much in their techniques, but in their willingness and readiness to assume responsibility. Ideally, every person in a group becomes a peacekeeper.

MEDIATOR

A mediator is a neutral, objective person who helps others resolve a conflict. A mediator is not a judge, she/he does not choose between two people or two factions, but rather helps each to listen and to resolve their differences. Mediation is a definite skill, and, usually, good mediators have had some training or much practice. Most communities, however, include many people who make good mediators. When conflicts arise within a group, members should not be ashamed to call for help from the larger community.

COORDINATOR

A coordinator can serve as a group center, a switchboard through which information is passed. She/he keeps track of what is being done, who is doing it, and what needs to be done. The coordinator's role is especially important in large projects involving many details and many helpers. It also tends to be exhausting and not as rewarding as many other tasks, but it provides a marvelous opportunity to make mistakes and learn how to take criticism. Coordinators should be more widely appreciated, and should exchange roles often.

The most interesting aspect of a group, however, is its hidden structure. All groups function according to both overt and covert rules. The unspoken rules often concern expression of feelings. In many families, for example, an unspoken rule says: you can't say anything negative about Mommy and Daddy. In many groups, a similar unspoken rule holds sway: don't say anything negative about anybody.

In the Reclaiming Collective, however, we run our meetings by this covert rule: if people laugh at you, insult you, and swear at you, they are showing affection; when people speak quietly and carefully according to the approved growth-movement formulas, watch out! Children run in and out, we eat and drink continuously, and the meetings resemble something between amateur comedy tryouts and a pitched battle in a nursery school. The meetings inevitably run for four or five hours, but we get through our agendas. I consider these meetings to be great group process.

The overt rule, which we are continually struggling to live down to, is: all feelings are real, and inherently valid; express them freely.

Another aspect of a group's hidden structure can be made visible by having members ask themselves the following questions:

How much do I feel connected to the group? How alienated do I feel? If the group were a circle — where would I be in it? At the center? On the periphery? Outside? How would I act differently if I felt central and connected?

A group that is having conflicts might ask each member to draw the group as a circle, and to mark her/his position, so that everyone can look at the drawing and talk about the various perceptions of the structure.

One easy way to give up power is by assuming we don't have it. There are strong cultural forces at work making us feel alienated and isolated, so it should be no surprise that group situations can be very painful for many people, who feel excluded or peripheral, never quite in with the in crowd. Someone who feels isolated feels powerless; and it is always easy to feel that others — the group — are doing something to that individual, imposing something that she/he doesn't have the right or authority to challenge. After all, throughout our lives various groups *have* been imposing conditions on us that (they claim) we do not have the right to challenge. We tend to assume, even in structures that are openly committed to egalitarian, antiauthoritarian principles, that we don't have the right to make decisions unless we are given specific permission. That is what our experience in authoritarian structures has taught us.

As an example, in the early days of the Diablo Canyon Nuclear Power Plant blockade, another woman and I felt a need for a general gathering in the evening, to sing, share announcements, and feel a sense of the camp as a whole. The blockade was clearly an open, anarchic structure; nevertheless, our first instinct was to seek out a trainer, someone who seemed to have a position of leadership to ask, "Who has the authority to call a meeting?" "You do," was the response. So we did — by simply walking around camp and calling out, "We're having a gathering."

We could easily, however, have assumed a position of power-lessness, and spent the evening grumbling about how insensitive the leaders were because they didn't see that we needed a meeting of the whole camp.

Let's imagine, for a moment, that the Abalone Alliance had a hierarchical structure, that when we asked, "Who has the authority to call a meeting?" we were told that we could submit a proposal in triplicate to the Board of Directors, and that the Chairman would decide.

We could still have walked around camp, called out, "We're having a meeting," and had one. The consequences might have been different — but the power was ours if we had recognized and been willing to take it. That's important to remember when we deal with the hierarchical structures we encounter constantly in daily life. Very often, we abandon our power even when the structure does not take it away from us. Or we ask permission to take it — putting ourselves in the position of dependent children, instead of assuming our right and authority to make decisions.

The formal roles in a group can be used consciously to help change its underlying structure. For example, during one meeting in the women's jail at Diablo Canyon, I was about to facilitate when another woman objected. "The same people always run the meetings — and I think there are some power issues going on."

We asked if she had ever facilitated a meeting, and when she said no we appointed her facilitator for that one. Instead of being an outsider complaining, she was given a formal role that placed her at center. Often now, in the collective groups I belong to, we begin meetings with a weather report, asking each person how central or distant they are feeling. Whoever feels most peripheral may be appointed facilitator. Whoever tends to monopolize the talk is asked to take notes. Whoever feels grumpiest and most irritated is asked to be vibeswatcher.

In any group, members have associations outside the group itself. These contacts may range from quick exchanges of news to deep friendships. The more two people communicate outside the group, the more information they may exchange, and the more they may influence each other. An outside coalition can increase the influence of its members within the group. A coalition, like an individual, can take the position of outsider, encapsulating its members and alienating them.

When a group is alive and thriving, coalitions are constantly forming, shifting, deepening, re-forming. When there is a great deal of crossover among coalitions, they become the stitching that binds the group together as a whole. But if they become frozen into factions, or if one or more members find themselves excluded from coalitions, the coalitions can become sources of schism.

There is no way to make people like each other if they don't. There are, however, ways to increase contact and communication among members. When two people work together, they generally draw closer, provided they are both responsible. Otherwise, they may end up hating each other. In that case, one or the other may leave the group, thus resolving the problem. If people from different factions within a group take on a task together, they are forced to communicate more with each other, and often a new bond is formed. In Reclaiming we have found that teaching in pairs and meeting often to plan classes causes us to grow very close to our co-teachers. That closeness becomes one of the rewards of teaching. Nevertheless, we make an effort to shift teams around, so that we maintain many ties with many members, and the group as a whole is strengthened.

People come to groups, as we have said, from many different backgrounds and with many different needs and experiences. The positions we assume in a group are often part of an ongoing pattern that each of us repeats in life unconsciously, unless we make a deliberate effort to become aware of it and to change. Some of us get used to being at center, important figures in any group. Others gravitate toward the middle, where they can be anonymous. Still others are always on the outside. It takes a lot of work to change the patterns we have learned in competitive groups and in other structures of domination.

Following are descriptions of ten such positions, ten informal roles I have seen people take on in nonhierarchical groups. Of course, no one plays only one role — we all switch, invent new characters for ourselves, grow and develop. Some of us are even able to function as solid, committed, loving, hard-working, real people.

Power-from-within encompasses the power to change ourselves. In my experience, people change not by being given answers, but by asking themselves pertinent questions. I have provided such questions for each of the roles I describe. The ten are arranged according to the place within a circle that each tends to assume, moving from the periphery to the center.

THE LONE WOLF

You don't commit yourself to the group, but love to criticize and compare the group with other groups, usually unfavorably. Ask yourself, "Why do I want to hang around people I consider inferior? Am I afraid of my equals?" Also ask, "How would my criticisms be different if I said, 'We should' . . . instead of, 'You should' . . .?"

THE ORPHAN

Often you come from a background of loss and deprivation. You may have been a prisoner, mental patient, or another one of the culture's Fallen. You desperately want the closeness the group offers, and are terrified both of the vulnerability that represents, and of the rejection you are sure you will get instead. You believe that if people really knew you, they would be disappointed or disgusted. So you slink around the edges of groups, never opening up or making close friends, and eventually others *do* start to dislike you, fulfilling your worst fears. Ask yourself, "What work can I take on for the group, preferably in company with one or two others? What can I contribute?"

GIMME SHELTER

You are constantly demanding something from the group: advice, reassurance, help. You want the group to make you feel welcome, important, loved, supported. After all, don't they say that's what it's there for? Ask yourself, "What actual work can I do for the group? What tasks can I take on — and can I do them in such a way that my work does not require anyone else to expend time or energy on the tasks?" Also ask, "How would I act differently if I felt I had power?" then act that way.

FILLER

You just take up space. You feel your opinions and ideas aren't very interesting or valuable. Perhaps you have been trained all your life to think that way. Wear brighter colors and encourage yourself to speak up at least once at every meeting, particularly when your ideas and perceptions differ from others'. Take on a task involving more than routine work — perhaps with the orphan. Make a date with someone from the group to do something together outside the group.

THE PRINCESS

You are so very sensitive that the group process is never smooth enough for you. You feel compelled to comment on slight tensions and minor nuances of conflict, often expressing great anxiety. The Princess (who may also be male) is often a therapist or a psychic, and often leaves groups unless she/he is running them. Ask yourself "Who am I competing with, and why?" Refrain from commenting on group process until you can do so by affectionately insulting another group member.

THE CLOWN

The clown or fool is an important figure in many tribal religions. The clown's job is to make fun of people and ceremonies, and to provide comic relief. You probably provide an important service to the group. Nevertheless, ask yourself, "Can I be serious when necessary? Do I know when to practice restraint? Is my clowning, at any given moment, furthering the work of the group? Am I afraid of open conflict?"

THE CUTE KID

You are charming and cute, and want approval from others badly. Your excuse, when you don't want to do something, is to plead helplessness or get sick. You would love to be taken care of, yet you are actually much more competent and strong than you are willing to believe. Ask yourself, "Do I really mean that I *can't*, or that I don't want to? Does the task perhaps need to be done whether I want to do it or not — and done by me? What new level of power or responsibility will I come to if I do it? Does that scare me?" Also ask, "What in my life — in the group — would I do

whether or not others approve?" Ask the group not to praise you
for doing those things.

THE SELF-HATER

You are a perfectionist, harder on yourself than on others.
Nevertheless, you are continually escalating your standards for
the group, and continually outraged at how much others fail to
live up to them. You don't understand why other people feel
guilty after talking with you, when you are truly only trying to
raise their consciousness about the issue of the moment.

Be nicer to yourself. Play. At least once a day, do something
irresponsible. Sandwich your criticisms between expressions of
appreciation. Ask yourself if you identify with Jesus. If the answer
is yes, get friends to sing hymns to you off-key before meetings.

THE ROCK OF GIBRALTAR

You take on thankless tasks and get them done. You remember
what everyone else forgets. Everyone comes to you with their
problems. Outsiders often see you as "the leader" of the group.
Indeed, you feel that the group would fall apart without you.

Ask yourself, "Am I afraid of showing my weaknesses?" Also
ask, "What tasks can I delegate?" Give away some of the juicy,
creative tasks as well as the routine work. Begin training your
replacement immediately, before burnout sets in.

THE STAR

You feel the meeting hasn't really begun until you arrive. You
talk a lot, and often interrupt people, because you know that you
will say exactly the right thing to save the situation. Really, you
are brilliant, and you enjoy impressing people.

Practice silence. Ask yourself, "Do I want to impress people or
to empower people? How do *I* feel about people who are constantly trying to prove to me that I can never equal *them?*" Recognize that others feel the same way about you. Change, and keep
your friends.

My tendency in groups is to play the role of Rock or Star. I was
trained for those roles from childhood. In my family, I was given
a great deal of responsibility. Because my father died when I was

five, I was often my mother's confidante, and learned that even adults took my views and opinions seriously. I grew up feeling special. In school, I was often the smartest kid in the class, the one who always knew the right answer when nobody else did. I was also smart enough to realize that being the constant winner in the classroom competition did not make me well-loved, and in fact, it could easily make me a target of jealousy and hostility. So I developed a kind of phony humility, a manner that said, "Aw, shucks, kids — I'm just one of the gang — those As were sort of an accident. And look how bad I am at softball (heh, heh)."

In groups, I felt comfortable taking on a lot of responsibility, facilitating meetings, taking the role of teacher, priestess, leader. In collectives and nominally leaderless groups, my outward manner was still "Aw, shucks, kids — I'm just one of the gang." Yet, actually, much of my own sense of identity depended upon being the one to step in with a brilliant answer at the crucial moment.

In *The Spiral Dance* I recorded some of the struggles around power and leadership that we went through in my first coven. My present coven, Raving, emerged from a class for women that I taught. We spent three years struggling to break out of the teacher-student framework and make our power relationships truly equal. For a long time I was genuinely confused. I thought I was bending over backward to give people power — I didn't understand why they weren't taking more of it. What I didn't see was the way I held tight to the reins while complaining loudly that the horses wouldn't guide themselves. As long as I saw myself *giving* people power, I unconsciously believed that that power belonged to me.

For example, for a long time we considered our rituals collective because we all performed such tasks as leading various parts, writing invocations, and guiding trances. That was certainly a step toward collectivity and away from the custom of one person leading everything. However, because the actual control of a ritual rests with the person who controls the transitions and the timing — who starts and stops things — it was a lot easier for me to give up leading anything overtly than to give up starting and stopping what everybody else was doing.

I also discovered — painfully — that as each woman in the coven finally came into her own sense of power, she and I would have a fight. I gradually understood that, having taken on a position of authority in the group, I, on some level, represented the principle of authority to each woman, a principle each of us must battle if we are to claim the authority in ourselves. As long as I was willing, even unconsciously, to play authority, each woman was going to have to battle me. Such conflicts may be productive between analyst and client, but in a circle they tended to be extremely draining, especially for me.

Somehow, Raving managed to muddle through. Eventually, we became a collective, called Reclaiming, as well as a coven, and decided to begin teaching classes and helping new groups to form. We also decided that there must be ways to structure the groups based on another model of power, so the new groups wouldn't have to repeat our struggles with authority.

One decision we made was to teach in pairs, so that from the beginning students could see power being shared and flowing easily. One teacher almost inevitably becomes an authority — two create more space in the center, so others can join them more easily. We also systematically turned over parts of each class and each ritual to the students, so that everyone got a chance to be the central focus, to take both power and responsibility. Finally, advanced students began teaching with us.

Another lesson we learned is that the roles people take on in groups are often related to their class backgrounds. Class is not just a matter of income, but of values and expectations, the subtle messages one gets from one's family and peers. My family valued intelligence and education — there was never a doubt in the atmosphere that I was bright, would go to college, and would succeed at something requiring brains. I could have been born, equally bright, into a family in which children were discouraged from speaking to their elders, or where there were too many children for any one to receive much attention. The family values might have centered around hard work instead of education, and the expectations might have been that we just weren't the sort of people who excelled in school, which wasn't an important arena of life, anyway. I might have grown up thinking I was dumb and should keep my mouth shut in groups of smart people.

Opening up a discussion of our class backgrounds is important in groups — not to make middle-class people feel guilty or defensive, but because we do not really know each other unless we know each other's histories. When class differences can be named, the sense of isolation, of being from another planet, that people from poor or working class backgrounds often feel in groups can be lessened. And we can learn from our differences in ethnic background, race, sex, physical limitation, and appearance.

Estrangement perpetuates itself by keeping us divided from each other. We are taught to fear people of different ethnic or class backgrounds, to turn our frustrations and resentment on each other instead of on the system that hurts us all. Talking about our differences, confronting our distrust of others who are different, is the first step in healing the pain we feel at our separation. Only through such healing can we create community that reaches across the lines of race, sex, and class, so that all our separate strengths can be joined together.

When we struggle to step out of roles, to confront our differences, we do so not to be politically correct, but to free ourselves and to enrich our experience. The culture of domination rewards us for being at center, for hanging on to attention, status, and control. The cult at the heart of American culture is that of personality, offering as its highest reward the narcissistic joy of Making It, of being applauded, admired, and looked-up-to from below as one straddles the top rungs of the ladder. But the top rungs are isolated and unstable. One can always fall. And being looked up to is very different from being supported by the real love and real trust of others upon whom we can also depend, because they are equals, because they can call forth their own power-from-within.

At center, we get attention. We wield power — but we are not free to move. When you are uniquely important and responsible for everything, you are also neatly trapped. When you let go, when you realize that others can do what you do equally well, although undoubtedly differently, you can move on, and undertake new responsibilities, without expecting what you have built to collapse when you leave.

About a year after we began teaching together, Reclaiming went through a period of crisis. Two of our five members had to move away from the area in order to find jobs in their fields. The remaining three of us were struggling to continue the classes and meet the commitments of the collective. Two of us went to the Diablo blockade, when the alert was called, leaving Lauren by herself to handle everything. At such moments, collectives often crumble. But because we had trained our replacements, other women were ready and eager to take over our responsibilities. Instead of dying the group expanded.

A healthy group is never stable. It is always changing, growing, re-forming. There are many theories about the stages of group formation, but in my experience with groups several stages are generally occurring at once. Nevertheless, a broad movement can usually be discerned, and knowing something of its pattern can, at least, reassure us that we are not the only group who ever went through these particular conflicts and survived. I prefer to conceive of the cycle as following the magic circle of the four elements:

CYCLES OF GROUP TRANSFORMATION
AIR

The group begins with a common vision and common perceptions. Often, members are excited when they meet others who think as they do, who share common goals. This is usually a honeymoon period, during which members feel close to each other and admire each other — because they don't really know each other. Energy is generated.

FIRE

The group struggles to discover how to use its energy. In hierarchical groups, members struggle for power-over. In nonhierarchical groups, members struggle for power more subtly, or struggle to define structures and processes that will empower individuals and allow them to share power equally. The group begins to discover its will, and deep feelings are generated.

WATER

The group struggles with the feelings members have for each other. Now that members know each other, they love each other and rage at each other. People in the group both want and resist more intimacy. They fight about their closeness or distance. Someone's feelings are continually being hurt. Sometimes group members become lovers — or, worse, fall in love with each other's lovers. This stage once drove me to formulate Starhawk's Three Laws of Small Groups:

1. In any small group in which people are involved sexually, sooner or later there will be grave conflicts.
2. In any small group in which people are involved, sooner or later they will be involved sexually, even if only in fantasy.
3. Small groups tend to break up.

EARTH

If the group survives its emotional conflicts, it tends to *crystallize*, defining itself and its boundaries more clearly. As its purpose and character emerge, the group can begin to undertake serious work. During this phase some members usually leave the group (if they haven't left before). New members join. The group functions in the wider world. Its successes, failures, and continued growth lead eventually to a new vision — and the cycle begins again.

In each stage, conflicts arise about the very areas which are potential sources of new growth. Conflict can be creative if we look upon it as telling us what tasks we need to accomplish. Some guidelines for each of the stages follow:

AIR

Conflicts arise about goals, perceptions, and differences. Visions and goals need to be expressed. Accept that people will have differing perceptions. Discuss people's differences in background, including class, race, culture, education, and conditioning to sex roles. Also discuss differences in people's present situation, including their special needs, the resources of time and money available to each, and their personal goals. Differing levels of experience should also be acknowledged.

Create a bonding ritual.

FIRE

Conflicts arise about power. Use all the processes described above that encourage the sharing of power. Exchange roles, train replacements, encourage silent people to speak up and talkative people to occasionally shut up. Practice consensus.

Competition is always present in groups. Acknowledge it: it can be used creatively. Create situations, such as rituals, in which people can show off and be admired.

Work directly with group energy through breathing, chanting, dancing, and grounding.

WATER

What are people feeling? Express the negatives. Speak the unspeakable. Name the group's unspoken rules. Be aware of how much time, energy and attention each member asks for, and receives. Give the group, and individuals, praise and appreciation as well as criticism — and encourage members to accept praise. Share food. Have fun.

When couples or coalitions develop, take care that those involved also strengthen ties with other group members — perhaps by working together on projects.

EARTH

Clarify the group's organizational structure and its boundaries: who is in and who is out. Wish those who leave well, but don't try to keep them if they want to go. Take on new people. Get the work done.

AIR

Reflect on the experiences that grow from the work. Arrive at new visions, perceptions, goals, differences. Start a new cycle.

METASTRUCTURES

And so groups grow and combine — but not into faceless masses. They grow as bodies do, into organisms consisting of many cells, many parts, each of which retains its own integrity. We make networks. We weave webs. We could also say that our organizations are like music — they should contain silences and many small phrases repeated with infinite variations, and they should join in strong rhythms, in moving themes.

Small groups network by using *spokes* (as they are called in the Abalone Alliance) as wheels use spokes to join the rim to the hub. These spokes, however, join wheels to wheels, circles to other circles. I am drawing this as I write and I make patterns that look like snowflakes, crystals, stars, diagrams of molecules, a bed of sea coral, a matrix of bone, something organic, or perhaps a demented child's tinkertoy construction.

Spokes are people chosen to speak for the group, to embody the group will and to connect it with other groups. Like people taking other formal roles, spokes should be changed frequently. Spokes from many groups can meet to discuss issues and, if their groups empower them to do so, to make decisions. When all groups work by consensus, every decision is a synthesis of many people's viewpoints and ideas, not an either/or choice decided by a majority. At the blockade, for example, affinity groups formed clusters and sent spokes to cluster meetings. Each cluster, in turn, sent a spoke to the overall council that made decisions affecting the camp. But the council held no power-over individual groups. Power always rested in the smallest unit. The affinity groups shaped the decisions of the larger groups. The council, after hearing from the clusters, who in turn had heard from each affinity group, could make the decision to begin the blockade. But it could not tell any individual group where to go or what to do.

Such structures are often criticized for being inefficient. They are easily ridiculed — especially in the media. Of course anyone who has recently dealt with a government agency, or tried to get a large corporation to redress a computer error might well question whether hierarchical structures are, indeed, as efficient as we like to believe. In fact, anyone who has ever worked in the lower levels of a hierarchy knows the amount of waste, theft, and minor sabotage that occurs daily. Hierarchies appear to be efficient only because they have enormous resources, money and the armed forces of the state to back them up.

A general can tell a soldier where to attack and what weapons to use. If the soldier disobeys, he may be shot or thrown into prison. Networks of circles cannot call on the national guard to enforce their commands, even if they want to. Covens, peace groups, antinuclear groups, and women's groups can neither buy nor command obedience. Indeed, if they tried to command it, they would arouse nothing but resentment. Our major (perhaps our only) real resource is people — their good will, their power-from-within. Efficiency can only be judged by the degree to which the will and the power of the people involved are tapped and strengthened. By that standard, egalitarian structures are highly efficient.

However, networks do not always convey information quickly. A network does not need a leader, but it often needs a *center* — some point where information can be collected and distributed to all the circles.

On some projects, the center might be a person or a small group of people. Inevitably, because we have all been conditioned to seek outside authority, network members will imbue the central people with authority, ask them to make decisions, and often see them as leaders. Central figures in egalitarian groups should be prepared to challenge others' assumptions, and to maintain a sense of humor.

A center does not have to be a person or group, however. It may be a physical place where people can meet; it may be a periodic event, such as the general camp meeting my friend and I called at the Diablo Canyon Nuclear Power Plant blockade. It may be a telephone tree, or a bulletin board located in a central place. It may be a radio station, a newspaper, a newsletter, a coffee house, or a neighborhood bar. It may be a festival or a ritual — but there must be some way to spread information quickly among members of a group, because without information, nothing can happen.

The Goddess manifests where we are. If we dream these networks, these snowflake structures, into a larger vision, we find that their texture differs from place to place. People begin to speak of politics of place, of bioregions.¹ My community is concerned with this neighborhood: with knowing the local dogs and their owners; the child of the couple who run the flower shop; the identical twin butchers; the black man who sits on his stoop and smiles as I walk up and down the street, and who likes to watch the comedy auditions at the Other Cafe. It has to do with history — with the wild boar that once ran on Sutro Hill, with the hippies who flocked here in the sixties, and with their sad remnants, the burnouts, the addicts, who still haunt Haight Street like the ghosts of acid trips past.

Our vision is of this neighborhood, this city, governed not from above but from below. What could we do, as neighbors, as city-zens, if we took our power — if we shaped the future of our city out of our love for these particular hills crowned with imported eucalyptus forests, these waters, these bridges, this clear air, these Victorian houses with their long halls and tiny rooms, this legacy of poets and gold dust and earthquakes? What if we also called our community this bay, this ocean? What if it were not some-thing separate from the pelican and the snowy egret and the gray whales passing in their migrations past our cliffs? Perhaps if we knew our neighbors we would not allow them to be forced out of their homes by the ever-rising rents; perhaps they would protect us. Perhaps together we would change the city's face, find ways to draw power from these winds, these tides, find ways to help each other through the losses, the hard times — because hard times come to us all.

When we say *community*, we might think about things in new ways — not with loyalty to "one nation, indivisible" (too big to grasp), but with loyalty to real people in a real place, where we live. Loyalty to a watershed that stretches from the high Sierras down the winding delta into the bay, and to all people who drink that water. In Europe, the old cultures arise again; we are not Bri-tish, they say, but Irish, Scottish, Welsh, Cornish, Manx; not French, but Breton; not Spanish, but Catalan. The empires come apart at the seams. In the Southwest of the United States, in the Black Hills, the Indian tribes still fight to survive. Perhaps it is time for all of us to reconsider our loyalties, to consider what might further human survival. Our work is not just sawing the legs off the ladders, but building the structures that can replace them.

We spin our circles. Some of them hold and many unravel; yet we begin again, knowing that this work of making community is weaving the mantle of the Goddess. May it be a cloak to shield each one of us from the cold; a net to catch us when we fall.

Chapter Eight

❧ ☙

Sex and Politics

August, 1979

Coven Raving is meeting. As always when we meet, we talk about our lives, about our needs, about our lovers or lack of lovers.

We are gathered under a high Victorian ceiling in a flat in the Mission district. The sashes are drawn as the time comes to work magic. We take off our clothes.

That is relevant, because our magic, our deliberate linking and focusing of minds, our raising and molding of subtle energies, our touching of each other, our intimacy, is not separate from our sexuality. Nor can our sexuality be separated from our magic. We are not lovers with each other, but we are five naked women in the small room, and as we breathe together, inhaling and exhaling in unison, becoming one—one breath, one organism—the air is heavy with odors that are earthy, spicy, fetid. We are exotic flowers; we are slowly-eroding-over-a-lifetime flesh.

We are Witches. We pursue together the Mysteries. And sexuality, not in its narrow but its broadest sense, is the essence of those Mysteries.

I am writing now beside a lake that is 7000 feet up in the Sierras. The still water is a perfect mirror, reflecting the rounded outcroppings of pink and gray granite, which have been molded into forms that undulate and are sexual. Cracks suggest vaginas and their stony, clitoral protrusions. The line where rock meets water becomes the body's line of symmetry. The Goddess stretches out Her arms: a fallen log and its mirror image, to protect Her hidden clefts. Her pendulous breasts, looked at from the opposite side, become uprising penises. Up here, it seems clear that earth is truly Her flesh and was formed by a sexual process: Her shakes and shudders and moans of pleasure, the orgasmic release of molten rock spewing forth in fiery eruptions, the slow caress of glaciers, like white hands gently smoothing all that had been left jagged.

Up here it seems clear—not that everything is sexual, but that sexuality is an expression of the moving force that underlies everything and gives it life.

Light penetrates the water. A fat log, weathered to silver, thrusts into the lake's green depths. We dive from it; our skin tingling with the sudden rush of cold, then slither on our bellies back along its surface, which is slippery underwater. Wrapping our legs around it, we lie on the warm, smooth wood; it is like lying upon a lover.

It seems that sexuality can be a process of mirroring. Self reflects self in the water; in the motions of hands, lips, tongue, genitals; in the thrust and arch of bodies; in attraction; in conversation; in growth and change. Mirroring, we take another into ourselves and become changed by that other. Being mirrored, we are acknowledged, our beings are recognized; we feel our own impact. Mirroring and being mirrored, we create a reverberation, the hum and throb of an energy that lifts us in waves of emotion and sensual pleasure. We create a dance.

No wonder, then, that the mirror was always an attribute of the Goddess of love. The word *mirror* is related (not etymologically, but in poetic resonances) to *mira!* (the Spanish "Look!"), myriad, and miracle; mer and mar (the "sea"), the seductive mermaid; merry, marry; and to the Goddess-names Miriam, Mariamne, Mari, Maria, Miria.

Mirroring begins with the self. It is our own reflection we see first and recognize as wonderful, as a miracle. All love begins as self-love. (This does not mean, however, that it stops there.) It is some reflection of oneself, some feeling of likeness or connection that first attracts us to a lover. (Here I could be dreary and quote Jung or Freud and theories of projection and transference, but I will not.) "Celebrate yourself, and you will see that Self is everywhere," is a saying in the Faery tradition of the Craft.

Yet the mirror is easily distorted. The culture of estrangement, which teaches us to denigrate sexuality, makes it impossible to look in the mirror and see a clear reflection of our own instincts and deepest desires. Instead we see a fun-house distortion, a parody. We become diseased.

The root of that disease is power. Sex is an exchange of power in the form of energy that flows between two beings. But the culture of estrangement distorts all power into power-over, into domination. Sexual relations become a field on which questions of power and status are played out. The erotic becomes another arena of domination and submission. Our own sexuality becomes something alien.

This alienation is no accident. Our economic and political systems, our science and technology, are rooted in our alienation from our own bodies and from the realms of deep feeling. The imposition of the puritan ethic in the seventeenth century and the denigration of sexuality that accompanied the Witchburnings created conditions in which capitalism was fostered and peasant classes were forced into alienating wage labor.[1] Today, as long as we remain cut off from the sources of deep feeling in our lives, we remain avid consumers of packaged substitutes for feeling that can be sold at a profit to a mass market. When we lose our feeling for beauty, we become willing to accept the ugliness our culture creates. We cut ourselves off from the horror and despair we might otherwise have to acknowledge.

Yet our sexuality can bring us another sort of power, as Audre Lord describes it, "That power which arises from our deepest, non-rational knowledge . . . The erotic offers a well of replenishing and provocative force to the woman who does not fear its revelation . . ."[2]

A true transformation of our culture would require reclaiming the erotic as power-from-within, as empowerment. The erotic can become the bridge that connects feeling with doing; it can infuse our sense of mastery and control with emotion so that it becomes life-serving instead of destructive. In the dialectic of merging and separating, the erotic can confirm our uniqueness while affirming our deep oneness with all being. It is the realm in which the spiritual, the political, and the personal come together.

> Once we begin to feel deeply all the aspects of our lives, we begin to demand from ourselves and from our lives' pursuits that they feel in accordance with that joy of which we know ourselves to be capable. Our erotic knowledge empowers us, becomes a lens through which we scrutinize all aspects of our existence . . . The demands of our released expectations lead us inevitably into actions which will help bring our lives into accordance with our own needs, our knowledge, our desires.[3]

The erotic is bound up with the push-pull conflict between union and separation — a conflict that does not disappear after childhood but remains throughout our lives, always present in our work and in our relationships. Eternally, Kore leaves Her mother, descends to the dark, and returns again. Eternally, the God dies and is reborn.

The Goddess who is the mother is the love Goddess, the Goddess of the erotic. This means that through our sexuality we can again connect to the realm of deep feeling we touched as children through our mothers. So the deep forces of life and death, which manifest in mothering and in our development of a sense of ourselves as separate, autonomous beings, also manifest in sexuality.

Sexuality is the way we, as adults, experience this particular dance, deep in the caves of the body. For in sex we merge, give way, become one with another, allow ourselves to be caressed, pleasured, enfolded, allow our sense of separation to dissolve. But in sex we also feel our impact on another, see our own faces reflected in another's eyes, feel ourselves confirmed, and sense our power, as separate human beings, to make another feel.

In the culture of estrangement, the great dance of life and death, of merging and emerging, is reflected in the fun-house-mirror-distortions of authority. And what we see in the mirror is the gulf our culture creates between feeling and doing, the split that ties women and nature and all oppressed groups to feeling (to being the ground that adapts) and links selfhood to men, to the dominators, the masters, those who perform and control.

So women are taught by this culture to be passive mirrors that reflect the selves of men. "My mother told me," a friend of mine recounts, "that I would be much more interesting to boys if I listened instead of talking." Our own selves are made problematic — our own ability, competence, and mastery are a threat to our promised female birthright of secure dependency. No wonder some part of ourselves may respond to pornographic images that depict the troublesome female self being destroyed — reverting to helplessness, to the silence, the dependence of infancy. Women become deluded that if they take in and take in, reflect and reflect, something will finally get through. Something will shake us to the core and awaken the sleeping spark of our own movement.

And men are inculcated with the same disease in reverse: an obsession with *impact*, with making oneself felt, even if the only impact one can have is destruction, the only feeling one can arouse is pain. The core of men's identity is their separateness. A separate self, cut off from the sources of its own feeling, must have its existence, its being, confirmed by the reaction it can cause in another. But when that other has been reduced to a non-being, then one's impact is not felt because there seems to be no one else there to feel it. In reality, the rapist's victim feels. She suffers, but the mind of the rapist cannot reflect that suffering, so the rapist's self, his existence, is not confirmed by his act. He annihilates himself with his inability to feel, as he annihilates his victim physically. He strikes out harder and harder, with more and more violence, yet his fist seems to strike a void; nothing happens, there is no response. The real pain, the real death of his victims remains unknown to him, because they were never alive to him. And so culture strikes out against nature, attempting to control, to master, to feel its impact, even though nature herself has not been real to Western culture since the triumph of the mechanist world-view in the seventeenth century (see Appendix A). We cannot hear nature's cries even when her distress threatens our own survival.

Estranged culture breeds sadists and masochists. We may reverse the roles: a man who wields great power in the hierarchy of the culture, who lives in a nonfeeling self that achieves mastery, may feel his self as a sexual burden, may play out its destruction in masochistic surrender. Women may fear dependency more than the problematic self (if they are smart women); some may search for their sense of mastery and control in the sexual arena, instead of or in addition to, seeking it in other areas of life.

Hierarchy itself is a sadomasochistic thought-form. If we examine the roles played in sadomasochism,[4] we can see clearly that what is being played out, over and over again, in the masks of guard and prisoner, teacher and student, priest and supplicant, adult and child, master and servant, is the relationship of power-over. And the perpetuation of hierarchy requires our willingness to play "bottom" in real life, to accept humiliation and subjuga-tion, to acquiesce in the cramping and corruption of our sexuality.

How, then, can we transform our distorted sexuality into empowering eroticism? How do we generate within ourselves the feeling self? If the erotic heals the split between flesh and spirit, can we use its power to heal our own splits, to bridge gaps between the spiritual and the political, to create a culture that serves not only life but joy?

First, we must reject spiritual systems that further the flesh/spirit split. We must reject asceticism, hierarchies, the confining of sex to marriage or reproduction. Spirituality can be voluptuous, sensuous. Religion can mean touching each other, allowing our-selves to feel moments of beauty, of energy, of joy fully. If the Goddess is immanent in flesh and nature, then our practice deepens our connection to flesh and nature. "All acts of love and pleasure are my rituals," She says.

We must also demand that our politics serve our sexuality. Too often, we have asked sexuality to serve politics instead. Ironically, the same movements that have criticized sexual repression and bourgeois morality have themselves too often tried to mold their sexual feeling to serve the current political theory. This tradition includes nineteenth century revolutionary asceticism, the New Left's demand that women practice free love (meaning sex without involvement), the fear of lesbianism in the early women's movement, and the mandatory separatist line taken by some in the later women's movement. Too many generations have asked: What do my politics tell me I should feel? The better question is: What do I, at my root, at my core, desire?

If we see that root of desire as the Goddess incarnate, as the source of power-from-within, if we honor it and explore it with eyes open, then we can ask: how do I create a society that furthers my sexuality? How can I live my politics erotically, so that they deepen my knowledge of the mysteries, so that they deepen my capacity for joy?

Such politics are dangerous. They are extremely threatening to patriarchal society, because they threaten the roots of hierarchical power relationships.

That is why the movements for lesbian and gay liberation are threatening — and why they are vitally important to any real movement for change. Sexual desire for a person of one's own gender challenges the idea that the only valid purpose of sex is reproduction; it means that sexuality is valued for its own sake, for pleasure, not as a means to an end.

Lesbians, women loving women, are threatening because they are women refusing to serve as ground for the male self. They withdraw the flow of nurturing upon which the cut-off male self depends, affirming, instead, selfhood in each other, nurturing and strengthening each other.

The gay men's movement has aspects that are threatening to patriarchy and potentially liberating, as well as aspects that may be oppressive and can reproduce the power relationships of patriarchy. Men who are cut off from feeling may substitute male bodies for female bodies as objects, and may treat each other as commodities. Yet men who truly love men, who are willing to be each other's ground and support, are potential sources of far-reaching change. The Faeries, for example, deliberately attempt to re-link the feeling and doing selves by identifying with the Goddess. Thus they reconnect with the ground of life and death. To see men who deliberately embrace the characteristics associated with women (softness, silliness, wearing costumes, decorating themselves, nurturing, being vulnerable) — may be terrifying to other men because so much male identity in the estranged culture depends on a difference from women, that is, it is negatively defined. Yet beyond the fear may be the power to redefine the male self positively as a rooted whole, not a severed part.

However, we should not fall into the trap of saying one can *only* be a true feminist if one is a lesbian, or that one must be gay to be a liberated man. Desire does not follow the mind's dictates. Women and men may have to struggle through more masks, more sets of expectations, as they attempt together to work out sexual relationships not based on power-over. But that struggle is vital. To honor sexuality is, ultimately, to stop defining ourselves in terms of our sexual partners, to realize that the richness of sexual attraction and expression lies in its hues, its infinite shadings, and only our cultural estrangement restricts us to the three primary colors.

I feel an obligation, at this point, to say a few words about committed, monogamous relationships, if only because that is what I practice. Commitment, even marriage, does not have to be based on the principle of power-over. It can be a deliberate choice to focus one's energy on another human being with depth and passion. In marriage, whether it is legal or informal, heterosexual or lesbian or gay, we go through stages that take us around the magic circle, much as we do in groups. We fall in love with a vision — often an airy projection of some idealized part of ourselves. We pass through fiery phases during which we fight over power, and stages of flowing and merging together. When we live together with someone, we must also ground the relationship by caring for all the mundane things of earth. Through the struggle, we begin to see our partner as distinct from our images and fantasies, as a real and separate human being who values what is real in us (not our idealized image, nor our reduction to an object that serves another's needs) as ourselves.

An erotic politics cannot be based on hierarchical structures. Any authoritarian structure, regardless of its party line or position, reinforces the power relationships of oppression and alienation. The circles we spin can become erotic structures, based on personal contact and connection. In small groups we can share feelings, we can touch and stroke each other, cry together or laugh together, as well as do business. Circles remain small so we see each other, reflect each other, and our unique personalities have an impact on others to whom we feel connected. A movement of small groups is strengthened by an underlying network of human connections, a weaving of close relationships that bind it like warp and weft. Community is inherently erotic.

Sex is energy. What gives the physical exchange its excitement, its intensity, is the movement of vital energy, an energy not limited to human beings, but present in earth, air, water, fire, in plants and animals, in all living things. Understanding that the erotic is energy opens up the potential for an erotic relationship with the earth.[5] We can love nature, not just aesthetically, but carnally, with our meat, our bones. That sort of love threatens all the proprieties of estranged culture. Love that mirrors the wildness of nature can move us into the struggle to protect her, and can give us the deep strength we need. That love is connection. When we feel it deeply, perhaps with an oak, when we feel the tree's aura move into our bodies, feel our energy flow through the ground into its roots, let ourselves merge and feel at one with its tree-ness, we are sustained in the fight to keep the ax from its trunk, the radiation from its leaves.

To recognize that the erotic is energy is to restore eros to the whole body, to escape its limitations to a few narrow zones of pleasure. The whole body becomes an organ of delight. With it we can respond with pleasure to the vast beauty of the living world.

Eros as energy shapes many aspects of culture and appears in many forms: raw, instinctive lust; personal, bonded love; and the power to heal, to learn, to create. In a culture of immanence, sexuality would be honored in all its diverse appearances.

Instinctive sexuality, animal lust, was recognized in other

cultures as a sacred force. Untamed eros was known to generate powerful energies connected with growth and with the fertility of plant and animal life. The so-called fertility rites in the ploughed fields, and the sacred orgies that so outraged the Biblical patriarchs, were religious celebrations that honored the sacredness of instinct, and the power of the life-force that pulses no less through our human bodies than through the bodies of other animals.

It is hard for us to imagine what such rites were like. In our culture, everything impersonal is exploited. If we experience impersonal, lusty sex, it is not in the context of connection — of knowing ourselves as nature or as animal — but in the context of the marketplace. So the young women who offered up their virginity at the gates of Babylonian temples are today termed *prostitutes*, yet in their own society they were acting as priestesses, learning to honor the Goddess instinct in themselves and the God Eros in whatever shape he chose to appear.

The erotic is also the personal. The interweaving of energies creates a bond — perhaps, indeed, that is the test of what is truly erotic — it creates a bond that is not based on exploitation.

The exchange of erotic energy creates patterns, forms, entities, an energy structure. Traditionally, it is the basis of the *family* (at least since the ideal of romantic love came to replace arranged marriages based on economics). Potentially, the erotic bond could be the model for all other associations, all connections in freedom. But in patriarchal culture, the family itself becomes another arena of authority, a hierarchical structure of dominance. The family mirrors the culture; the culture mirrors the family. And children, growing within a family, reflect its structure in the formation of their innermost selves. So our psyches grow in patterns of authority and domination. And the families we create, the relationships we establish, become corrupted by our struggles for power-over each other. Love is rarely as clear as the reflection of a log in the water.

Yet that same energy can be the source of a new bond. It can link our circles together — not because we rub genitals together but because we allow our meetings to be steeped in feeling, to contain acts of beauty and touching.

In a culture of immanence, the erotic infuses all the relationships that in our culture are based on power-over. Healing, in that context, becomes an act of shifting energies, not one of control. It is based on caring, not mechanics, whether it is a healing of the heart, the mind, or the body. It takes place in a context that is not sterile, but sensual, infused with beauty and emotion. In healing we can experience our profound terror of annihilation, of the betrayal and decay of our bodies, and our psyches. Through this experience we can know the depths of our desire for life, for health, for connection.

Teaching and learning, too, become erotic endeavors — not sterile exercises in mastery of facts, but journeys together. In Reclaiming (our feminist spirituality collective) when we teach the arts of magic, each class, each workshop is itself a ritual. We do not just explain the Goddess, we invoke Her; we create the bond, arouse the power so that each student knows it in her or his own body, in an individual way. Our purpose, as teachers, is not to demonstrate our knowledge or our power, but to create a context that evokes power-from-within each person in the circle.

Work, too, can become alive with erotic power. The purpose of the ancient fertility rites was not only to awaken the earth's energy and draw it into the prepared ground to infuse the year's seed. It was to charge even the labor of planting, of weeding, of picking the harvest with evocative memories, and to link each act of work with the deep forces of life and death.

Not all work, of course, is pleasurable or potentially sensual. Yet even in routine work, we can feel our impact on the world, see ourselves mirrored in a change we have brought about — as we fix something that is broken, clean something that is dirty, build something that didn't exist before.

What makes work alienating is the hierarchical structure in which our efforts, our pace, our needs, our sense of timing, our connection with our own bodies' rhythms and with our friends and coworkers, are all shaped to serve somebody else's ends. When we are valued only as objects, for the most mechanical of our abilities, when our work serves the ends that seem meaningless or even harmful to us, we are alienated.

To change the nature of work would be to change the underlying basis of society. We are challenged to find or create jobs and ways to work that restore value to the work itself, instead of the profits extracted from it. For work that has inherent value becomes erotic in the sense of *connecting*, enabling us to bond to the world in meaningful ways, to use our power, our abilities, and to see their results.

SEX MAGIC

Esoteric teachings about sex describe a quality called *polarity*. Polarity is a quality of energy, a flow, like the electric field that is generated between the positive and the negative poles of a magnet. The currents of polarity are very powerful forces, and magical training often focuses on learning to recognize and channel those currents.

The simplest aspect of polarity is the energy that flows between women and men. In many traditional Craft groups, tantric groups, and some Native American traditions, female/male polarity is the juice, so to speak, that makes the magic work. So, some covens insist on an equal number of males and females in the circle, and some male Shamans must have a close connection with a woman in order to raise power.

Polarity can also be created internally, however. If a woman creates an inner male, or a man creates an inner female, polarity can flow between the person and what we call the *companion self*. It is important, however, not to associate the companion self with qualities, such as aggression or passivity, that are traditionally considered male or female. The companion self is *not* the Jungian anima or animus, and it does not complete one's personality. Instead, it is a source of energy. To resort to a mechanistic metaphor, creating a companion self is like building a generator in the basement instead of plugging into outside power lines.

And polarity does not have to be generated either between two partners according to the heterosexual model. There are female/female and male/male polarities, each of which can also be generated or within a person by the creation of a same-sex *double*. These currents may have a different flavor but be equal in power and sometimes stronger than heterosexual polarities. Which form of polarity one chooses to work with is a matter of personal taste and inclination. But within a healthy community, all forms are necessary if a balance is to be sustained.

But polarity cannot be described, only experienced. Readers who feel ready for the experience might try some of the following training exercises:

THE MIRROR

In a warm, private place, stand naked in front of a full-length mirror. Place a bowl of salt water at your feet. Ground and center. (See the description of the Tree of Life exercise on page 30 for one method of doing this. Others are described in *The Spiral Dance*.)[6]

Look at your body and like it. Let yourself take pleasure in looking at every part of it.

If you don't like your body, you are not alone. Most of us in this culture are trained to hate our bodies — to wish they looked some other way.

Imagine that your feeling of dislike for your body is a murky stream that flows out of you on your breath into the salt water. Pick up the bowl and breathe into it. Let yourself make sounds that help to carry the bad feelings away.

When you feel ready, relax. Breathing deeply, from your belly, draw energy up from the earth, like a clear stream of water that flows into the salt water and clears away all the negativity. When the water is clear and begins to glow, take a sip — because you are not trying to get rid of your negative feelings; you are transforming them to free the energy they contain.

Repeat this ritual at regular intervals until you can love your body. It is also helpful to try some new activity, such as dance, massage, hiking, or some sport that allows you to feel strong and take pleasure in your body. Do not diet or attempt to change the way your body looks — work on learning to love it the way it is.

THE DOUBLE

Again, stand before the mirror. Ground and center. Look at your body and like it.

Now imagine that the image in the mirror is your twin. She/he is your dear friend, someone who loves you. Let a feeling of warmth and affection flow from you to your double. Breathe into it from your belly — make sounds that strengthen the energy and movements that help it flow. Let it build until it becomes a powerful current.

Notice the *feel* of that current. Find a name for your double, and an image or word you can use to evoke the feeling you are experiencing now.

You can talk with your double, or, if you like, make love with her/him.

When you are done, thank your double and ask how you can call her/him back again. Ground the energy by placing your hands on the earth (or on the floor, as the case may be) and visualizing the currents returning into the ground.

THE COMPANION SELF

Stand before the mirror. Ground and center. Again, look in the mirror and like yourself. Let a feeling of warmth and affection flow from you to the image in the mirror.

Now imagine that the image in the mirror begins to change. If you are a woman, it becomes more male. If you are a man, it becomes more female. The change moves slowly downward, from your hair to your face, your eyes, nose, mouth, jaw, throat and neck, shoulders, chest, breasts, arms and hands, waist and belly, hips, genitals, thighs, calves, and feet. If you have trouble visualizing the change with your eyes open, close them. Feel affection and attraction for the person you have created in the mirror. Breathe that feeling into the image, let it build. Make sounds and movements that help it grow, until it becomes a strong current flowing between you.

Notice how it feels. Again, name your companion self, and find an image or word you can use to evoke the current you are feeling now.

Have a conversation. Play. Make love.

When you are finished, thank your companion self, and ask how you can call her/him back again. Then ground the energy.

LOVING NATURE

Go outside. Find a plant. (You can also do this with a tree, a stream or some other natural object.) Sit or stand comfortably. Ground and center.

Call up the current you felt with your double or companion-self. Use your word or image of power.

Let the current flow into the plant until you feel its energy radiating back. Enjoy it.

When you are done, ground and center.

This exercise is healing — both for you and for the plant. Try it regularly with your plants and see how your garden grows.

FOR LOVERS

Both of you should be familiar with the workings of polarity. Retire to a warm and private place.

Sit opposite each other. Look into each other's eyes. You and your lover should each hold your hands up in front of you, palms outward. Your hands and hers/his should be about a quarter of an inch apart. Ground and center. Let yourself feel warmth and affection for each other.

One of you should now call up the current you felt with your double or companion self, whichever you prefer. Let it flow through your hands into your lover's hands. When you feel ready, trade. Let your lover send while you receive.

Lie down next to each other. Place your hands on each other's bodies — in whatever places please both of you.

Call up the current of polarity (whichever type you like) using your word or image of power. (You may want to share this with your lover, or you may prefer to keep it secret.) Then you can both send and receive simultaneously.

As the currents build, make sounds or movements that help them. Let the process reach its natural conclusion.

Note: This practice builds a deeper-than-superficial bond between lovers. Choose your partners carefully.

It is especially good for reviving passion in a long-standing love affair or partnership, in which love is strong but the fire is dying out.

If you try this and nothing happens, at least one of you is probably angry. Talk about it. Fight. Try again.

It is important to work with the currents of polarity in this exercise, *not* the visualization of the double or the companion self. Love is already complicated by enough projections.

This exercise is also a healing one for both partners.

Use your imagination to expand on these exercises or to invent your own. The power you have now learned to know as your own can be called up whenever you need it. Let it inspire your creativity, strengthen you in your work, grow your garden, heal your sicknesses, awaken your heart. Call it into your hands when you touch another person, call it into your eyes and your breath, into your voices when you raise it to challenge domination. Call it into your circles.

And do not be afraid to let it go. Like all energy, the erotic power of polarity moves in cycles, it ebbs and flows. It is always available, yet after it comes to us it will always recede. The ebb is the time of quiet, of rest — the silence between pulses in the rhythm of the dance.

A fear runs like a thread through Western culture — from the Church Fathers through Freud — that sexuality, if unleashed from the control of the internalized authority, the self-hater, would run wild and destroy civilization. But sexuality has its own regulatory principle, its own rhythm of expression and containment, arousal and satiety. Knowing that rhythm, honoring it in our own flesh, in our hearts, we invoke the love Goddess, who beckons. The father God who commands fades away. The stories of estrangement lose their punch lines. In place of them we can create new myths with images that arise from another context. The work of myth-making; the work of creating new forms, new structures not based on hierarchy; the work of securing and defending our right to keep our bodies and sexuality free from restrictions and intrusions by the agents of authority; the work of encountering and transforming our inner structures; the work of love — connecting, knowing another intimately, equally, honestly — all these are linked. They are the same struggle. There can be no escape into a private world of love and romance; because no one can love freely in a society based on domination. Yet the public struggle against domination cannot be waged with joy and spirit unless we bring to it a sense of personal power, a strength based on the electric, erotic spark of the earth's energy running freely through our bodies.

That spark can sustain our struggle until we can learn to meet as equals, free in our bodies and in our imaginations, until we learn to love, not reflections of ourselves that obscure each other, but one another's true faces as we mirror each other's passion and delight. Until we can become, in our lovemaking, oak trees whose branches intertwine, sequoias whose trunks slowly grow together, cats on the back fence, jaguars, tigers, jungle birds — until our teeth are wolves' teeth and our tongues, like bear's tongues, taste the honey of each other's bodies — until our blood and our semen again become sacred substances of power that we use to consecrate our tools, our holy places, each other.

The rising of the erotic force is the rising of a great transforming power. When the erotic is strong, domination falls away, the pornographic must retreat, and authority can no longer maintain its hold. The story that follows is true. I present it as a parable:

THE WOMEN DANCE NAKED IN JAIL

The women arrested at the Diablo Canyon Nuclear Power Plant blockade are detained in an old gym at the California Men's Colony, a prison. We are watched, day and night, by male as well as female guards. The guards sit in the corners, looking over the floor of wall-to-wall mats. The women must undress in front of male eyes. There are no screens, no doors to shut. Late at night guards walk up and down the rows, shining flashlights onto the faces and bodies of the women, who lie cold under the one blanket which has been provided. It is a situation of deliberate humiliation, a small, calculated harassment, part of the punishment inflicted by the state for challenging its authority with our women's bodies.

Outside is a small exercise yard. The central California sun is hot. And we begin to take off our shirts to lie in the sun bare-breasted. Some of the women decide to wash their clothes; they wrap themselves in towels, or wear nothing. We feel good about our bodies; we enjoy looking at each other. In that setting of corrugated iron and concrete, we are soft and alive and beautiful.

"I never knew how many shapes and sizes women come in," says a friend, whose life has not previously allowed her to hang out in the company of two hundred naked women. "And we're all beautiful. Look at that woman there. She's like a sculpture — like a Venus of Willendorf, a Goddess."

We are all the Goddess in her multitude of forms: an Aphrodite, an Artemis, a Maiden, a Mother, a Crone. We are all Persephone, dragged into the underworld by the authorities of patriarchy. But our living bodies transform hell. The situation is pornography brought to life, a constant humiliation that enacts a classic sadomasochistic guard/prisoner fantasy. Yet it is transformed by the presence of the erotic. We are connected with each other, and in our love for each other there is no footing for shame.

It is the guards who must adjust to us. Some are embarrassed; some delighted. Some deliberately feed us false information; some are genuinely friendly. They have no vested interest in the nuclear power plant. They have been transferred from San Quentin and Soledad prisons; for them, this is a paid holiday. No one has asked them whether men should guard women, whether we should be given extra blankets, hot food, or toothbrushes. Most of the women are white and middle-class; the guards are working-class, black, Latino. They have come to this particular job because it was the best of the choices their lives presented to them; as we have come to the blockade for the same reason. In that sense, none of us is free. None of us has the power, except as we demand it and take it, to determine what choices we are offered.

The women discuss the issue of bare breasts. Some feel it undermines the seriousness of our action, that it will look bad to the media. But we choose not to impose a restriction on each other.

At night we dance naked in jail. One woman plays the single guitar they have allowed in. We beat on tin cans; the corrugated iron walls become a drum. We clap our hands; we sing "Jailhouse

Rock." We paint tuxedos on our bodies and make corsages out of waste paper. We pretend we are having a prom. The music rises and the rhythm rises; we sweat together, the room is filled with the odor of two hundred women. And we dance, knowing that we are allowed this as a privilege, as so much of what has been good in our lives is a privilege; knowing that women who are in jail alone, who are not white, who do not have a movement and a legal team behind them, whose stories are not of interest to the newspapers, cannot dance, cannot go naked, may be raped and brutalized — not smiled at — by the guards.

Yet we dance, because this is, after all, what we are fighting for: this life, these bodies, breasts, wombs, this smell of flesh; this joy; this freedom — that it continue, that it prevail.

Chapter Nine

❧

Ritual as Bonding:
Action as Ritual

There is a fire. The people are gathered on the dancing ground. The priestess sings a chant; the drums begin. The people respond, with their voices, their bodies; chanting and moving in the pattern of the dance. From their voices, their bodies, arises the power to call down the Orishas, the Gods. Moving together, singing together, the people are one. The drums and the power unite them in a common bond, relinking them with each other, with the ancestors who down through time have chanted, have danced in this way, with the land that supports the people and the spirit that enters into them.[1]

There is a circle. The people hold hands; they chant together to the Goddess, the Gods. Now one is inspired to begin a chant; now another. They move together in a dance. The power moves through them, uniting them in a common bond with each other, with the land that supports them and the spirit that enters into them. Perhaps they are meeting on a beach near San Francisco or in a farmyard in Wisconsin. Perhaps they meet in the living room of an apartment in Manhattan. Their immediate ancestors probably did not dance or chant like this. Nevertheless, their circle is like the dancing ground of Africa, the kiva of the Southwest, or the Sundance of the Plains.

154

They are experiencing the power of ritual.

Rituals are part of every culture. They are the events that bind a culture together, that create a heart, a center, for a people. It is ritual that evokes the Deep Self of a group. In *ritual* (a patterned movement of energy to accomplish a purpose) we become familiar with power-from-within, learn to recognize its *feel*, learn how to call it up and let it go.

The pattern of the movement of energy in a Craft ritual is based on a very simple structure.[2] We begin by grounding — connecting with the earth. Often we use the Tree of Life meditation (see page 30). Then we cleanse ourselves, perhaps with a meditation on salt water or a plunge into the ocean, taking time to release our pain and tensions through movement or sound. (This may also be done after casting the circle.) The circle is cast: separating the ritual space and time from ordinary space and time, as we invoke the four elements. We invoke the Goddess and the God, and whatever other powers or presences we wish to greet.

Then we raise power by breathing, meditating, dancing, chanting. The power is focused through an image, an action, or a symbol. We may enter a trance together, taking a journey together into the underworld. After the power has reached its peak, we return it to the earth, grounding it through our hands and bodies. Then we celebrate with food and drink and take time to relax and be together. Finally, we thank all the powers we have invoked and open the circle, returning to ordinary space and time.

RITUAL AND GROUP ENERGY

Rituals create a strong group bond. They help build community, creating a meeting-ground where people can share deep feelings, positive and negative — a place where they can sing or scream, howl ecstatically or furiously, play, or keep a solemn silence. A pagan ritual incorporates touch, sensuality, and humor. Anything we truly revere is also something that we can ridicule respectfully. The elements of laughter and play keep us from getting stuck on one level of power or developing an inflated sense of self-importance. Humor keeps kicking us onward, to go deeper.

We break eggs over the initiate's body as she lies in the ritual bath. The eggs are symbols of her rebirth. She is a woman who loves calm, peace, order.

"This must be eggs-scruciating!" says a priestess.

"Oh shut up. This is a serious business."

"Eggs-zactly!"

"Would you stop it?"

"Don't egg her on."

Her coven becomes embroiled in a staged fight. They are pushing her to her limits — and past them. Soon everyone is laughing, close to tears, at silly puns. But under the laughter is the power — shining, throbbing. When we fall silent, as she is dried, and laid on towels, and stroked with feathers, and told a sacred story, we feel the power rise, strong because the laughter has pushed down our barriers.

Rituals can, of course, be planned and led by one person. But in a collective they are best worked collectively. In a small group, in which the bond is strong, where everyone knows the ritual structure and members trust each other, most ritual requires no planning at all.

Coven Raving meets. We spend a long time talking about our lives, catching up on gossip, taking care of business. At last we are ready to begin the magic.

We set a bowl of salt water in the center of the circle. We begin making sounds, naming aloud for each other — because we know and trust each other — what it is each of us needs to release. Diane speaks softly; Kevyn is dramatic, making loud noises and wide gestures. Each of us has an individual style.

When we are done, there is silence. In the silence, it becomes apparent to one of us that she is called to invoke the East. She takes the athame (the knife) from the altar, and stands facing her direction. Breathing deeply, she says whatever she is inspired to say, moves, sings, chants, cajoles, or softly whispers as the energy inspires her. Sometimes more than one of us will invoke the same direction, our voices blending, merging, playing against each other in counterpoint, while the rest of the coven moves, or chants, or makes soft sounds that help our energy.

After the East has been invoked, another woman moves to the South. Someone will be called to the West, and someone else to the North. Perhaps one of us will lead the invocation to the Goddess — or perhaps we will all begin to sing spontaneously, or we may chant sounds together. Maybe we will call the God with a poem, or a rhythm. We have no set plan when we start, and we don't need one because we have learned, over the years, how to flow with each other.

We have learned that if we can wait in the silence without a plan, inspiration comes. We know that if we stand facing a particular direction and see that element in our minds, words will come — or perhaps a sound or a motion. We have learned to wait for the up-welling of that inspiration, and we have learned to express it when it comes, to let it out without censoring it or feeling shy. So we stand, and when we hear the voices in our minds we say what we hear. If we try to judge it, or hold it back, the voices stop, or the words repeat over and over again, so nothing else gets through. Yet this process, which seems so simple, so unconscious and easy, has taken us years to discover, or remember, or invent. It required years to realize that we do not need hierarchy among ourselves, that we do not need to feel shy, that we can trust each other. But having learned this, within this safe, small group, our knowledge is sustained in other areas and in large groups. We find that in our writing, our work, our lives, we are able to wait in silence for the inspiration to arise. We have changed.

We can work the magic in the same way. Perhaps we are doing a healing. Our friend who is eight-months pregnant has been told she has a virus in her bloodstream that may make her baby deformed or diseased; the baby might be born dead. We put our friend in the center of the circle, place our hands on her belly, her arms, her face, her breasts. We begin to chant. Each of us closes her eyes. We visualize the baby healthy. Our voices rise and fall. They weave a new fabric of power for the baby — they re-weave its fate. We sing to it, call it. Now the power strikes one of us —

now it rises in another. But in the moment of working magic we are all facets of the Deep Self of the group; we do not get in our own way.

When the power peaks and falls, we all know it because we are all sensing the same power. Together we ground it. None of us has to direct, or even point out the transitions. So the ritual moves as smoothly as a well-directed play in which each of the actors knows her or his part. Yet it is utterly spontaneous, created in the moment. We could say that it is the Deep Self of the group that writes the lines, casts the parts, calls the cues — all as the ritual happens. Nothing blocks the rising of power, so it can be channeled to work, to cause change. The baby — who is the focus of many healing circles that work in the same way — is born in perfect health. Working together, with a common focus, all the circles, the community itself, grows stronger.

LARGE RITUALS

In a large group, especially one consisting of people who do not know each other well, we cannot reach the same level of closeness — nor can the power flow as smoothly — as in a small group. Yet larger rituals can also build community, and they have an excitement and an air of festivity that small coven meetings cannot attain. When bonding occurs in a larger group, and a Deep Self is formed, the energy may move by itself in the same way it moves in a small group.

In the early years of both Raving and Compost (my first coven), one or two people generally planned the larger rituals and I led them. Later, the whole coven would plan the ritual, and different individuals would lead different parts.

Our rituals then were, in a sense, more formal. We often wrote beautiful invocations and memorized them. We invented ritual dramas and led guided meditations and trances.

As Raving moved away from hierarchy to function more collectively, our interest shifted from leading and performing beautiful rituals to facilitating a flow of energy that could evoke power and inspiration in each person who came. We realized that energy would not flow collectively unless the rituals were planned collectively, so we invited our sister and brother covens, our students, and other interested friends to help plan the rituals as well as to participate.

To plan a ritual collectively, we begin by going around the circle asking people what the time and season mean to them, and what they need or want from the ritual. From their answers we develop common themes and images. Generally, someone gets an inspiration for a symbolic act that can focus the ritual.

For example, a year ago, members of the Reclaiming collective planned a ritual for the fire festival on February 2 called *Brigid*,[3] which is sacred to the Goddess of smithcraft, poetry, and healing. At that time, we felt as a group that we had a strong need to confront our feelings of political despair and powerlessness. Different needs surfaced as we went around the circle:

"I need a banishing — a purification."

"I need the ritual to move somewhere — I don't want to get stuck in my helplessness."

"I need some way to connect with people — I have a hard time feeling close in a group of a hundred people."

"To me, Brigid means fire. I really want a cauldron."

"Candles. For me, Brigid means candles."

The ritual we finally created began with about eighty or a hundred people gathered in a large circle in an open room. Different covens had prepared the invocations, to the four directions, the Goddess and God. Then we began a banishing dance, moving counterclockwise, with different people yelling out the phrases that had kept them powerless. The group repeated these in mocking, screeching tones until the energy of each phrase had died away.

"I'm Mommie's good girl."

"I'm Mommie's good GIRL."

"GOOD GIRL!"

"GOOD GIRL!"

"Big boys don't cry."

"BIG BOYS DON'T CRY!"

"DON'T CRY BIG BOY!"

"DON'T CRY!"

"DON'T! DON'T!"
"DON'T YOU DARE!"
"You can't do anything anway."
"You can't DO ANYTHING!"
"YOU CAN'T!"

A banishing dance is sometimes deeply moving — and sometimes hilariously funny. That night it was funny, partly because the circle was so large that its energy tended to scatter. Still, humor is always good for bonding, and the group as a whole felt closer after the banishing.

In another part of the ritual we asked people to move into four small groups, according to their preference for one of the four elements. In the small groups we could feel closer to each other than we had in the large mass. Within each of the smaller circles, we passed a bowl of salt water counterclockwise. Each person, in turn, told of the times when they felt powerless.

"I felt powerless during the war in Vietnam."

"I feel powerless when I lie, or when I can't say what I'm feeling."

"I feel powerless when I go to work and have to spend the whole day filing somebody else's memos."

"I feel powerless when I can't reach out to people."

Then we passed the salt water clockwise. Each of us spoke of the times when we felt powerful. When we finished, we sprinkled salt water on our heads, naming ourselves and saying, "I bless my power."

"I feel power when I make contact with people — when I can be there for somebody else."

"I feel powerful when I sing, when I let my voice be heard."

"I feel powerful when I write."

"I feel powerful when I act."

"I felt powerful giving birth, weaving, planting my garden."

"I felt powerful joining together with other people to act."

"I feel powerful when I tell the truth."

To me, this was the most moving part of the ritual. It taught me that power is truly within our reach — that the things that take it away, and the places in which we find it, are very simple things and places. To find our power we need only look at the ways in which we give it away.

We danced, we chanted together, we raised a cone of power and dropped down into a guided trance/meditation to find a vision of our power — and one way in which we could use it in the world. A central cauldron was lit, and each of us lit our candles from this fire as we spoke of our vision, our commitment. Afterward we celebrated with food and wine, and then we opened the circle.

Another aspect of collective planning is the post-mortem, the discussion of which elements different people liked and didn't like in the ritual, and how the ritual could be made better next time. When rituals are fluid, open to change, they can be improved constantly — unlike traditions with set rites and liturgies.[4] The consensus was that we had put too much into this ritual — that it was exhausting, but that moments within it had been deeply moving.

It also worked — in the sense of empowering us, moving us beyond grief and despair into action. Many of us who were confronting our feelings of defeat and futility a year ago, today are committed to ongoing political work.

There are many factors we have learned to be aware of in planning large, open rituals. A ritual can alienate as easily as it can empower.

The first element to plan carefully is grounding. For a ritual to be powerful, we must start grounded, stay grounded, and end grounded, because the power that we raise comes into our bodies through the earth, and then returns to the earth.

We always begin a ritual, or any act of magic, by breathing together, by visualizing our connection to the earth and our connection to each other. (Most often we use some variation of the Tree of Life.) One of my favorite visualizations follows:

TREE OF GENERATIONS

Breathe deeply, from your belly. Let yourself stand loosely but firmly planted on the earth. Straighten your spine, and release the tension in your shoulders.

Now imagine that your spine is the trunk of a tree that has roots that go deep into the center of the earth. Let yourself breathe down into those roots, and let all the tensions and worries you bring with you flow down with your breath and dissolve into the earth.

Feel the way our roots connect under the earth, how we draw power from the same source. The earth is the body of our ancestors. It is our grandmothers' flesh, our grandfathers' bones. The earth sustained the generations that gave birth to us. As we draw on their power, the power of the earth, as we feel it rise through the roots in our feet and through the base of our spines, let us speak the names of our ancestors — of the ones who came before us, of the heroines and heros who inspire us . . .

And feel the energy of the earth rising into our bellies as we draw it up with our breath, feel it rise into our hearts and spread out from our hearts up through our shoulders and down through our hands. Feel it move around the circle through our hands — feel how it connects us through our breath. As we breathe together — breathing in, breathing out — we link ourselves together, and we speak our own names . . .

And feel the power rising up through our throats, and out the tops of our heads like branches that sweep up and return to touch the earth again, creating a circle, making a circuit. And the branches are our children and grandchildren, the generations that come after us, and we feel them intertwining above our heads, and we know that they are not separate from us, and that, like us, they too will return to earth. And we speak their names . . .

And through the branches, through the leaves, we feel the sun shining down on us, and the wind moving and the moon and the stars shining down. And we can draw in the power of that light, draw it in as a leaf draws in sunlight, and feel it spread down through all the twigs and branches, down through the trunk, down through the roots, until we are filled with light, and as the light reaches the roots, we feel them push yet deeper into the earth.

And as we relax, we feel the connection, the ground beneath our feet, and we know that we cannot lose that ground.

Whenever energy is raised, we ground it, return it to the earth, by touching the earth. Sometimes we place our palms on the ground; sometimes we crouch down and release the power through our entire bodies. We may ground the energy periodically during a ritual, and we are careful to ground it thoroughly after the cone of power is raised. Otherwise, we are left feeling nervous, anxious, unfinished — and the excess energy easily turns to irritation with each other.

The cone of power is raised at the point in the ritual when the energy we have drawn up through our bodies spirals upward into a cohesive whole, reaches a peak, and then dies down. In a large ritual, the energy needs a clear focus, something easily seen or heard, and understood. In the Brigid ritual described above, for example, we chanted for power and focused on the cauldron, symbol of the Goddess's transformative power.

Not everyone in an open ritual will be familiar with the techniques of moving energy. However, if a few strong people shape the power, others will sense its rise and fall. The cone can be directed visually if we throw our arms up in the air. When some people do this, others will instinctively do the same thing, and the energy will follow everyone's body movements. When we touch the earth to ground the energy, others will naturally imitate these actions too. Again, the flow of energy will follow our movements.

In a large, open ritual, language is also crucial. Words that are abstract and New-Age buzz-words drain power, and they cause people's lips to curl. Far better to say, "Let's hold hands and breathe together" than, "Let us have an attunement." William Carlos Williams's famous dictum to poets, "No ideas but in things," is a good guide for ritual-makers as well — since magic is the language of *things*. The metaphors we choose reveal both our spirituality and our politics. We should be careful not to reinforce dualism by focusing on light to the exclusion of dark.

If we wish people to participate in chanting and dancing, then the songs we use must be so simple that they can easily be picked up on the spot. The words must be understandable; nothing drains energy more than a large number of people fumbling with an unfamiliar name, unless it is stopping the momentum of the ritual to instruct people. (A selection of chants is given in Appendix C, Chants and Songs.)

When ritual is used in a situation that is not religious, such as a political demonstration, we need to be sensitive to the different needs and perspectives of all the people who may be involved. Religious trappings, the Goddess's names, even the word *Goddess* itself may offend many people and cause dissension. But if we speak of the *things* and people that embody the Goddess, that are manifestations of power-from-within — the earth, air, fire, and water, natural objects, each other — we speak a common language that can touch everyone, no matter what her/his philosophy or ideology.

The rituals Matrix facilitated in camp and in jail at the Diablo blockade put everything I knew about open rituals to the test. We wanted to share the power of ritual to create a group bond, but we were also aware that most people in camp were not Goddess-worshippers, or interested in becoming Witches. We were very sensitive about not *imposing* our religion on anyone — yet we did want to *share* the experience of magic.

Rose and I were the first members of Matrix to arrive at the blockade, the day after the alert was called. For several days, affinity groups gathered at the campsite, waiting until enough people were present to begin the blockade in force. During the waiting period, we took part in nonviolence trainings, helped with the work of the camp, and facilitated informal workshops in ritual. At one workshop, we planned a ritual collectively for the night of the full moon. It was very simple in structure. The main symbolic act would be to join our hands together in the center of the circle, reflecting the image on our camp buttons: joined hands across a stylized nuclear power plant, surrounded by a red circle that was crossed by a diagonal line (the international symbol for *no*).

We knew that because the underlying structure of the blockade was circular and nonhierarchical, no ritual we attempted to lead could work. Although we had a plan, we knew that, at most, we could facilitate and channel the group's strong, spontaneous energy if it arose.

As always happens, things did not go according to plan, yet everything we intended happened. The full moon rose while people were cooking and eating dinner. It was so fat and beautiful over the hills that everyone began howling, chanting, and banging on pots and pans. We had planned the ritual for much later, but friends came and told us that people were gathered down in an open field, waiting for the ritual to begin.

We went down, announcing the ritual as we went. I found myself deeply grateful for Rose's presence. In a structure so strongly oriented toward collectives, no one person alone could have worked a ritual. I am by nature a shy, introverted person, (although I have often been accused of overcompensating) and my first instinct in large crowds is to wish I could disappear. Rose, however, has flair for the dramatic. She combines a warm heart with a striking appearance. She has very short, hennaed hair, clothing in bright, contrasting colors, and a resonant voice. Together, we made an effective team.

In the field a crowd of more than a hundred people was gathered, singing, and some musicians played guitars. We had, of course, no lights, no sound system. We could not even have candles because of the extreme danger of fire — there were no props.

Our plan had been to start with a Tree of Life meditation, and build this into a visualization of a circle of protection that would surround each person, each affinity group, the camp as a whole, and even the police and workers we would face on the blockade. We were going to invoke the elements with a simple chant, do a spiral dance, and build power.

However, the power was already built before we began. We asked the musicians to get people into a circle, thinking that this would quiet them so we could begin. But as soon as the circle formed, people began dancing inward in a spiral. I looked at Rose, and she looked at me. We both realized that we needed to abandon our expectations. I knew that if I could put myself in the silent place that I can find in my own coven, and let the inspiration arise, the ritual would work. I also knew that I couldn't relax that much. But the dance was moving inward — and we had to do something. So we joined it. As it became a tighter spiral, and the musicians ducked outside it to avoid being squeezed to death, we began a Native American chant to the elements:

The earth, the water, the fire, the air
Returns, returns, returns, returns.

People picked up the chant; it grew in power, becoming an expression of our purpose at the blockade, our commitment to a return of the balance of the elements. Someone picked up the beat with a drum. Suddenly, spontaneously, *everyone* joined hands and moved together, just as Rose had envisioned in our planning. We were swaying and chanting with our hands entwined, and I slipped into the twin consciousnesses that a priestess develops, let myself go into the power, lose myself in it — in the exhilaration of it — and yet consciously remaining grounded in order to keep the power grounded. In fact, I finally began to sing a Tree of Life vision above the chanting. Rose also began to sing a vision, and soon others' weaving voices carried words and melodies above the chant.

At last we grounded. As people sat on the ground, we led the meditation we had planned, and then we asked people to speak of their visions for the blockade. Although hearing people's visions can be moving, after a while the descriptions usually begin to deteriorate into spiritual or political catch-phrases. When we felt the energy begin to dissipate, we thanked the powers we had invoked, and started the group singing. The faithful musicians kindly led the singing as we slipped away. The ritual was over.

Chaotic and backward as it was, Rose and I loved it. While some people who took part were frightened by the intensity of the energy, I suspect that most people also loved it as one loves a big, shaggy, clumsy dog who is terribly good-natured but cannot be trusted near breakable china. Certainly, people seemed to want more exposure to ritual. Weeks later, after a long, painful, all-day meeting, the decision by consensus to end the blockade included an agreement to have a closing ritual.

The closing ritual took place at the new moon. Members of the nonviolence trainers collective asked me to facilitate. Most of the original members of Matrix had gone home, including Rose. This ritual followed the usual structure more closely, although three weeks on blockade had made me an expert at letting go, and I was prepared, I thought, for anything.

We met in an open space under the central parachute. The trainers rigged solar-powered lights so we could see each other. We sang while people were gathering, and then grounded with a Tree of Life meditation.

"In my tradition," I said to the gathered crowd, "we begin by calling in the four directions and invoke the elements of earth, air, fire and water. I'd like to do that if it's okay."

The group murmured its agreement.

"Shall we do it formally, or just by chanting?" I asked.

"Formally," several people cried out. I then called for volunteers to call in each direction. These four people spoke the invocations. Two seemed to be from pagan traditions, and two from Native American traditions. Yet together they cast the circle. Again, I realized how easily the traditions fit together. The words and symbols may differ, but the thought-forms are the same.

We began a spiral dance, singing:

She changes everything she touches,
And everything she touches, changes.

As I began to unwind the spiral, I felt an impulse to make it a kissing spiral, one in which we kiss each person with whom we come face-to-face as we dance. We rarely do this in large, open groups, because many people find it threatening. That night it seemed right because I thought there were about fifty people gathered — a good size for a kissing spiral.

However, while we were invoking and dancing, the spiral had grown. What I didn't realize, until we began unwinding, was that there were about two hundred people in the dance.

We danced, and chanted, and kissed and danced and kissed until we were nearly dizzy or half-way into some other state of being. The situation was funny, but the hilarity only seemed to deepen the power. The spiral unwound, snaked, opened out, and threaded back. The chant went on and on. I began to fear that the energy would dissipate before it could be drawn into a cone. Then it changed. We began to sing:

> We are changers,
> Everything we touch can change.

The chant affirmed our purpose, affirmed the strength of the groups going out the next morning, on the last day of the block-ade. The power built. We drew together in a tight spiral again, swaying, chanting, and singing in free-form melodies and word-less harmonies until the power peaked. After we grounded, we sang the names of the affinity groups who were present. Again the singing was both funny and beautiful. Chanting, "Mother Earth," can be solemnly spiritual; chanting, "No Nukes, Hold the An-chovies," demands an appreciation of the absurdities of life.

ACTION AS MAGIC

Three hundred women are gathered on a San Francisco Street out-side the Bohemian Club, an exclusive playpen for heads of corporations and heads of state. The men who frequent the club make decisions to build nuclear power plants, to produce weapons, to cut back on social programs. Here the decision was made to produce the atom bomb.

"Weaving spiders come not here," is the motto of the Bohemian Club. It is a quote from Shakespeare. The women have come to weave. We are making a web that shuts the club's doors, that surrounds its ivy-covered walls and extends across the sidewalk into the street. All along the walls we have planted cardboard tombstones bearing the names of women who are victims of violence. As we weave, we chant:

> We are the flow, we are the ebb,
> We are the weavers, we are the web.

We raise power.

But this is not a ritual; it is a political demonstration by a group called the Women's Pentagon Action West. On the East Coast today thousands of women are marching on the Pentagon. They too will enact their mourning, anger, empowerment, defiance. They too have created an action that is also a ritual, an act of magic.

If magic is "the art of causing change in accordance with will," then political acts, acts of protest and resistance, acts that speak truth to power, that push for change, are acts of magic. Political organizers are fond of drawing distinctions between direct actions — those that literally attempt to stop some harmful process (as the Diablo blockade attempted to stop workers from loading fuel rods, or a strike attempts to shut down a factory or corporation) — and symbolic acts, such as marches, demonstrations, street theater productions, and rallies which make statements but have an indirect effect.

I once defined a spell as "a symbolic act done in a deepened state of consciousness." When political action moves into the realm of symbols, it becomes magical. If we apply the principles of magic to politics, we can understand political actions better and make them more effective.

A demonstration is a ritual because it has elements that are repeated. People gather and they process along a route. Their chants are usually simple, rhythmic slogans that raise a certain kind of power. Then they gather for a rally at which there are speakers — some interesting and some boring, and often there is music or some other entertainment. Finally everyone goes home.

Two years ago a group of artists and pagans decided to organize a demonstration in which the ritual elements would be heightened and would appeal to all the senses. It would be a moving ritual. We called it the Three-Mile-Island Memorial Parade, and it marked the first anniversary of the Three-Mile-Island nuclear accident.

The march itself had a score like a performance that was divided into two main acts. The first illustrated the negative future we can expect if nuclear power development continues. It was led by survivors from Hiroshima who chanted a Buddhist liturgy, and by Native Americans whose homelands in the Southwest were being destroyed by uranium mining. It was followed by a company of wailing women dressed in gray and black robes. A twenty-foot-high wood and papier-mache mockup of a nuclear cooling tower was carried on a flatbed truck. A street theater group dressed as scientists, government officials, and businessmen continually climbed to the top of this and tossed in babies, bodies, and piles of money. Another theater group followed; they were dressed as the mutant sponges rumored to be growing off the Farallon Islands where nuclear wastes have been dumped. A veteran, spokesman for a group who had been exposed to radiation in the early years of nuclear testing, told (from the back of another truck) of death and disease among his fellow servicemen. Finally, a medieval plague cart piled with bodies was drawn along by a crier who rang a bell and called out through the streets:

Bring out your dead!
Bring out your dead!

The second act of the march was heralded by a beautiful batik banner[5] showing a rainbow of people of many colors that stretched over a natural landscape within a circle of enclosing hands. It was followed by contingents of people representing the four elements. They were dressed in appropriate colors and carried representations of the renewable power that each element offers. Local affinity groups created wonderful effects — including water-dragons and a huge bird mounted on a bicycle wheel, with a windmill on its head. Other groups brought a giant Goddess puppet. In general, the procession featured the color and costumes San Franciscans love.

The Parade was designed to speak in the language of things — to convey its message in sensual, creative, and funny ways instead of having speakers at the rally. We compiled facts and printed them in a booklet that we handed out along the way. Our somewhat cynical idea was that no one listens to speeches anyway, and, certainly, few people remember facts. How much better to have them all written down for easy reference, in plain English, with no catch-words, no slogans, no leftist jargon to get in the way.

The Parade attracted about five thousand people. They marched a three-mile route from San Francisco's Civic Center through Japan Town (in memory of Hiroshima and Nagasaki) to the Panhandle of Golden Gate Park. There, we created a simple ritual. Ropes were drawn out from the cooling tower, and the people representing the four elements pulled it apart in a tug-of-war. As it collapsed, it released a flight of balloons with white origami doves attached, that sailed up over the Panhandle. With great enthusiasm, the crowd stomped the remains of the cooling tower to pieces. Several of us began a chant. Nobody could hear us because we were not using a sound system, but we started dancing amidst the litter of the cooling tower, and crowds of press photographers pointed lenses at our faces. Somehow, a few of us raised enough power so that it caught the assembled crowd. Suddenly, people were chanting sounds together. As one, everybody threw their arms above their heads and turned towards the sun.

The chant went on for a long, long time. It was smooth, peaceful, strong. Thousands of people became, for a moment, one voice. The chant ended all at once. When some of us sat down and grounded the power the rest followed suit. The day ended with small groups picnicking in the Panhandle, where they could circulate among information tables that many groups had set up.

The Parade was a powerful, joyful experience for those who took part, because it was structured as a ritual and honored the principles of magic. It had a clear focus that was linked to a particular time — the anniversary of the Three-Mile-Island nuclear accident. It had a beginning, a climax, and an end that grounded the power we had raised. It was collectively planned and organized; we spent a great deal of time networking, going to meetings of other groups, exchanging endorsements. It generated a great deal of enthusiasm and energy at a time when the antinuclear movement in San Francisco was at a low ebb. It has become an event that people remember.

In planning a magicopolitical event, the importance of having a clear focus cannot be over-stressed. If the purpose of an action is vague or the target is obscure, no spark is kindled in potential participants. An action speaks to Younger Self, not Talking Self; if a target must be explained, it may not be clear enough. Such explanations may have educational value, but will probably make organizing more difficult.

THE EQUINOX RITUAL

The oak trees of the back country around Diablo Canyon are the oldest oaks in the world. I don't know who told me that, or where the information came from, but I believe it. The oaks stretch around us and above us, high and sheltering. There are about eighty of us hiking on a secret path in the back country near the plant, a path that our guides have scouted. We are dressed in our darkest clothes, greens and blues, so that we can blend into the brush when helicopters fly over.

I am tired. Or rather, I am in a state beyond tiredness, between waking and sleeping, brought on by broken sleep and bad food. I am sustained now by energy that is no longer physical. In this state, the trees, the earth, come alive. They speak. They are angry, and we can let ourselves be pulled by the currents of their deep earth power. This must truly have been a sacred place to the Indians, for it feels like an open crack between the worlds, a place where even in bright daylight we are half in the underworld.

In my haze, I begin to see the whole blockade as a giant hex on the plant, an elaborate ritual. It has its own rite-of-entry, nonviolence training. Our way to the camp was secret — like the secret of the labyrinth. First we checked in at a site in the nearby town; then we were handed a map that guided us in a round-about, circular fashion to camp.

The action takes place on a mythical landscape.

Strangely, the camp and the women's jail were in parallel valleys, separated by conical hills. From each valley you saw the same mountains — only different sides — the opposing sides: as if the Goddess, as cosmic set designer, was saying to us, "Now, see the two contrasting principles of power and choose." For in the jail everything embodied power-over. The basis of that power — the guns in the guards' hands — was always clearly evident. And the location where the women were held was an old gym, once part of the California Men's Colony prison. The building, made of corrugated iron and concrete, was so bare and institutionally ugly that it seemed an affront to the human spirit that some creative person had been required to design it. Yet it was not very different from any school gym.[6] The men's jail had been a gym at Cuesta College. The men were incarcerated on campus, across the street from playing fields where cheerleaders and football players practiced. The college and the Men's colony had both been part of the same military base. They all interconnected, as if all these institutions — the school, the military base, the football field, and the prison were simply different facets of the same institution. (As they are.) Everything was grey, drab, or off-white.

But in the camp everything was bright and colorful. Although the land itself is in a square bounded by fences, the camp center was a circular meeting ground, and the surrounding areas were laid out in wedges, like a giant pie. People pitched their tents in clumps and circles; the tents were orange, yellow, bright blue, green, and all the happy colors favored by the makers of camping equipment — colors meant to be visible across vast stretches of mountain terrain (in case their owners get lost) and the tents hugged the yellow-gray straw on the ground. Everything was close to the ground: the tallest structure was a white tepee. There were banners and flags and pinwheels. Anyone seeing the camp from far away had to feel happy. It seemed magical — like a medieval fair from the past or a premonition of a better future. When we were in it, the space had the kind of order found in a messy room (where you can find anything because you know where you put it) — an order like that of an Arabian bazaar, a gypsy camp, or an Indian village. Everywhere there were circles of people meeting, talking, singing, standing with their arms around each other. The camp itself embodied the thought-forms of immanence. The space warped time around it, so that it got harder and harder, as the blockade wore on, to schedule anything, especially things like rituals — by the clock.

The camp lacked only one thing, a center. We needed a central fire, a hearth, a heart. In the hot, dry central California autumn everyone fears fire, but one could have been made safely. And of course, the people who planned the camp had their minds on logistics and serious problems, not on singing around the campfire or doing rituals — not until the end. But if the camp had had a center, a sacred fire to feed and house the Deep Self of the group, it might have been easier to keep the group's energy focused.

In the action we became Persephone, as we were dragged off by the forces of patriarchy to do our time in the underworld and then emerge again. We became Demeter, who sits at the gate, who rends her clothes and says, "This cannot go on!"

"It is categories in the mind and guns in their hands that keep us enslaved."[7] Somehow, facing the guns in their hands makes clear to us which categories in our minds are their agents. We go against the dictates of the self-hater, we ignore the voices that warn, "You'll get in trouble," and the constellations of fears that reflect the way power-over keeps us intimidated. We speak our truth to the police and the guards. We express it to the judge, to all who enact the role of authority. And the power of the internalized authority, the self-hater, is weakened. We see it for what it is, and we are confirmed in our ability to confront it with a deeper truth. We are changed — more deeply than any growth workshop, or therapy, or packaged adventure-tour could change us — because we are confronting something real, and our transformation of consciousness is integrated with our transformation of the reality that surrounds us.

And now a group of us hike into the back country. In a surprise action on the morning the Nuclear Regulatory Commission is scheduled to grant the low-power testing license to the plant, some of us will block the seven-mile-long road that leads from the main gate to the plant at its midpoint. This will catch both the workers and the police off-guard. When the first contingent of thirty people is rounded up, another thirty will appear suddenly a little further down the road.

Some of us are climbing up the hill because the next day is the eve of the autumnal equinox, and we are determined to celebrate it within sight of the plant. Our ritual will be a political action, a threat to the plant's security, an expression of defiance. It will assert — on a day when we know hundreds of our people will be arrested — that we are still here, that we are loud, and strong, and will come back in force.

And it will be an act of the magic-that-works. I will go with others from Matrix, from Sabot (a group that takes its name from the saboteurs, workers who tossed their wooden shoes into machines in the nineteenth century) and another group, TMI (Trainers, Monitors, Itcetera) About twenty of us will go together.

It is very hot, even under the trees. We keep on, and now we are become a spirit army, the people of the land returning. The land has become the ancient oak forests of Europe, the jungles of Central America, the New England woods — or the echo of some-place I have been but cannot quite remember.

"Copter!" someone says quietly. We step quickly into the sha-dows. Movement is noticeable; but if we stand still with our greens and blues fading into the forest cover, we will not be seen.

Someone catches my eye, and we smile. For a moment, I feel as if I were ten years old, playing spies with my friends Barry and Randy in the hot back alley behind our apartments. Now we are a big gang of kids who have somehow hooked the Highway Patrol and the National Guard into a giant game of cops-and-robbers, complete with real guns, real helicopters, real jails. The truth is — the blockade is fun. I hadn't expected that. I had expected to be tired, to be hurt, to be scared. I had expected to be home already, having done my bit — gone to the front gate, gotten arrested once, and done my four days in jail. I hadn't expected the physical action to feel so good.

It does feel good. It is a release. My life at home is embedded in words. I spend hours, weeks, months, putting words on paper at the typewriter. I spend hours every day listening to people as they talk about their pain, trying, with some combination of words, touch, and vision to repair the damage. All the time the frustra-tion keeps building, building — why should this be? What we experience as individual pain is the failure of our way of life. Yet everything I do, eat, enjoy — if I make a cup of coffee or drive to the movies or turn up the heat — somehow contributes to the gathering destruction. The truth is that we are always under the gun. My city is a target of missiles carrying bombs that are thou-sands of times more powerful than the one that destroyed Hiro-shima. Yet it is not the Russians but my own government that gives me this constant uneasiness, an omnipresent fear, but one I can rarely touch, a rage so deep it has settled into the bone.

Yet here frustration is gone. I feel like a victim released by a vampire — my blood is my own again. What has freed me is action. I have acted with my body, using not just words, but my whole being. I have become fully a part of this community of resistance, putting forth effort and taking risks. To be present with skills and patience I have for listening, for evoking feelings, for soothing hurts, for saying the right thing, and for knowing when to shut up is healing; it is the only spiritual discipline that makes sense to me in a nuclear age.

I feel better on that trail. Though I am hot, dirty, exhausted, and painfully aware that it is not really a difficult hike, it is that I am out of shape — I feel better than I have in years. Maybe ever. The blockade is well worth the price of admittance.

One gift of the blockade is clarity. All the issues that seemed amorphous, all the interconnections that were so painful to puzzle out in the abstract, have become real. At home, I neither deal nor use illegal drugs. I don't shoplift, make phony credit-card calls, or indulge in petty crimes. I drive at or below the speed limit and lead, in general, a blameless law-abiding life, so I have grown used to thinking of policemen as my friends. Here, however, it is very clear that the powers of the police, the courts, and the military are at one with the nuclear-power industry, with all the forms of power that threaten to poison these oaks, this ocean, our living human bodies. That is obvious when the police have dragged me away and locked me up — obvious to my sore wrists and scraped knees. Not that I mind having skinned knees — it adds to that sense of being a child again, even though the stakes here are not playful, but all too real. With every step into the power of these woods I am beginning to care about them in a way I didn't before. Even sitting in front of the main gate, even riding past the twin domes in the police bus, the danger the plant represented was still somehow unreal to me. It was an intellectual threat, a hypothetical enemy. But now, as I feel the power of this earth, these trees, this *place*, and envision it contaminated, off-limits, ruined forever, I begin to get unspeakably angry. The anger twists out of my bones — with each breath, each step, the anger twists into my *will*. Changing anger to will is one useful magic trick I have learned in all these years of training and practice. I will that this land remain clean.

Not my will alone. Something deeper is pushing us all up the hill. Let us call it the deep will, the will of the Deep Self of the blockade, of all of us. In terms of magic I could say that for two days and two nights I have been riding on that will — since the last night I spent in jail.

Some of us from Matrix, and some of my friends from Moonstone — an affinity group from the nearby town of Cambria — wanted to do a ritual together on the fourth night in jail. After lights out, we filtered unobtrusively out the door to the smoking patio, and formed a small circle between the walkway and the honeyhuts (the outdoor toilets). We cast a circle, concentrating heavily on invisibility — or at least on not being noticed. In eerie whispers, we invoked Hecate of the waning moon, and began to chant. We worked magic while women passed behind us on their way to and from the honeyhuts and the guards smoked on the patio ten feet away — and nobody did seem to notice. We raised our cone of power by pounding straight into the earth, bending down and chanting in the dirt, pounding with our fists on the hard ground, our drum.

"Isis. Astarte. Diana. Hecate.
Demeter. Kali. Innana."[8]

As we chanted the words suddenly became: "Diablo Canyon will never open," and we were filled with a conviction that this was true.

The conviction was scary because it was not rational. Even though the blockade was continuing and our supply of people was continually being replenished, it seemed that the likelihood of our actually stopping the plant from operating was slim. More than a thousand people had been arrested, but we just didn't have the enormous numbers it would have taken to keep the roads blocked with our nonviolent tactics. One hundred or two hundred people could be removed by the police in a very short time, whether they cooperated by walking with the officers or went limp. At most, we could delay the busloads of workers by an hour or two.

But the feeling was there. It was strong, in the way it is when a spell is working. And if we didn't believe we could stop the plant, what were we doing anyway?

We grounded the power and went to sleep. At three in the morning, the Moonstones woke me. They had put our names down on a list to cite out. This was an opportunity offered to those of us who had been held past the legal time limit without being arraigned. We could be released if we promised to appear for arraignment at a future date, and those of us who planned to return to the blockade accepted.

And so I find myself out of jail and back in camp just in time to be enticed on this new adventure, moving into the back country to celebrate the eve of the Equinox in sight of the plant.

For two days, we hike intermittently, eating cold foods because fires are both a security and a fire hazard in the back country. We sleep huddled together under thin blankets because the police are confiscating property and not returning it, and we do not want to lose our good sleeping bags. We hike in the dark and in the hot sun, as the logistics of our secret journey requires.

Finally, as dusk is falling on the eve of the Equinox, the guides lead us over a hill onto an open ridge. The fog-dipped coastal hills roll softly away from us. Below us lies the plant, square, hard-edged, and out of place, like a bad science fiction fantasy cartoon imposed on the landscape. In this place where the earth stretches out her arms and rears her soft breasts, this plant is the emblem of our estrangement, our attempts to control, to impose a cold order with concrete and chain links.

The sun is setting. We sit on the hill and eat our meager dinner, chanting:

We are all one in the infinite sun
Forever, and ever, and ever.

A helicopter flies by. It does what can only be called a double take, and returns. On the third pass, some members of the group moon it. That seems to be the signal to start the ritual.

We gather in a circle on the ridge. The helicopter flies around it, as if to seal it for us. In the center is a living tree the Sabotniks have brought to plant in the back country for a member of their group who was killed during the summer in a highway accident. We plant a flag they have made — a black one for anarchy, for the power of the dark, that is embellished with the pentacle of the Goddess. Some of us have brought offerings — I leave an abalone shell on the hillside.

The ritual is loose and wild. Dark falls, and as we feel our power and our anger rise, we break from the circle, line up on the ridge, shine our flashlights down on the plant, and scream. We yell out curses. We want them to know we are here, shining our flashlights down, to draw their searchlights playing over the hills. We are banging on pots and pans, pointing our anger like a spear.

Hiroshima.
Nagasaki.
Three Mile Island.
No Diablo!

We can think of no worse forces to invoke.

The power peaks, at last, as power always does. We send it down to find the plant's weakest spots, the fault lines within its structure-of-being. We ground, and open the circle, and pick our way slowly, silently, in the dark, back to where we have made our camp.

We wake at three in the morning and hike down the hill in the dark, to plant the tree and to climb over the fence onto the grounds of the plant, breaching their security. Again, the police arrest us.

As Kore returns to the underworld, we return to jail. We celebrate the Equinox once more, among women. But just as Kore emerges in the spring, we know that we shall also return to the hills, to this blockade or another one, to whatever action we must take to bring about the renewal of the earth.

Our Equinox ritual was only one small action in the larger ritual of the blockade. It was another step in a dance of many actions, many rituals, many focused powers.

After the blockade ended, new problems were suddenly discovered in the plant. Blueprints had been reversed; structures had been built wrong; equipment had been inaccurately weighed. The safety violations were so grave that the Nuclear Regulatory Commission took back the license it had earlier granted. At this writing, the power company is embroiled in audits and litigation. No fuel rods were loaded, and still the land is uncontaminated.

So the blockade succeeded — not by physically stopping the workers, but by changing the reality, the consciousness, of the society in which the plant exists. Not the blockade alone, but the years of effort and organizing that preceded the blockade, created that victory.

The ritual, the magic, spins the bond that can sustain us to continue the work over years, over lifetimes. Transforming culture is a long-term project. We organize now to buy time, to postpone destruction just a little bit longer in the hope that before it comes, we will have grown somehow wiser — somehow stronger — so that in the end we will avert the holocaust. But though power-from-within can burst forth in an instant, its rising is mostly a process slow as the turning wheels of generations. If we cannot live to see the completion of that revolution, we can plant its seeds in our circles, we can dream its shape in our visions, and our rituals can feed its growing power.

As we see the Goddess mirrored in each other's eyes, we take that power in our hands as we take hands, as we touch. For the strength of that power is in the bond we make with each other. And our vision grows strong when we no longer dream alone.

Epilogue

The journey draws close, not to an end, but at least to a resting place. I am glad, because it is very late at night. The fat moon hangs in the sky, waxes over the San Francisco Hills. Five days of rain have given way to a clear sky. The kittens that played on my desk when I began this book have grown into cats. They file themselves in my drawers and knock papers off my desk. It is winter now, but moving toward an early California spring. I am waiting to see if the bulbs I planted will sprout and bloom. I am waiting to see the buds swell on the winter-flowering magnolias, to see the rhododendrons unfold, fragrant and pink, once again. I am waiting to see all the fragile beauty of the world renew itself.

And if there have been losses, acid rain on the Sierras, a constant whittling away of the choices — the possibilities of pleasure open to the poor, the possibilities open to any of us; if there has been narrowing of friendships and growing mistrust; if it seems that domination and hatred grow in strength daily as we read the daily news, and the shadows of the bombs grow longer in our imaginations; if a four-month-old baby has a brain tumor and the holocaust has already begun, still we have not yet lost hope.

That hope sways on an edge so delicate that it is possible that the choices any one of us makes could tip the balance. If these words at moments seem to have power for you, take it as a measure of the power you have if you reach for it, if you draw it up from the dark, if you will risk it. And perhaps it is you, your reaching, your voice, your work, your joy, your love, that will make the difference. Perhaps it is up to you to reclaim the world.

Or perhaps it is up to us all, to join our hands, our voices, to reach into the dark and reshape it into a clear night sky where we can walk without fear, into a well of healing from which we can all drink, into the velvet skin of life, the newly fertile ground.

It is very late, and I am very tired. Yet I know that I can lie down and sleep and rise up fresh in the morning, as the heavy moon will set and rise. That is our magic; our power to return, as something always pushes up from underground that can feed us.

So tonight I find myself feeling hope. I am feeling that exhilarating, scary sense of certainty, of a spell brewing, as if we were all part of a ritual that is now beginning to work. For the force that pushes us toward each other, flesh to flesh, heart to heart — that moves us to dance, to work, to birth and to weave — is a power that never stops reaching out for life.

The night, the moment — each moment — presents us with a chance to meet that power, to grasp it, to dream it into being.

It is in your eyes. It is in your hands.

Appendix A

❧ ❧

The Burning Times: Notes on a Crucial Period of History

She is afraid. Her own fear has a smell more pungent than the needles of pine that her feet crush on the forest path. The earth steams after spring rain. Her own heart is louder than the lowing of cattle on the common. The old woman carries a basket of herbs and roots she has dug; it feels heavy as time on her arm. Her feet on the path are her mother's feet, her grandmother's, her grandmother's grandmothers'; for centuries she has walked under these oaks and pines, culled the herbs and brought them back to dry under the eaves of her cottage on the common. Always, the people of the village have come to her; her hands are healing hands, they can turn a child in the womb; her murmuring voice can charm away pain, can croon the restless to sleep. She believes she has faery blood in her veins, blood of the Old Race who raised standing stones to the open sky and built no churches. The thought of the church makes her shiver; she remembers her dream of the night before — the paper pinned to the church door. She couldn't read it. What had it been? The proclamation of a Witch-hunt? She passes her hands over her eyes. These days, the Sight is a trouble; her dreams are haunted by the faces of women in torment; their sleepless eyes, the lids forced open as they walk up and

183

down, night after night, weak from hunger, their bodies shaved and displayed to the crowd, pricked deep to find the evidence they call devil's marks, then taken for the private amusement of the jailors. And they were mild here in England, where Witches were only hung. She thought of the tales, whispered at Meetings, of Germany and France, of devices to crush bones and tear limbs out of their sockets, of veins ripped apart and blood spilling on the dirt, and of flesh charred as flames rose about the stake. Could she keep silent under that — or would she break, confess to anything, name anyone they wanted as her fellow Witch? She doesn't know; she hopes she will never know.

The old woman makes a banishing sign with her left hand and walks on. Perhaps the paper in the dream was something else entirely. But the bad smell clung to it. Enclosure? Were they going to divide the common land, build fences, tear down the little cottages like her own? She feels a stab under her bodice and sits down, hardly able to breathe. Yes, that was it. What will she do? Who will speak for her or take her in? She has no husband, no children. Once the village would have protected her, but now the priests have done their work well. The sick fear her even when they come to her for help. The villagers fear each other. The bad harvests, the rents, and the always increasing price of food — there are too many rats scratching at the same little pile of grain, and the priests and the preachers are always at them to scratch at each other. Still, there were uprisings in the West and in the North against enclosure. There could be risings here.

She turns and looks deep into the forest. For a moment she is tempted to turn around, to follow the pathway further than she has ever been. Some have said the Old Race still lives in the forest's hidden center. Would they shelter her? Or would she find the camps of the master-less, the tinkers, the outlaws, those who had been driven, like herself, off the land? Would it be a freer life under the trees? Could they use a healer? And would they someday swarm out from the woods and wastes, an army of the dispossessed, to tear down the fences of the overlords, the manor houses, and the churches, to reclaim their own land for freedom?

She is still. But finally she shoulders her basket and starts off, back toward the village. Young Jonet at the mill is near her time, and the old woman knows it will be a difficult birth. She will need the herbs in this basket.

She is afraid but she walks on. "We have always survived," she tells herself. "We will always survive."

She repeats it, over and over again, like an incantation.

* * *

We survive, still, in the culture of estrangement, for how much longer no one knows. Yet to change that culture intelligently, we must understand it, trace its roots, know its history — not because estrangement is the lineal descendent of one particular historical event or time, but because the past is still alive in the present.

The drama of estrangement is a long and complex story, and perhaps it can never be fully retold. To tell it fully would be to retell all of history. But at least we can raise the curtain on the first scene of what may well be the last act, and look closely at the old woman's period, the sixteenth and seventeenth centuries, a time when Western Culture underwent crucial changes that produced the particular brand of estrangement that characterizes the modern world.

"Two descriptions are better than one," states Gregory Bateson in *Mind and Nature*, because "the combination of diverse pieces of information defines an approach of very great power to what I call . . . the pattern which connects."[1] When we look at the sixteenth and seventeenth centuries with binocular vision, we can see in sharp relief the many facets of our present dilemma.

One eye gives us the view with which we are familiar. We see the period of the Renaissance and Reformation as the great flowering of art, science, and humanism — a time when constricting chains of dogma were thrown off, a time of questioning and exploration, of the birth of new religions and the reevaluation of corruption in old institutions, a time of discovery and enlightenment.

But close that eye and look through the other — the left eye, the Witch's eye, and the sixteenth and seventeenth centuries are the Burning Times when persecution of Witches, and of women as Witches, reached its peak; the times of terror and torture; the times of the rack and the strappado; of forced confessions; of children used as witnesses against their mothers; of public death at the stake.

With binocular vision, the question that stands out is not: why did they persecute Witches? Church history is a history of persecution. The Witch burnings were not an isolated phenomenon; they must be seen in the context of centuries of blood and terror.[2]

For the Jews, the Middle Ages were a period of continually escalating restrictions, humiliations, expulsions, and wholesale slaughter. In Spain, the forcibly converted Marranos, who continued to practice Judaism secretly, were tortured by the Inquisitors and, if unrepentant, were burned like Witches at the stake. Christian heretics, both individuals and whole communities such as the Waldenses and Albigenses, were also victims of the rack, of the sword, and at the stake.

Rosemary Ruether points out in New Woman, New Earth: Sexist Ideologies and Human Liberation, that "many of the ideas later projected upon Witches, such as nocturnal orgies and child sacrifice, were directed by the Inquisition first against heretics. . . . The image of the Jew as a demonic alien was similar in many ways to that of the Witch . . . The Jew was seen as a devil worshipper, equipped with horns, claws, and tail, riding on a satanic goat. Like the Witch, the Jew was believed to steal the Eucharist and to perform other blasphemous caricatures of Catholic rituals."[3]

The Witch persecutions were, however, different in several important ways from persecutions of Jews and heretics. To begin with, they were directed primarily, although not exclusively, against women — particularly during the sixteenth and seventeenth centuries. Witches were not an alien ethnic-religious group, like Jews, set apart from Christian society. Nor were they a clearly delineated alien sect, like the Albigenses, with a clearly defined doctrine and organization. It is true that Witches were accused of worshipping the devil, but not in the same sense that the Marranos, for example, were accused of continuing their traditional Jewish worship.

The devil, in the mind of the witchhunters, was an actual being, and Witches were charged with having actual social and sexual intercourse with him. They were accused of feats that were fantastic and bizarre, that contradicted our ordinary grasp of reality: night flights, turning people into animals, and charming away penises and hiding them in birds' nests.[4] We are tempted to conclude that somebody must have suffered from full-blown paranoid delusions.

Throughout the late Middle Ages, sporadic Witchhunts occurred, as the Renaissance bloomed in the late fifteenth century, they become widespread.[5]

In 1484, a papal bull by Innocent VIII declared Witchcraft a heresy and extended the power of the Inquisitors to hunt Witches in Southern Germany. In 1486, the Dominican Inquisitors Kramer and Sprenger published the *Malleus Maleficarum* (called "The Hammer of the Witches"), which became the witchhunter's manual for the next two and a half centuries. Persecutions increased throughout the sixteenth century and reached their greatest extent and ferocity in the early seventeenth century. (The Salem Witch trials, in the late 1600s, were a localized outbreak that will not be considered here.)

Estimates of the actual number of Witches executed range from 100,000 to 9,000,000.[6] The higher estimates include many who were not officially executed but died in prison. The true number is difficult to estimate, and this fact is less important than an understanding of the climate of terror that was unleashed. Anyone — especially any woman — could be accused of being a Witch. Witchcraft was defined as a special crime to which the ordinary laws of evidence did not apply. Jean Bodin, a noted French witchhunter and intellectual, actually favored the use of children as witnesses because they could be persuaded more easily to give evidence against the accused.[7] Once accused, the suspected Witch was subjected to tortures such as those in the following contemporary description:

> There are men who in this art exceed the spirits of hell. I have seen the limbs forced asunder, the eyes driven out of the head, the feet torn from the legs, the sinews twisted from the joints, the shoulder blades wrung from their place, the deep veins swollen, the superficial veins driven in, the

victim now hoisted aloft and now dropped, now revolved
around, head undermost and feet uppermost. I have seen
the executioner flog with the scourge, and smite with rods,
and crush with screws, and load down with weights, and
stick with needles, and bind around with cords, and burn
with brimstone, and baste with oil, and singe with torches.[8]

Sometimes torture went on for days and nights, as in Germany,
and sometimes it was limited to an hour at a time, as in Italy and
Spain.[9] So-called torture was banned altogether in England,
where starvation, deprivation of sleep, and gang-rape did not
count as torture. Whether the accused yielded to intolerable pain
and named others or confessed to whatever her torturers suggested; whether she was mercifully strangled at the stake before
burning, or burned alive, or hung, or banished, or whether she
committed suicide, accusation meant ruin.

In practice, accusations of Witchcraft were mostly directed at
women in the lower strata of society.[10] Especially at risk were
widows, spinsters, and those who were unprotected by a man.
When wealthy or prominent persons were accused, "the credibility of the confessions extracted under torture broke down and
influential public opinion began to suspect that the previous confessions did not represent real experience."[11] The Witchhunts,
then, were directed against women as a sex and against the
peasant-laboring class.[12]

The question that emerges in my mind about the Witch persecutions is not: why? It is: why *then?* Why at this particular time in
history did the hierarchies of both the Catholic and the newly
formed Protestant Churches sanction and encourage the persecution of Witches? Whose interests were served?

A society is not a static thing, an object, a single entity. It is a
system, an ever-changing network of interlocking relationships
wherein the whole is more than — and sometimes qualitatively
different from — the sum of its parts. The ways in which necessi-
ties and luxuries are produced, the shares of both to which different classes within society are entitled, the level of science and technology, the distribution of power, the sexual arrangements, the
child-rearing practices, the individual psychology and ideologies

embodied in religion, in philosophy, in education, and in institutions — all these shape each other. Interactions among them are not simple; they are nonlinear, circular loops of cause and effect that feed back on one another, acting as mutual pressures and restraints. A change in one aspect of society changes the dynamic balance among all its aspects. Other aspects then must change in an attempt to preserve a constancy in the relationship between human beings and their environment, so that this relationship will allow group survival.[13]

During the sixteenth and seventeenth centuries, Western Society was undergoing massive changes. The Witchhunts were an expression both of the weakening of traditional restraints and of an increase in new pressures. It was a revolutionary time, but the persecutions helped to undermine the possibility of a revolution that would benefit women, the poor, and those without property. Instead, the changes that occurred benefited the rising monied-professional classes, and made possible the ruthless, extensive, and irresponsible exploitation of women, working people, and nature.

As part of that change, the persecution of Witches was linked to three interwoven processes: the expropriation of land and natural resources; the expropriation of knowledge; and the war against the consciousness of immanence, which was embodied in women, sexuality, and magic.

THE EXPROPRIATION OF LAND

Feudalism was an authoritarian, hierarchical system, but it was based on an organic model. Carolyn Merchant, in *The Death of Nature: Women, Ecology and the Scientific Revolution*, gives many examples of Medieval thinkers who used the human body as a model and metaphor for the societal body.[14] In a work published by John of Salisbury in 1159, the prince, together with the clergy, functioned as the soul of the commonwealth. The lawmakers were its heart; judges and governors were its sense organs. Soldiers were its arms and hands; one arm protected the people from without, the other disciplined them from within. Financiers were the states' bowels. Peasants, laborers, craftspeople and menial workers were the feet that supported all the rest.[15]

Feudal society was, in reality, a system of complex, interlocking rights and responsibilities that functioned, in many ways, like an organism.[16] Its basic unit was the local community, the manor, village, or, in late Medieval times, the town. The economy was agrarian, based on subsistence farming. Roads were poor and transportation was slow. Agricultural goods were perishable, so each community depended primarily on what it could grow and produce itself.

Agriculture was based on the village as an organism, rather than on the labors or profits of the individual or the nuclear family as independent agents. In many areas, the fields were held and worked in common. The introduction of the heavy plow in the Carolingian period had made it necessary for peasants to band together in order to acquire and maintain a plow and a team of oxen or horses needed to pull it. Instead of having small individually owned fields, the village as a whole might own enormous open fields. Decisions about when and what to plant, what land to leave fallow, how to rotate crops, and how to allot the harvest fairly would be made communally. Instead of owning a compact plot of land, a peasant owned or rented "a right to part of the profits of the soil."[17] In some cases, the peasants received from the produce several strips of land of different types: arable fields, hay meadows, and pastures. The peasant owed a corresponding contribution to the communal work of ploughing, planting, harvesting, and husbandry.

Even in areas in which land was owned independently, vast tracts of pasture, forest, fen, and wasteland were covered by a complex network of *rights of common*.[18] Although the local lord might be said to own a wood or pasture, the common people would have the right to graze cattle on the fallow fields, to run pigs in the forests, and to gather wood for fuel or for repairing buildings and fences. In some areas, large tracts of forest land were set aside as the king's private game preserve. (This is the legal meaning of the word *forest* in the medieval period.) Peasants were forbidden to kill deer. (Remember the Robin Hood stories?) And they could not even drive them away from their fields, but the peasants might have compensatory rights to downed wood, or to other benefits from the forest.[19]

Even in villages where land was farmed independently, it was bound by the rights of others. One family might, for example, have the right to graze cattle on another family's fields after the harvest.

The lords possessed the land but they did not *own* it as we own private property. They were restrained by traditional common rights from changing the use of the land. A lord could not, at his pleasure, cut down a forest in which common people held rights. Even in the middle of the sixteenth century, the "City Doctrine" that "men could 'use their possessions as they list' seemed tantamount to atheism."[20] Land was expected to provide a livelihood, but profit was not its primary purpose:

> In the Middle Ages, land was looked on as a source of dignity or as a nursery of soldiers, or as a means of maintaining a governing class in the social position appropriate to it. To exploit an estate in order to get from it the highest monetary revenue was considered almost an abuse of property rights, especially if such exploitation involved the misery or degradation of the cultivators of the soil . . . The growth of a money economy made inroads on manorial custom behind which the tenants had found shelter, and allowed the lord to indulge to the full his profit-searching proclivities.[21]

Feudal society was still guided by an economic principle of use, not one of gain. Land, for example, had value because it provided subsistence; this fact was the basis of its power to determine social standing. It supported armies, and was thus the base of political power. But it was not yet seen as a resource to be exploited for maximum gain.

Feudal laws and customs guaranteed peasants — whether free or serfs — access to the land, to the means of subsistence. The same laws and customs denied the peasant-laboring classes the right to anything more than subsistence. Whatever the peasants succeeded in scratching from the land beyond what was needed for keeping themselves and their families alive was distributed upward, as rents, feudal tribute, church tithes, and mandatory work tributes. That surplus wealth of grain, fruit, milk, meat, wool, and other produce supported the classes that fought and governed, and that also ruled the church.

The upper classes were supported at the expense of a gradual, long-term depletion of the land's fertility:

> The landlords' practice of extracting from unfree peasants (those not subject to fixed rents) any income above subsistence meant that those peasants were unable to give back to the land what they took. They had insufficient reserves to reinvest in animals for plowing and manuring the soil. In many regions, soils became quickly exhausted and badly eroded.[22]

The prosperity of the upper classes was a false prosperity based on the accumulation of an ecological debt, much as today we maintain an artificially high standard of living by depleting the land and our nonrenewable resources.[23]

Declining fertility of the land was one source of pressure to change traditional agricultural patterns. Other pressures came from the rise of a market economy that superseded the feudal economy. The feudal economy, of course, had always included markets. In the late feudal period and the early Renaissance, they began to dominate. The rise of a market economy meant a shift from use-values to gain as a value. Instead of producing one's own food, and selling what was extra, landowners began to produce for the market, not what was needed, but what could be sold for a profit.

American gold flooded Europe in the sixteenth century, causing terrible inflation. Landlords found their traditional rents were worth less and less. Inflation provided the pressure, as the opening of markets provided the opportunity, to maximize profits from the land.

In England, many landowners turned from raising grains and vegetables for local consumption to raising sheep for the expanding wool market.[24] Wool was England's first major export, and the textile industry was the first one organized along capitalist lines. Grain was restricted from export in 1491 and its price and profitability were kept low by law. The export of wool was encouraged, and unlike perishable agricultural products, wool could be shipped, even in an age of poor roads and slow transport. English woolens found a ready market in the Netherlands and elsewhere on the continent.

Raising sheep required fewer laborers than raising crops. It was also done most efficiently when the land was enclosed, i.e., fenced off. Profits also tended to be more secure when decisions were made by one owner or his agent (who would have only one set of interests to keep in mind) rather than by a communal body that might have to weigh, balance, and compromise among the interests of many villagers.

Landowners began to pressure for enclosure. Enclosure, in effect, turned the land into private property under a single person's control, destroying the network of mutual rights and obligations that had characterized the medieval village.

In the seventeenth century, enclosure increased and spread from forests and wasteland to fields and farmland. Towns now provided a market for crops and dairy produce. Landowners who could consolidate large holdings and put into practice the new so-called scientific agriculture could make large profits. Defense of enclosure was based on the fact that increased production and new agricultural methods succeeded in improving the yield of the land — in part because landholders of the upper classes could retain the surplus wealth the land produced and could return some of it to the land by investing in methods that renewed fertility.

The laws and customs that secured rights of common could be changed in several ways. If the common land fell into disuse because the land changed or the population was destroyed, the lord might acquire unilateral rights. In times of disturbance, such as the religious wars of the sixteenth century, or when massive amounts of land changed hands for political reasons — for example, when Henry VIII dissolved the monasteries' holdings, the common people often lost their traditional rights.[25]

Land that was not held under ancient common rights, such as wilderness, wasteland, forests, and marginal land, could be appropriated more easily than the legally entangled fields and meadows of the villagers.[26] So the wilds and wastes were often enclosed earlier than arable farmlands were. Forests, already shrinking because fuel and wood were demanded for building, especially shipbuilding, now were further diminished. The natural environment was changed beyond recognition, and much wilderness was destroyed. The view of land as private property was linked to the new world-view that saw nature as non-alive, and as something valuable only when it could be exploited.

Land could also be enclosed by agreement of those who held common rights, and who were paid in proportion to their holding. A single payment of money, however, was inadequate compensation for loss of access to the means of providing an independent livelihood. And, as Paul Mantoux states:

> The mighty had means at their disposal to suppress any opposition: "Unwilling commoners are threatened with the risks of long and expensive lawsuits; in other cases they are subject to persecution by the great proprietors who ditch in their own demesne and force them to go a long way round to their own land, or maliciously breed rabbits and keep geese on adjoining ground, to the detriment of their crops."[27]

Enclosed land, instead of serving multiple needs and purposes, served only one. When a forest was cut down and enclosed for grazing land, it no longer provided wood for fuel and building, acorns for pigs, a habitat for wild game, a source of healing herbs, or shelter for those who were driven to live outside the confines of town and village. When a fen was drained to provide farmland, it no longer provided a resting place or nesting sites for migratory birds, or a source of fish for the poor.

"Enclosures," as Bacon put it, " 'bred a decay of the people.' Whole villages were depopulated; the houses tumbled into ruin; the roofless church became a sheep-pen; a few herdsmen lived where once had been the abode of a thriving agricultural community."[28]

Enclosure was hardest on those who lived marginally: the squatters on the common, the poorest of the peasants who supplemented scanty crops with the produce of forest and fen; the laborer whose wages did not provide a livelihood.

Those who lost their source of an independent livelihood became totally dependent on wages. In the seventeenth century, maximum wages for agricultural workers were fixed by the magistrates at the Quarter Sessions.[29] These varied according to the price of corn, not the cost of living. Wages in industries, such as the textiles, were also fixed by laws that protected the manufacturer, not the worker. Men could earn barely enough to support themselves; there was little or no margin for feeding a wife and children. Women's wages were much lower than men's.[30]

A family who held and worked a small plot of land could provide most of their own food, and money earned from wages could provide necessary extra cash. Generally, wives tended the family gardens and raised cows, pigs, or chickens. Their women's work was of utmost importance to the family's survival. When a family lost its land, it became dependent on meager wages, the whims of an employer, and the ups-and-downs of the economy. The poor sank into deeper poverty and helplessness. The result was most devastating for women. When a family had too little food to go around, the husband could work on a neighboring farm, where at least he was fed. "The woman with a baby to care for and feed, could not leave her home every day to work and must share the children's food. In consequence, she soon began to practice starvation."[31]

Infant mortality was rampant among laborers. Those who depended on wages for a living were considered likely to end up "a charge on the parish" — which institution was, by law, required to provide relief to the poor. Parish officials, in order to keep the number of poor people to a minimum and to keep "rates" (taxes) down, prevented unemployed laborers as well as other destitute people from settling in new areas in search of work. Pregnant women of the poorer classes were especially undesirable, for they would soon produce new mouths for the parish to feed.

The fact that a woman was soon to have a baby, instead of appealing to (parishioners') chivalry, seemed to them the best reason for turning her out of her house and driving her from the village, even when a hedge was her only refuge.[32]

Enclosure destroyed the peasant village as an economic unity. Power over important decisions, which affected the well-being of the whole community, was no longer vested in the village or its representatives. Instead, it became fragmented and privatized, appropriated by the landholders along with the land.

The poor were no longer seen as entitled to the means of a livelihood — even a bare one. Instead they were forced into wage labor at wages that did not provide even a subsistence income.[33] The organic community was destroyed, and individuals became like atoms — separated, no longer bound by mutual obligation.

In many areas, the peasants resisted.[34] There were riots against enclosure in many areas of England, such as Somerset, the Taunton wool district, Wiltshire, Gloucester, and North Devon. In Germany, the Peasants' War of 1525 was an open rebellion against the landlords' usurpation of the peasants' traditional common rights. In the 1630s, fen dwellers in England destroyed drainage projects. Enclosure was one of many underlying issues in the English Civil War.

The persecution of Witches undermined the unity of the peasant community and contributed to its fragmentation. Such a climate offered an outlet in which any local quarrel could escalate into a lethal attack. Moreover, the peasants began to live in fear of each other. Any old woman who got mad and muttered under her breath might be a Witch uttering a curse. And any neighbor, herself accused and taken, might name her closest friends or her own relations under torture.[35] The persecutions encouraged, spawned, paranoia. Among people who for centuries had been in a powerless position, the persecutions could only exacerbate the difficulties of cooperating to challenge the oppressive power of others.

Witches also made convenient scapegoats, diverting the anger and rage of the poorer classes to these other members of their own class. They provided an accessible target for men's hostility to women. They encouraged women to blame each other for misfortunes instead of looking for the conditions that caused suffering and misery. If a child died or wasted away, one could feel power in accusing a Witch and seeing her hanged, instead of admitting one's powerlessness.

Festivals, feasts, and folk customs, either overtly pagan or pseudo-Christian, had always provided a source of communal unity. The maypole, the bonfires on the ancient Celtic feast days, the traditional dances and customs were tied to the seasons and the changing round of the agricultural year.[36] They expressed the integration of the community with the land, and the changing cycles of the seasons in a never-ending round of renewal. While in many places their original meanings were undoubtedly forgotten, they continued to encourage feelings of local pride and bound the participants to each other:

> Many of the folk customs which had previously been ignored by the high culture of the church leaders had now come to their attention . . . The first stage of Witch persecution functioned as a purge by the orthodox Catholic culture of the ethnically distinct folkways of villagers and highlanders.[37]

These customs were the expression — in actions, songs, costumes, celebration — of the organic unity of the human community and of the oneness of the peasant with the land and its gifts. Their destruction ripped apart the unconscious fabric of peasant life. Those leaders who remembered the deep meanings of festivals and customs no longer dared to share their knowledge. The rituals that had bonded villagers together were destroyed as the communal bond was destroyed. The celebrations that tied the peasant to the land were branded as evil and satanic when the peasants began to be driven off the land.

Enclosure was also devastating for Witchcraft. The sacred places and meeting grounds of the Old Religion were the wastes and forests that were now fenced off, cut down, or destroyed. Many of the Witches were themselves among the marginally poor who were hit hardest by the loss of their traditional rights of common.

Oral traditions tell us that many Witches, along with the remnants of the pre-Celtic peoples know as Faeries, left Britain at this time. Legends differ about their destination, some say it was Portugal, others says Eastern Europe, still others say the New World or the mythical lands of the Otherworld (The Land of Youth, the Isle of Apples, the Summerland). Although the Craft survived in isolated pockets and in family traditions, the ancient customs and rituals, as well as the bond with the land as a living being were destroyed as a social force.

This period also marks the begining of colonial expansion. Those who emigrated were cut off, in some cases only by a generation, from the experience of a tie to the land that honored the inherent rhythms and being of nature. These emigrants brought the ethic of private property and the absolute right of ownership to the New World; they imposed it on Africa, India, and the Far East, and they extended it to the ownership of people. Slaves were viewed as subhuman — savages and devil-worshippers, without inherent value except potential profitability. This property ethic supported a ruthless slave-trade, just as it justified expropriation of land from the Native Americans.

The English settlers' own great-grandparents may have honored nature in their fields as harvest Goddess or fertile spirit of the Maypole. They may have marked the sun's cycles with bonfires to rouse in themselves the God's quickening fire, and they may have made love in the ploughed furrows in the spring, uniting the fecundity of both human flesh and soil. Yet now, cut off from the immanent religions of their past, they viewed with total incomprehension the Indians' respect for the earth as a Grandmother, and their reverence for animals and plants as fellow creatures. They looked on the African religions — which saw all things as alive, as houses for spirit — as rank superstition and suppressed them among slaves, outlawing the dance and the drum because white masters feared that the common bond of religion would spark slave rebellion. The masters enforced conversion to a Christianity that reconciled the slave to her/his condition and a continuing rationale for slavery was that as slaves Africans were Christianized.

The ethic of ownership has shaped every feature of the landscape of reality today, from the food that I eat, grown by mammoth corporations using a so-called scientific agriculture that poisons the soil and ultimately strips it of its fertility, to the property speculations that have driven blacks and working-class white families out of the neighborhood where I live, to the acid rain that falls even on protected wilderness.

That reality shapes our consciousness. To oppose its destructiveness effectively, it is not enough to oppose piecemeal the most virulent abuses of ownership. We need to change our understanding, to recognize that destruction is inherent in the very concept of ownership, which robs the earth of its life and inherent value. We need to join with the Indians to restore a sense of sacredness to the land, and to greet the earth again as Grandmother, sister, mother.

THE EXPROPRIATION OF KNOWLEDGE

The Witch persecutions were tied to another of the far-reaching changes in consciousness that occurred during the sixteenth and seventeenth centuries. The rise of professionalism in many arenas of life meant that activities and services that people had always performed for themselves or for their neighbors and families were taken over by a body of paid experts, who were licensed or otherwise recognized as being the guardians of an officially approved and restricted body of knowledge.

The Catholic Church had for centuries served as a model for an approved body that dispensed approved grace. Many of the charges against Witches and heretics can be seen as charges of giving or receiving "Brand X" grace, one that lacked the official seal of approval; of transmitting knowledge without approval. Witches' powers, whether used for harming or for healing, were branded as evil because they came from an unapproved source. In a dualistic world-view in which Christ has subsumed all good, every other source of knowledge and grace must be an aspect of his opposite — the evil Satan.

In the sixteenth and seventeenth centuries, many forms of knowledge began to take on a new economic importance. The Reformation destroyed the Catholic Church's absolute monopoly on the approval of knowledge. At the same time, the market economy was spreading into more and more areas of life. Knowledge itself began to be an "intangible commodity".[38] It was something to be sold only to those who could afford to buy it.

Ivan Illich, in an essay called "Vernacular Values," discusses the politics behind the standardization of language. Nebrija's Castilian grammar, the first grammar of a vernacular tongue, appeared in 1492 — the year in which the Jews were expelled from Spain, and in which Columbus set off upon his voyage of discovery. The standardization of the unbound and ungoverned common speech became a tool of discrimination and a weapon of conquest.

The language that people had always learned on their own and used as their own was appropriated by a professional elite of educators who could impart the approved version to the fortunate, for a fee. Those who spoke with an unapproved accent or nonstandard grammar were, and still are, branded as inferior, and excluded from access to wealth, status, and power.

> When language becomes a commodity, it is no longer a vernacular that spreads by practical use, [that] is learned from people who mean what they say and who say what they mean to the person they address in the context of everyday life. . . . With taught language, the one from whom I learn is not a person whom I care for or dislike, but a professional speaker. . . . Taught colloquial is the dead, impersonal rhetoric of people paid to declaim with phony conviction texts composed by others, who themselves are usually paid only for *designing* the text. . . . This is language that implicitly lies when I use it to say something to your face. . . ."[39]

Elsewhere, Illich points out that the word *education* was not used before the Reformation: "By the early seventeenth century a new consensus began to arise: the idea that man was born incompetent for society and remained so unless he was provided with 'education'."[40]

Institutionalized education differs from the learning of skills and concepts. *Education* is a thing to be acquired. Anyone with a brain can learn, but an educated person has, like the Scarecrow in the *Wizard of Oz*, more than a brain. The educated person has a *testimonial* — a degree, a license, an official seal.

Women were excluded, in this period, from the institutions of formal education. They had no opportunity to acquire degrees or licenses. The growing importance of institutionalized education meant that women were increasingly excluded from fields in which they had previously worked.

Foremost among the rising professionals eager to consolidate their power were doctors. Healing was an area in which women had always played a vital role. As mothers they cared for their families. As noble ladies, they dispensed care to their dependents and nursed the wounded after battle. In medieval times, women practiced as physicians and apothecaries. Among the poorer classes, the village wise woman, or Witch, who preserved the traditional knowledge of herbs and natural healing, was often the only available source of medical care.[41]

Licensing is supported by the premise that it protects the consumer of services from incompetents, charlatans, and unethical practitioners. In reality, licensing protects those with approved credentials from competition by allowing them to limit their own numbers and raise their fees. It is one of the primary ways in which "functions that a dominant group prefers to perform . . . are carefully guarded and closed to subordinates."[42]

In London, the College of Physicians monopolized medical practice. They restricted their membership to twelve physicians in 1524, when the population of the city is estimated to have been 60,000. By 1640, when the population is variously estimated to have been from 360,000 to 420,000, the physicians had increased their ranks to a total of forty-three members. Obviously, the vast majority of people had no opportunity to receive approved medical care. "One object of keeping the number of physicians down was to keep fees up; at 6S 8D to 10S[43] for a visit, only the well-to-do could afford to call a doctor."[44]

"In so far as the less well-to-do had any medical treatment at all, they got it from surgeons, apothecaries, and a nameless host of freelance practitioners, some chemists, some herbalists, some cunning men or white witches, some quacks."[45]

"The College objected most of all to those unlicensed practitioners who were not quacks but had some medical knowledge, especially if they gave their services to the poor gratis."[46]

Those who turned to the uneducated but knowledgeable village Witch probably received more sound advice than those who could afford the high fees of a licensed physician. Then, as now, the approved medical profession favored the heroic style of treatment: bleeding, purges, emetics, and cauteries were the licensed physicians' stock-in-trade. The Witches, and radical critics of the medical profession who often drew on the Witches' knowledge, favored preventive medicine, cleanliness, the use of herbs, gentle, natural treatments, and building up the patient's strength.[47] Many of the so-called old wives' remedies are still used today — both by those who are returning to a more holistic view of healing and rediscovering the value in herbs and in nature's medicines, and by those who use these remedies as the basis for pharmaceutics. Foxglove, which yields the drug digitalis, useful for heart ailments, is a well-known example.

> [The Witches had] pain-killers, digestive aids, and anti-inflammatory agents. They used ergot for the pain of labor at a time when the Church held that pain in labor was the Lord's just punishment for Eve's original sin. Ergot derivatives are the principal drugs used today to hasten labor and aid in the recovery from childbirth. Belladonna — still used today as an anti-spasmodic — was used by the Witch-healers to inhibit uterine contractions when miscarriage threatened.[48]

The wise women or Witches were also midwives. As the male medical profession began to drive out unlicensed healers, male doctors began to encroach upon what had always been the female preserve of midwifery:

> Only by the seventeenth century do we find the man-midwife appearing on the scene, and he appears at the moment when the male medical profession is beginning to control the practice of healing, refusing "professional" status to women and to those who had for centuries worked among the poor. He appears first in the Court, attending upper-class women; rapidly he begins to assert the inferiority of the midwife and to make her name synonymous with dirt, ignorance and superstition.[49]

Adrienne Rich, Mary Daly, Barbara Ehrenreich, and Deirdre English have written comprehensive and moving accounts of the takeover of midwifery by the male medical profession, and of the resulting toll of suffering exacted from women.[50]

The Witch persecutions were used to destroy unlicensed healers and midwives. They were a direct attack on those who offered unsanctioned healing. Physicians were often instrumental in bringing charges of Witchcraft or suggesting that Witchcraft was operational in a difficult case.[51] Doctors were consulted as experts by the Witchhunters, much as psychiatrists are consulted as expert witnesses in legal cases today. "In the Witch-hunts, the Church explicitly legitimized the doctor's professionalism, denouncing non-professional healing as equivalent to heresy: 'If a woman dare to cure without having studied, she is a Witch and must die.'"[52]

"Witch hunts did not eliminate the lower class woman healer, but they branded her forever as superstitious and possibly malevolent."[53] In so doing, they further fragmented the communal bonds of the peasant-laborer cultures, and they weakened women's power to resist male domination.

Healing is a vitally important part of culture. In traditional communities, healers are focal figures. Today in the Third World, "The midwife is, and always has been, a key figure in the lives of rural women. She is part doctor, part counselor — in some places still part sorceress — and, mostly, a confidence-inspiring person at the time of childbirth."[54]

To destroy a culture's trust in its healers is to destroy that culture's trust in itself, to shatter its cohesive bonds and expose it to control from outside.

Healers provide models of knowledge, competence, and worth. Yet healing is also a power relationship. If, at a vulnerable time of sickness or childbirth, I put my body and life in the care of someone of my own sex, class, and culture — someone whom I see as being of *my own kind*, I give power-over to that person. But I can also identify with her, and internalize the image of her strength so that it feeds my own confidence and strength. If I am forced to give power-over my own being to someone who represents an elite from which my kind are excluded, my confidence in myself, in my own ability and right to control my own destiny is weakened.

As a woman, if my society withholds from me the approved knowledge about my body, and forces me to turn to men for care and help with the most female of experiences, I hear the clear message that I am incompetent, incapable of caring for myself. When women healers are downgraded and portrayed as filthy and malevolent, women as a group are forced to internalize a sense of shame, self-loathing, and fear of their own power.

When lower-class healers are branded ignorant and superstitious, and are excluded from approved knowledge, other members of that class begin to see themselves as ignorant, and to doubt their ability to assert control over their own lives. Their ability to resist the external forces that exploit them is lessened.

Colonial powers knowingly and deliberately use Western medicine to undermine the faith of Third World people in their own healers and in cultural traditions that stand in the way of industrial development that benefits the corporations and economies of the West. In 1892, Indian healers were called "An influence antagonistic to the rapid absorption of new customs. . . . Only after we have thoroughly routed the medicine men from their entrenchments and made them an object of ridicule [could whites] hope to bend and train the minds of our Indian wards in the direction of civilization."[55] Today, so-called improved medical care justifies the destruction of indigenous culture. This occurs as the resources of remote areas are more and more exploited. Approved Western medicine is the hypodermic that injects Western values of ownership and profit and the Western world-view that supports those values into cultures that are still based on intimate connections with nature, and on organic ties among human beings.

Traditional healers were, and are, religious leaders. As such they upheld the values of immanence, of the spirit present in the world, of worth inherent in nature and all living creatures — values that opposed exploitation of natural and human resources. They were focal figures around whom communities might organize. In America, before the Civil War, black healers such as Harriet Tubman and Nat Turner "played important roles in helping blacks resist the slave system."[56] Native American healing methods, religions, and culture are today central in the Indian struggle to regain and protect their rights and their lands.

The Witch persecutions and attacks on unapproved healers in the sixteenth and seventeenth centuries were also an attack on a value system, a campaign in the ideological war that continues today.

THE WAR ON IMMANENCE

The Witch persecutions, the enclosures and the expropriation of land, the attacks on traditional healers and midwives, and the seizing and withholding of knowledge, were powerful factors in changing people's attitudes, beliefs, and feelings. The effect of these events was not limited to the suffering of specific victims:

> These events were aspects of something more: the revolution in man's thinking and feeling that imposition of the protestant ethic involved. Protestant preachers in the late sixteenth and early seventeenth century undertook a cultural revolution, an exercise in indoctrination, in brainwashing, on a hitherto unprecedented scale. We only fail to recognize this because we live in a brain-washed society: our own indoctrination takes place so early, and from so many directions at once, that we are unaware of the process.[57]

This indoctrination had deep consequences in forming our views about work, time, and pleasure; about women and sexuality; and about the intrinsic nature and value of the world.

The Reformation and, in England, the Revolution and Restoration in the middle of the seventeenth century, can easily be portrayed as conflicts between two opposing classes and their religious and philosophical ideologies. The first could be termed the *Old Order*: the static hierarchy supported by the Catholic (or Anglican) church that upheld custom, tradition, and authority. The underlying power and wealth of the Old Order was based on land.

The New Order, represented by the mainstream Protestant sects — Lutherans, Zwinglians, and Calvinists (Puritans in England) — challenged hierarchy and authority, and upheld the authority of the individual conscience. They were based primarily in the rising commercial-professional classes, and their eventually triumphant power and wealth was based on money, i.e., on the ownership and use of capital in a market economy.

Both the Old Order and the New Order located God, as the source of true value, outside the living world. In the Old Order value was brought back into the world through the formal hierarchy of the church and the landed aristocracy it supported.

In the New Order, value was brought back into the world — that is to say, God spoke — through the individual conscience, without the need of an intervening hierarchy. Max Weber in his classic work, *The Protestant Ethic and the Spirit of Capitalism*, has shown how the Protestant ideology of individualism gradually became a new ideology of work and gain. The doctrine of predestination held that only a chosen few were, from the beginning of time, destined for salvation. Those few, the elect, were the *content* of the world. The rest, the vast majority, were filler, irretrievably damned and not inherently important. This doctrine both reflected and supported the unequal distribution of graces and comforts in this world; it legitimized inequality. Work and material gain became signs of one's membership in the elect. Money was imbued with a new symbolic value. It became the token of grace, the conduit through which God's value was returned to the world — and therefore it was far more important than any other value.[58]

The rise of markets provided an arena in which *gain* as a value could flourish. The rise of the Protestant Ethic reinforced the transformation of the European economy into one that was increasingly controlled by markets. These were based not on the value of things-in-themselves or the comfort, enjoyment, or usefulness things provided, but on gain and profit, on things-as-instruments-of-gain. The New Order was one of yet deeper estrangement.

There was, however, a third force, in conflict both with the Old Order and the New: the peasant-laboring classes, whose wealth, if any, was limited to a plot of land for subsistence, whose numbers were great, and whose sources of power were few. History may record their risings and rebellions, but rarely does it record their beliefs, philosophies, and ideals.

In England, during the Revolution, from 1641 to 1660, censorship was lifted.[59] The writings that surface from the lower-classes at that time reflect a wide variety of religious and political philosophies. But a common thread among them is the recognition of true value in this world and this life — the world-view that I have termed *immanence*.

How much of this world-view stemmed directly from the remnants of the Old Religion is difficult to document. The most radical of religious sects still presented themselves within a Christian framework, however Pagan their practices or ideas. The Witch persecutions carried on by representatives of both the Old and New Orders, under the auspices of both King and Parliament, created a climate in which an overtly Pagan movement would have faced both popular prejudice against it, and severe and immediate repression by the authorities of Church and state.

Many of the dispossessed peasants and laborers without land squatted in the forests and wastes where there was "freedom from parson as well as squire."[60] In the extensive forests such as Sherwood, Arden, and the New Forest, a mobile and volatile society of "squatters, itinerant craftsmen and building labourers, unemployed men and women seeking work, strolling players and jugglers, peddlars and quack doctors, vagabonds and tramps . . ."[61] lived. "They were lawless, nobody to govern them; they care for nobody, having no dependence on anybody."[62]

These same areas were both the regions of greatest peasant revolt in the early seventeenth century (according to Christopher Hill) and the areas where, according to our Oral Tradition, Witchcraft maintained its hold the longest. (It was in the New Forest that Gerald Gardner discovered a Witch coven in the 1930s that claimed to descend in an unbroken line from the time of William the Conqueror.)[63]

> Squatters in forest or pastoral regions, often far from any church, were wide open to radical religious sects — or to witchcraft. (Hostility to the clergy had been a striking ele-

ment in the Robin Hood ballads) . . . The densely populated forests of Northamptonshire were centres of rural puritanism, strange sects and witchcraft. The "cheese" district of Wiltshire, the scene of violence resulting from disafforestation in the early seventeenth century, was also an area of poorly-paid part-time clothing workers and of religious heresy. Ely . . . had long been a centre of plebian irreverance and resistance . . . In the Isle of Axholme the inhabitants were said to have been virtual heathens until the draining of the Fens . . .[64]

Matthew Hopkins, the witchfinder, found two villages in Northamptonshire that he described as "infested" with Witches in 1645 or 1646.[65] A year later, he or his coworker may have sparked execution trials at Ely that resulted in several executions.[66] Wiltshire, the county in which Stonehenge and Avebury are located, was the ancient center of pre-Christian religion. Robin Hood is identified, both by our oral tradition and by records of trials, with the God of the Witches.[67] His band of merry men and Maid Marion form a coven of thirteen. "Maid" or "Maiden" was (and still is) the honorary title for one of the female leaders of a coven, and Marion was one of the common names of women tried in England as Witches.[68]

The witch-cult, which had survived for so many centuries as an underground popular religion, may have contributed more to radical protestantism than has yet been appreciated. "The witches," said Cotton Mather in a significant phrase, "are organized like congregational churches." Some aspects of the witch-cult have indeed much in common with medieval heresies, as well as with protestant sectarianism. The connections, if any, are obscure and difficult to establish: much more investigation is needed before we can speak with certainty. What is clear is the lower-class basis of the cult. It was a secret organization, anti-state, anti-state church. . . . Many leaders of peasant revolt in this period claimed to be sent by God. Some of them may have been sent by the God of the Witches rather than by Jehovah.[69]

More investigation certainly is needed before direct connections can be established firmly. But an underlying similarity of ideas can be demonstrated. Radical sects, like Witches, preached immanence (God manifest in the world). Familists, one of the earliest sects, were followers of Henry Niclaes, born in 1502, who taught that heaven and hell were to be found in this world.[70] A related sect, the Family of the Mount, "questioned whether any heaven or hell existed apart from this life: heaven was when men laugh and are merry, hell was sorrow, grief and pain."[71] Christ, they held, was within every believer.

Ranters, who could easily be seen as seventeenth-century hippies, "set up the light in nature under the name of Christ in man."[72] They called God *Reason* which, in the seventeenth century, had a meaning closer to *consciousness* than to mechanistic logic.

"One of them said that if there was any God at all, he himself was one. 'God is in everyone and every living thing,' said Jacob Bauthamly (in a pamphlet dated 1659). 'Man and beast, fish and fowl, and every green thing, from the highest cedar to the ivy on the wall. He does not exist outside the creatures.' 'He is me and I am him.' "[73]

Ranters addressed each other as "fellow creature," a phrase reminiscent of ritual salutations in the Craft. They referred to themselves collectively as "my one flesh": God was a member of the community of my one flesh, one matter. "Ranters insisted that matter is good, because we live here and now."[74]

The Diggers, another radical sect, attempted to abolish private property, hold land communally, and turn the commons and wastes over to the common people for their livelihood. On April 1, 1649, a group of laborers began digging the commons on St. George's Hill, on the edge of Windsor Great Forest, an area with both radical and Pagan traditions.[75] Gerrard Winstanley, their philosophical leader, "had a vision in a trance telling him to publish it abroad that 'the earth should be made a common treasury of livelihood to whole mankind . . ."[76] A second formulation was: "True religion and undefiled is to let every one quietly have earth to manure."[77] "Collective manuring of the common lands was a religious act for the Diggers . . ."[78] The manuring, making the earth fertile, takes precedence over cultivation. The

Diggers may or may not have been connected with the Witches, but they were certainly earth-religionists.

Winstanley also equated God with universal reason that "dwells in every creature, but supremely in man."[79] "This idea of God as immanent within the whole material creation . . . is connected with a respect for natural science as the means of becoming acquainted with God's works."[80] "To know the secrets of nature is to know the works of God . . ."[81] He identified the traditional Christian God, who legitimizes private property, with the Devil, and The Fall with the rise of property ownership.

Sectarians were noted for practicing sexual freedom. Ranters and Quakers occasionally went naked as a sign of grace. The Ranter Lawrence Clarkson anticipated Freud and Norman O. Brown by identifying sin, not with an act — but with its repression. "None can be free from sin till in purity it be acted as no sin, for I judged that pure to me which to a dark understanding was impure: for to the pure all things, yes all acts were pure . . . Without act, no life, without life, no perfection."[82] "What act soever is done by thee in light and love, is light and lovely . . . if that within thee do not condemn thee, thou shalt not be condemned."[83]

These words are comparable to the modern Charge of the Goddess from the present-day liturgy of the Craft (of unknown origin): "All acts of love and pleasure are my rituals . . . and if that which you seek you find not within yourself, you will never find it without. For I have been with you from the beginning, and I am that which is attained at the end of desire . . ."

The sects also contained women in high positions. They allowed women to participate in Church government. Women preached, traveled the country in company with men, spoke out against unequal marriages, and demanded divorce by simple declaration. Mary Cary, a minister, wrote a utopian pamphlet in 1651 declaring that, "The time is coming when not only men but women shall prophesy; not only aged men but young men, not only those who have university learning but those who have not, even servants and handmaids."[84]

The triumph of the New Order with its Protestant ethic and the defeat of the radical sects, was a political, economic, and religious triumph of the commercial-professional classes over the peasant-laboring classes, of male domination over women. The imposition of the Protestant ethic involved a campaign against ideas of immanence in three realms: work, sexuality, and philosophy.

Max Weber has shown the way the rise of the Protestant ethic provided a new ideology of work, one that reflected the shift in value from *use* to *gain*, and served the rise of capitalism. The concept of a *calling* placed a new sort of value on work and gain, which became signs of one's membership in the elect, and were not valued for their real benefits, the material benefits they conferred, but because they were now the channel through which one approached God, who was not of this world. Work and gain, paradoxically, were valued as if they were not of this world, as if they were inherent goals, good in-and-of themselves. Work became an ascetic discipline and "this asceticism turned with all its force against one thing: the spontaneous enjoyment of life and all it had to offer."[85]

For the rising monied classes, hard work and ascetic self-discipline, however piously motivated, did pay off in material success. They prospered; and prosperity as the visible sign of God's grace could be enjoyed, even though other spontaneous enjoyments — sex, dancing, sports, games, festivals, and nature — were still seen as works of the Devil.

For the peasant-laboring classes, however, discipline and hard work led, at best, to bare survival. The work ethic was used by the monied classes to impose discipline on the laborers and the poor. Idleness was sinful; charges that cottagers were idle were made in support of enclosure.[86] Charges of idleness also justified low wages, which ideally "should allow the labourer but just wherewithal to live; for if you allow double, then he works but half so much."[87]

A man does not "by nature" wish to earn more and more money, but simply to live as he is accustomed to live and to earn as much as is necessary for that purpose. Wherever modern capitalism has begun its work of increasing the productivity of human labour by increasing its intensity, it has encountered the immensely stubborn resistance of this leading trait of pre-capitalism."[88]

Traditional festivals, saints' days (which were often Christianized versions of ancient Pagan holidays), dances, and games were attacked by mainstream Protestants. The Witch Persecutions were an attack on the celebrations, beliefs, and customs that had supported the peasant-laboring classes in their desire for comfort and enjoyment — for pleasure in life as well as work.

As work became an ascetic discipline, women were pushed out of many kinds of productive labor. We have seen how enclosure divested women of the land they had used to provide food for their families, and how the rise of the male medical profession, in company with the Witch persecutions, forced women out of the domains of healing and midwifery. In late Medieval times, women played important roles in many crafts and industries. Marriage was in many ways a business partnership, and wives of merchants or craftsmen often worked alongside their husbands. Widows usually continued their former husbands' businesses. Women had been brewers, bakers, shipowners, publishers, printers, glovers, peddlars, merchants, accountants, pinmakers, and shopkeepers. They had also worked in agriculture and in the textile industries.[89]

As long as the family remained the basic unit of production in the economy, women retained an important role in many sorts of work. But as industry moved out of the home and workshop, into factories and large-scale enterprises, women were excluded. The productive unit became the individual worker, who was more easily manipulated, more conveniently mobilized, and more fully exploitable when *work* (not family, personal pleasure, or communal obligations) was defined as the only true purpose of this life.

The Witch persecutions were, above all, attacks on women. The propaganda that supported the Witchhunts stressed women's inferiority and defined their nature as inherently evil.

When a woman thinks alone, she thinks evil . . . They are
more impressionable than men and more ready to receive
the influence of the disembodied spirit . . . Since they are
weak they find an easy and secret manner of vindicating
themselves in Witchcraft. They are feebler both in mind and
body . . . As regards intellect or understanding of spiritual
things, they seem to be of a different nature than men . . .
Women are intellectually like children . . . Women have
weaker memories, and it is a natural vice in them not to be
disciplined, but to follow their own impulses without a sense
of what is due . . . She is a liar by nature . . . Woman is a
wheedling and secret enemy . . ."[90]

Hatred of women was not limited to any one area or religious
body: "This misogynist pattern was not peculiar to the Dominican's work. It was standard to refer to witches as women in the
witch hunter's treatises and to include a section showing, from the
'nature' of women, why witches are female. This pattern is found
equally in sixteenth- and seventeenth-century treatises written by
Protestants."[91]

Women bring life into the world. In a culture in which women
mother, women's bodies provide our first experiences of warmth
and comfort, of a deep sensual pleasure untainted by
restrictions.[92] To turn against women, then, is to turn against life
itself, to deny flesh, pleasure, and comfort. And an asceticism that
denies the flesh must, of necessity, denigrate women.

Women are also, however, our first frustrators, source of the
first will that opposes our own, that denies as well as gives, as well
as the source of our mortality, of the vulnerability of body-bound
creatures to disease, pain, and death. Norman O. Brown in *Life
Against Death*[93] argues that we are willing to relinquish the deep
pleasure of sensual life in the body in order to deny death. In so
doing, we turn to the substitute pleasure of enterprise — culture-
building work in the world.

In order for the realm of work and enterprise to be free from the
taint of mortality, women and all we represent must be excluded.
So, as the Protestant ethic raises work to the status of a transcendent endeavor, women, who embody immanence, are driven
out. Immanence is attacked through women's bodies: the immor-

tality of spirit-estranged-from-flesh is exalted through the torture and destruction of women's flesh. Men revenge themselves on the mother who failed to satisfy completely by destroying mother-kind. They repair the childhood humiliation of bowing to the mother's will by destroying women's wills. The blame for women's destruction must fall, not on the conflicts inherent in mothering, but on the religious and economic systems that deepen those conflicts, that encourage men to act them out by victimizing women.

When a woman is excluded from productive labor, she is forced into the role of object. Both lower-class and upper-class women are relegated to the realm of reproduction, intensifying both men's and women's tendencies to identify all women with mother — someone both more than human and less than human, but never simply human.

A lower-class woman also reproduces the labor power[94] of her man. Her work is unpaid, but necessary. It is she who takes the commodities earned by the worker and transforms them so that they can be used; she cooks the food, washes the clothes, and cleans the house. The cold abstract, money, is transformed again in her hands, restored into the realm of what has value in-and-of-itself, what can be used and enjoyed. But because her work is unpaid, it does not partake of the new value now accorded to gain and profit. She cannot profit from it, cannot bargain for higher wages or attempt to gain from it more than she puts into it. Her work gradually comes to be considered less real than a man's work, and the woman herself becomes unreal, a two-dimensional screen upon whom a man can project his fantasies.[95]

Working women are relegated to the least attractive jobs, and excluded from those occupations offering hints of transcendence or the nobility of a calling. Lower-class women are an expendable labor force, cheaper to hire than men, and easier to fire in a slow season since they are not considered real workers.

Upper-class women become commodities, exchanged in marriage as tokens of men's power, status, and success. The upper-class woman learns to package and market herself. She too is an object, not a subject; the other, not the self, of culture.

As the others, the objects, women have been made screens upon which men's latent fear and hatred are projected. The Witchhunts inflamed and legitimized that hatred, aiding the economic forces that attacked her physical and existential self.

In women, the persecutions reinforced self-hatred and suspicion of other members of their sex. To both sexes, the role of victim was made to seem the woman's natural and deserved role.

Hatred of women extends to hatred of all flesh, all sensual life. The Witchhunts, as a campaign in the war on immanence, were also directed against sexuality, especially women's sexuality and homosexuality.

"All Witchcraft comes from carnal lust," states the *Malleus Maleficarum*, 'which is in women insatiable." Witches were accused, as their primary acts, of consorting with demons, of lewd and lascivious acts. Witches' Sabbaths were portrayed as orgies where unnatural lusts were indulged.

Lesbianism and male homosexuality were often associated with Witchcraft; Arthur Evans, in *Witchcraft and the Gay Counterculture*, cites numerous instances of this.[96] Homosexuals and lesbians were subject to torture and execution as civil criminals, but so-called unnatural sex was also evidence of Witchcraft. The Witch persecutions denigrated sexuality and enforced heterosexuality. They punished women for sexual aggressiveness and enforced passivity, punished women for enjoying sex and enforced frigidity.

Sexuality was a sacrament in the Old Religion; it was (and is) viewed as a powerful force through which the healing, fructifying love of the immanent Goddess was directly known, and could be drawn upon to nourish the world, to quicken fertility in human beings and in nature. The Goddess was known, not through hierarchy or ascetic discipline, but through ecstacy, through deep connection with another human being. The ritual cycle in the Craft centers around themes of the interweaving of life and death; through confronting death, acknowledging and accepting our mortality, we are free to experience life deeply in its full sensuality. "Sing, feast, dance, make music and love, all in my presence, for mine is the ecstasy of the spirit, and mine also is joy on earth."[97]

If the woman, symbolically, is the body of immanence, then sexuality, valued in-and-of-itself, is its soul. Gay sexuality, affirming in its very nature the primacy of pleasure over reproduction, and religious sexuality, upholding the deep value of the body and its experience, both threaten the ascetic discipline of labor, which requires denial of the body. Aggressive female sexuality is incompatible with the role of women as victims, as objects. The Witch persecutions used torture and terror to scar the Western psyche by identifying sex with evil.

Finally, the Witch persecutions aided the war on immanence as it appeared in the sciences and in the intellectual life of the time.

In the seventeenth century, the mechanist view of the world as composed of dead, inert, isolated particles was still being challenged by views expressed in systems of magic, such as alchemy, astrology, hermeticism, Cabbalism, and ritual magic. Many of these systems had, by this time, become very different in practice from Witchcraft. These formal magical systems tended to be hierarchically structured and rule-bound, and by this period, they had adopted Christian and Jewish, as well as classical Greek and Roman symbolism and terminology. However, they shared with the Old Religion, and with many of the radical Protestant sects, a view of the world as inherently alive, dynamic, and relational — valued in and of itself. Their logic was dialectical, not a dualism without synthesis; opposites were interdependent; from each entity arose its opposite, and the resulting tension caused change.

David Kubrin describes mechanical philosophy as follows:

> Matter itself . . . existing in empty space . . . is all there is, all that underlies the whole of the sensate world of phenomena. Changes in the phenomenal world all arise out of the "matter and motion" of the underlying molecular or atomic world, each of the atomic or molecular particles in itself having *only* size, shape, and its state of motion — all quantitative entities — as its attributes. The world, in essence, is colorless, tasteless, soundless, devoid of thought or life. It is essentially dead, a machine . . .[98]

Mechanism, in our minds, has become identified with reality and truth, and magical philosophies are identified with error and superstition. Yet mechanism has, in the long run, proved invalid. Physicists now tell us that there are no solid atoms — only interactions among particles, which themselves may be patterns of probabilities, none of which can be observed objectively because observation requires interaction with the observed.[99] Systems theory teaches us to move beyond simple cause-and-effect logic, and look instead at patterns of interactions. Magic can be seen as the philosophical precursor of relativity and probability theory.

Mechanism triumphed, not necessarily because it was the best description of reality, but because of its political, economic, and social implications. Magic, the science and philosophy based on the principle of immanence, was identified with radicalism and lower-class interests. "The animist concept of nature as a divine, self-active organism came to be associated with atheistical and radical libertarian ideas. Social chaos, peasant uprisings, and rebellions could be fed by the assumption that individuals could understand the nature of the world for themselves and could manipulate its spirits by magic. A widespread use of popular magic to control these spirits existed at all levels of society, but particularly among the lower classes."[100]

After the Restoration of Charles II in England, such ideas were termed *enthusiasm*, and a vigorous campaign was carried out by the state, the established Church, and the new scientific institutions against them. Enthusiasm was associated with radical activism and rebellion. "[A] conception of the world's being inherently active, full of Gods, and constantly changing helped develop people's self-confidence, and perhaps better encourage them . . . to step forward *to act, to transform the world*, rather than to remain passive in the face of the great social transformations then sweeping England."[101]

The expropriation of knowledge, which we have seen operating in the area of healing, extended to science as a whole. Mechanism, which supported exploitation of nature because nature was inherently dead and valueless, and which furthered the removal of value from things-in-themselves, from everything that could not be quantified and counted, became the approved knowledge.

Other views were branded as dangerous, wrong-headed and foolish. Kubrin demonstrates that even Newton, whom we commonly think of as the father of mechanism, was deeply involved with the study of alchemy and Hermeticism. His magical writings, however, were never published because he feared being linked with radicalism and freethinkers.[102]

The Witch persecutions helped assure the triumph of mechanism. Ironically, mechanism, by undermining belief in demons, devils, and all noncorporeal beings, as well as belief in all systems of magic, eventually destroyed the rationale for Witchhunts. However, by that period (the eighteenth century), mechanism itself had become an entrenched ideology that legitimized the rising capitalist economy, the exploitation of women and workers, the plundering of nature — and one that exalted the quantifiable over the qualitative elements of life. "Mechanism, as a metaphysics and an epistemology, not only spread from physics to chemistry and biology, but also to physiology, psychology, religion, poetry, ethics, political theory and art."[103]

THE PAST ALIVE IN THE PRESENT

The old woman is gone now. Whether she was hanged as a Witch, or escaped to live in the wastes with other refugees and vagabonds; whether she ended her life in the comfort of her own small cottage, or was driven out to lie cold and hungry under hedgerows, she is dead. But something of her lives on, in the children of the children of the children she delivered. Her fears, and the forces she struggled against in her lifetime, live on.

We can open our newspapers, and read the same charges against the idle poor. The expropriators move into the Third World, destroying cultures, purveying approved Western knowledge, plundering the resources of land and people. The ethic of ownership supports them. Scientific agriculture poisons the earth with pesticides; mechanist technology builds nuclear plants and bombs that may yet make the earth a dead thing. If we turn on the radio, we can hear the crackle of flames in every broadcast. If we watch the news or walk out into the streets, where the transcendent value of gain raises rents and real estate prices, forcing people out of their neighborhoods and their homes, we can hear the dull thud of the enclosure notice nailed to the door.

The issues seem endless. Everywhere we turn for comfort or for healing, we are met by the approved guardians of a knowledge that alienates us from our bodies and our souls. The smoke of the burned Witches still hangs in our nostrils; most of all, it reminds us to see ourselves as separated, isolated units in competition with each other, alienated, powerless, and alone.

But the struggle also lives on. Understanding the history of that struggle allows us to undertake it with a clear vision, one that recognizes the interwoven nature of the issues involved, that knows that our interests are not separate, whether we are women struggling to regain our place in the work force, or migrant workers demanding a living wage, or Indians whose lands are poisoned by uranium tailings, or ecologists trying to preserve a wilderness area Whether our immediate needs are for food, health care, jobs. childcare, housing, or open spaces, our ultimate interest is the same — restoring a sense of the sacred to the world, and so restoring value to our own lives and to the community of beings — human, plant, and animal — that share life with us.

That common vision, that common value, can be the base of a power no one can wield alone — the power to reshape our common lives, the power to change reality.

Appendix B

❧ ❦

Tools for Groups

MEETING PROCEDURES

Breathe together. Connect. Choose facilitator, vibeswatcher, timekeeper, and notetaker. Check-in.

Review agenda and make changes, or call for agenda items, establish priorities, and set times for each.

Go through the agenda.

Take breaks. Stop to periodically check how members are feeling, and to breathe.

Evaluate the meeting.

Set the next meeting date, time, and place.

Close.

RITUAL PROCEDURE

Gather people and explain the ritual. Introductions. Check-in.

Ground and center. Hold hands and breathe together. Tree of Life.

Purify.

Make sacred space. Invoke the four directions.

Invoke the Goddess and God.

Create the image upon which the energy will focus

Raise the cone of power.

Ground the power.

Share food and drink.

Say goodbye to the Goddess and God, and to the four directions.

Open the circle.

QUESTIONS FOR KEEPING TRACK
OF GROUP STRUCTURES AND PROCESS
(These are useful in self-cricticism sessions.)

1. Why did I come to the group and what do I want from it?
2. What is the group doing well? Poorly? How do I play a part in each?
3. How much time do I take up as compared with others?
4. How much attention do I get as compared with others? Compared with what I want?
5. How much do I listen to others? How present am I?
6. Am I getting the information I need in order to participate in the work of the group? If not, why not?
7. What am I seeing, thinking, or feeling that I'm not saying?

8. How central am I to the group? How much influence do I have? How much do I want? Over which decisions?

9. With whom do I talk most outside the group?

10. How much structure do I want or need in the group?

11. How much closeness do I want or need? How much can I tolerate?

12. How important is the group to me? What priority does it have in my life? How committed to it am I?

13. What are the unspoken rules of the group?

14. Is what I am doing or saying serving the interest of the group or my personal hidden agenda?

SOME TOPICS FOR ROUNDS OR ACTIVE LISTENING

There are an infinite number of possible topics, but these may get you started. Note that broad topics are tackled from a specific, personal angle. We don't do a round on "sexism," we do a round on how being a woman or man has limited us.

1. How has being a woman/being a man limited me? What possibilities has it offered me that I wouldn't otherwise have had?

2. What are the strengths I bring to the group from my specific racial, ethnic, or cultural background? What needs do I have from the group?

3. How has my experience of life been limited or enriched by my class background? What strengths and weaknesses has it given me?

4. How has violence affected my life?

5. In what situations do I now feel powerless? When do I feel empowered?

6. How would my life be different without the threat of nuclear war?

7. What do I do to make money? What do I have to give up to do what I do?

8. What do I do with my anger?

9. What problems do I have with love relationships?

10. How do I expect to die? What feelings does this question evoke?

Appendix C

Chants and Songs

The Fire Song

Words and music by Starhawk

We can rise with the fire of freedom
Truth is a fire that burns our chains
And we can stop the fire of destruction
Healing is a fire running through our veins

I wrote this chant especially for a blockade at the Livermore Weapons Laboratories, which took place on February 2, 1982. The second of February is the Celtic holiday sacred to Brigid, Goddess of smithcraft, poetry, and healing.

We can rise with the fire of free-dom___
Truth is a fire that burns our chains. And we can
stop the fires of des----truc--tion___
Heal-ing is a fire run-nin' through our veins

The Return

Native American

The earth, the water, the fire, the air,
Return, return, return, return.

One version of this song is sung by Michael Tierra on a tape of chants called *The Giveaway*.

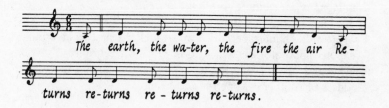

The earth, the wa-ter, the fire the air Returns re-turns re-turns re-turns.

The Flow and the Ebb

Words and music by Shekinah Mountainwater

We are the flow, we are the ebb,
We are the weavers, we are the web.

I learned this chant in the women's jail at the Diablo Blockade. As we were ending our ritual on the Equinox in a moment of sweet silence, the guards told us we had to go back into the main room. Someone quietly began chanting this, stood up, took the hand of the woman next to her, and led a snake dance into the room where the other women were. We circled the room and everyone in it, making the perfect end to the ritual. I thank Shekinah Mountainwater for sharing this chant.

We are the flow___ We are the ebb___
We are the wea-vers We are the web___

She Changes Everything She Touches

Words and Music by Starhawk

She changes everything she touches and
Everything she touches, changes

Change is   Touch is
Touch is   Change is

We are changers
Everything we touch can change

Change us   Touch us
Touch us   Change us

Verses are not sung in order, but simultaneously by different people, as they occur to each person.

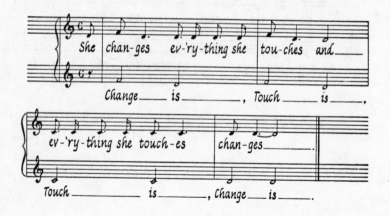

Goddess Chant

Words by Deena Metzger and music by Caitlin Mullin

Isis, Astarte, Diana, Hecate
Demeter, Kali, Inanna

Sung by Charlie Murphy in the song "The Burning Times"
recorded in 1981 on the album *Catch The Fire.*

All music transcribed by Newbury Music Library and Publishers.

Notes and Sources

NOTES AND SOURCES

The notes for this book include both traditional footnotes and listings of general sources and resources. Often my thinking has been influenced by a particular writer, or by conversations with a particular individual, and I feel credit is due them even if I do not cite any specific passage in the text. On certain subjects, I suspect the reader may also appreciate a short list of resources for further reading. The lists I have provided are not exhaustive but can serve the interested reader as a beginning.

Prologue

1. I use the word *matristic* ("mother-oriented") rather than *matriarchal* because for many people matriarchy implies a reverse image of patriarchy. Academics debate endlessly about whether cultures ever existed in which women exercised power over men. But the point that I am trying to make about Goddess-centered culture is that power was based on a principle different from that under patriarchy.

Judith Ochshorn argues convincingly that in early, polytheistic cultures, power was not based on gender in the same way it is under patriarchy. Ochshorn, Judith. *The Female Experience and the Nature of the Divine*. Bloomington, Ind.: University of Indiana Press, 1981

2. Ancient Goddess religion is an enormous subject. Two good resources, presenting different perspectives, are: Ochshorn, Judith. *The Female Experience*; and Stone, Merlin. *When God Was a Woman*. New York: Dial Press, 1976.

3. Resources on witchcraft include:

Adler, Margot. *Drawing Down the Moon*. Boston: Beacon Press, 1981.

Gardner, Gerald. *Witchcraft Today*. Cavendish, Suffolk, Great Britain. Ryder, 1954.

Murray, Margaret. *The Witch-Cult in Western Europe*. New York: Oxford University Press, 1970.

Starhawk. *The Spiral Dance: A Rebirth of the Ancient Religion of the Great Goddess*. San Francisco: Harper and Row, 1979.

Chapter One

An earlier version of this chapter was published under the title, "Consciousness, Politics and Magic," in Spretnak, Charlene, ed. *The Politics of Women's Spirituality: Essays on the Rise of Spiritual Power Within the Women's Movement.* New York: Doubleday, 1982, pp. 172–184.

1. Griffin, Susan. *Woman and Nature: The Roaring Inside Her*. San Francisco, 1979, p.1.

2. These circles describe the effects of a one-megaton hydrogen bomb. Most weapons in stockpiles are far more powerful.

3. San Francisco Chronicle, 23 June 1980. (This description was given in an interview with a mother from Love Canal, an area contaminated by chemical wastes.) Byline Beverly Stephens.

4. DiPrima, Diane. *Revolutionary Letters*. San Francisco: City Lights Books, 1979, p. 98.

5. This is a term I borrowed from Marx, although I use it in a broader sense. *See* Marx, Karl. "Private Property and Alienated Labor," in Selsam, Howard, and Martel, Harry, eds. *Reader in Marxist Philosophy*. New York: International Publishers, 1963, pp. 296-303.

6. Engels, Friedrich. "Humanism Versus Pantheism: On Thomas Carlyle," in Selsam and Martel, *Reader in Marxist Philosophy*, pp. 234-235.

7. White, Lynn, Jr. "The Historical Roots of our Ecologic Crisis," in Spring, David and Eileen, eds. *Ecology and Religion in History*. New York: Harper and Row, 1964, p. 25.

8. See the essays, "Timber: What Was There for Them," pp. 56-64; and "Forest: The Way We Stand," pp. 220-221, in Griffin, Susan *Woman and Nature*.

9. Merchant, Carolyn. *The Death of Nature: Woman, Ecology and the Scientific Revolution*. San Francisco: Harper and Row, 1980.

10. Marcuse, Herbert. *Eros and Civilization*. New York: Vintage Books, 1955, p. 41.

11. For a more complete critique of Jung's work, *see* Goldenberg, Naomi. "Jungian Psychology and Religion," in *Changing of the Gods*. Boston: Beacon Press, 1979, pp. 46-71.

12. For a deeper psychological understanding of why we blame women for death and decay while we see men as clean, pure, and abstract, *see* Dinnerstein, Dorothy. *The Mermaid and the Minotaur: Sexual Arrangements and Human Malaise*. New York: Harper and Row, 1976.

13. "Witch" and "Witchcraft" denote the Pagan, pre-Christian religion of Europe based on the immanent Goddess and Her Consort. This should not be confused with Satanism, Devil worship, so-called black magic, or any other Christian heresy.

14. The Handbook Collective. *The Diablo Canyon Blockade Encampment Handbook*, p. 45. This may be available from Abalone Alliance, Northern California Preparers/Trainers Collective, c/o Pandora's Box, 127 Rincon Street, Santa Cruz, CA 95060.

Chapter Two

1. Stone, Merlin. Personal communication based on unpublished research. Two Aryan Texts that specifically describe light as good and dark as evil are the *Zend Avesta* of the Aryans in Iran, and the *Book of Manu* of the Aryans in India.

2. Rubin, Lillian. *Worlds of Pain: Life in the Working Class Family*. New York: Basic Books, 1976, p. 19.

3. Daly, Mary. *Gyn/Ecology: The Metaethics of Radical Feminism*. Boston: Beacon Press, 1978, pp. 75–79.

4. The next seven paragraphs describe the Tree of Life meditation, often used to begin a ritual.

Sources:

This chapter was strongly influenced by my reading of several works on systems theory, of which the most valuable are:

Bateson, Gregory. *Mind and Nature: A Necessary Unity*. New York: Bantam, 1979.

Bateson, Gregory. *Steps to an Ecology of Mind*. New York: Ballantine, 1972.

The male/female, culture/nature split is developed as a theme in the following book: Griffin, Susan. *Woman and Nature: The Roaring Inside Her*. San Francisco: Harper and Row, 1980.

Griffin, Susan. *Pornography and Silence: Culture's Revenge Against Nature*. New York: Harper and Row, 1981.

Two useful resources on the convergence of the new physics with mysticism are: Capra, Fritjof. *The Tao of Physics*. New York: Bantam, 1975, and Zukav, Gary. *The Dancing Wu Li Masters: An Overview of the New Physics*. New York: William Morrow, 1979.

My thoughts on hierarchy were influenced by reading this book: Bookchin, Murray. *Post-Scarcity Anarchism.* Montreal: Black Rose Books, 1971.

Important investigations into structures, stories, spirituality, and politics are found in:

Christ, Carol. *Diving Deep and Surfacing: Women Writers on Spiritual Quest.* Boston: Beacon Press, 1980.

Goldenberg, Naomi. *Changing of the Gods.* Boston: Beacon Press, 1979.

Rossman, Michael. *New Age Blues.* New York: E.P. Dutton, 1979.

For an excellent discussion of how ideas and concepts have shaped American cities, *see:* Jacobs, Jane. *The Death and Life of Great American Cities.* New York: Vintage, 1961.

A wonderful collection of Goddess stories is found in: Stone, Merlin. *Ancient Mirrors of Womanhood: Our Goddess and Heroine Heritage,* Vols. I & II. New York: New Sibylline Books, 1979. This book is available from: New Sibylline Books, Box 266, Village Station, New York, NY 10014.

My thoughts on language owe a debt to years of friendship and ritual-making in company with Lauren Liebling.

Chapter Three

An earlier version of this chapter was presented as a paper entitled, "Ethics and Justice in Goddess Religion" at the Annual Conference of the American Academy of Religions in New York City in 1979.

That paper was published in *Anima: An Experimental Journal.* 7:1, pp. 61–68; in Forfreedom, Ann and Julie Ann, eds. *Book of the Goddess.* Sacramento, Calif.: Temple of the Goddess Within, 1980, and in Spretnak, Charlene, ed. *The Politics of Women's Spirituality: Essays on the Rise of Spiritual Power Within the Feminist Movement.* New York: Anchor/Doubleday, 1982, pp. 415–422.

1. Conversations with Donna Warnock, whose perceptive development of integrity as a unifying concept helped shape and focus my own thinking in this area, were influential in the preparation of this chapter.

2. Commoner, Barry. *The Closing Circle.* New York: Knopf, 1971, pp. 45–46.

Chapter Four

1. In most esoteric traditions, what I call the *underworld* is named *the astral plane* or *the higher plane.* Sometimes it is called *the inner plane.* I have deliberately chosen metaphors that stress going deeper into the world, rather than getting out of it, to remind us that our framework is immanence.

2. Obviously, being in professional training myself, I have a certain amount of ambivalence about this point.

3. Lessing, Doris. *The Four-Gated City*. New York: Bantam, 1970, pp. 518–519.

4. Green, Hannah. *I Never Promised You a Rose Garden*. New York: New American Library, 1964, pp. 55.

5. Lerner, Michael. "Surplus Powerlessness." This is an article available from *Social Policy*, 33 West 42nd Street, Room 1212, New York, NY 10036.

6. You may prefer to use another term, such as *parents, guardians, primary caretakers*.

7. My thoughts on despair are influenced by unpublished writings on "Despair Work" by Joanna Rogers Macy of the Inter-Help organization.

8. Dinnerstein, Dorothy. *The Mermaid and the Minotaur*. New York: Harper and Row, 1977. She uses the phrase "animal-poetic" throughout.

In general, the psychology in this chapter is derived from that obscure branch of knowledge known as object-relations theory. In particular, it is influenced by Margaret Mahler's theory of child development, as presented by Gertrude and Rubin Blanck in: *Ego Psychology: Theory and Practice*. New York: Columbia University Press, 1974, and *Ego Psychology II: Psychoanalytic Developmental Psychology*. New York: Columbia University Press, 1979.

I have also found some of Jean Piaget's formulations useful, especially as presented in: Ginsburg, Herbert, and Opper, Sylvia. *Piaget's Theory of Intellectual Development*. Englewood Cliffs, New Jersey: Prentice-Hall, 1974.

My thoughts on fear were influenced by conversations with China Galland. Joy, herself, of course, was a primary source for the material in this chapter, and I am grateful for her willingness both to travel the dark paths of the underworld, and to let me publish an account of her journey.

Chapter Five

1. *See* Ochshorn, Judith. *The Female Experience and the Nature of the Divine*. Bloomington, Ind.: University of Indiana Press, 1981.

2. This invocation approximates the one done at the Summer Solstice Ritual (at the Pagan Spirit Gathering in Northern Wisconsin organized by Circle Network) held from June 18 to June 21, 1981.

3. Spretnak, Charlene. *Lost Goddesses of Early Greece*. Boston: Beacon Press, 1981, pp. 21–41.

4. Marcuse, Herbert. *Eros and Civilization: A Philosophical Inquiry into Freud*. New York: Vintage, 1955, p. 147.

Other sources for this chapter are:

Brown, Norman O. *Life Against Death: The Psychoanalytical Meaning of History*. Middletown, Conn.: Wesleyan University Press, 1959, pp. 202–304.

Chodorow, Nancy. *The Reproduction of Mothering*. Berkeley: University of California Press, 1978.

De Beauvoir, Simone. *The Second Sex.* New York: Bantam, 1970.

Dinnerstein, Dorothy. *The Mermaid and the Minotaur.* New York: Harper and Row, 1976.

Freud, Sigmund. *Civilization and Its Discontents.* Translated by James Strachey. New York: W.W. Norton, 1961.

Griffin, Susan. *Pornography and Silence: Culture's Revenge Against Nature.* New York: Harper and Row, 1981.

Perera, Sylvia. *Descent to the Goddess: A Way of Initiation for Women.* Toronto, Canada: Inner City Books, 1981.

Rich, Adrienne. *Of Woman Born: Motherhood as Experience and Institution.* New York: Bantam, 1976.

Chapter Six

1. Visual cues may help when incurable bores are present in a group. For example, suggest that everyone in the group quietly raise their hands when they stop listening to someone. The message is soon clear. Try this in classes and at public lectures, too.

2. A good resource for understanding communication styles and group interactions is Virginia Satir. She writes about families, but her material can also give insights into the way people behave in small groups. *See* Satir, Virginia. *Peoplemaking.* Palo Alto, Calif.: Science and Behavior Books, 1972.

3. Mander, Jerry. "Kit Karson in a Three-Piece Suit: Forced Relocation of 9634 Indians—Happening Now," *Co-Evolution Quarterly.* No. 33, 1981, p. 59. (Box 428, Sausalito, CA 94966)

An excellent and exhaustive resource on creating non-hierarchical community is: Couver, Virginia; Deacon, Ellen; Esser, Charles; and Moore, Christopher. *Resource Manual for a Living Revolution.* Philadelphia, New Society Press, 1977. This is available from Movement for a New Society, Baltimore Avenue, Philadelphia, PA 19143.

The body of material in this and the following chapter comes from experience rather than written sources.

Mickey Sanders introduced me to Quaker Dialogue in the Santa Rita Country Jail, after the Blockade of the Livermore Weapons Lab on February 1, 1982.

Comments and perceptions expressed about the Diablo Blockade or any other actions or groups are purely my own, in this and succeeding chapters.

Chapter Seven

1. An excellent resource with an ongoing discussion of these ideas is the maga-

zine, *Co-Evolution Quarterly*, Box 428, Sausalito, CA 94966. Subscriptions are $14.00/year. Especially pertinent articles are:

Hess, Karl. "The Politics of Place," *Co-Evolution Quarterly*. No. 30, 1981, pp. 4-16.
Bookchin, Murray. "The Concept of Social Ecology," No. 32, 1981, pp. 14-22.
Berg, Peter. "Devolving Beyond Global Monoculture," No. 32, 1981, pp. 24-28.
Dodge, Jim. "Living by Life," No. 32, 1981, pp. 6-12.
Mills, Stephanie. "Planetary Passions," No. 32, 1981, pp. 4-5.

See also: Berg, Peter, ed. *Reinhabiting a Separate Country: A Bioregional Anthology of Northern California.* San Francisco: Planet Drum Foundation, 1978. Planet Drum Foundation also publishes a newsletter, available by writing to Box 31251, San Francisco, CA 94131.

A good resource on class is: Rubin, Lillian. *Worlds of Pain: Life in the Working Class Family.* New York: Basic Books, 1976.

A fine source on racial and ethnic diversity is: Moraga, Cherríe, and Anzaldua, Gloria. *This Bridge Called My Back: Writings by Radical Women of Color.* Watertown, Mass.: Persephone Press, 1981.

My perceptions of Reclaiming express my personal perspective, not that of the Collective. Other members would, and will, undoubtedly disagree on many points. As a group, we are constantly struggling and evolving in many areas touched on in this chapter.

Discussions with Kevyn Lutton have helped me understand the importance of class differences better.

Chapter Eight

1. See Appendix A for a fuller exploration of this subject.
2. Lord, Audre. "The Erotic as Power," *Chrysalis*, No. 9: Fall, 1979, p. 29.
3. Lord, Audre. "The Erotic as Power," p. 30.
4. Califia, Pat. "Feminism and Sado-Masochism," *Heresies: A Feminist Publication on Art and Politics.* 4:1 (Issue 12), pp. 30-34. Heresies Collective, Inc., 225 Lafayette Street, New York, NY 10012. This entire issue focuses on sexuality, and is an invaluable resource.
5. Carol, a Wind Hag (the name of a coven), suggests that many people may find it easier to begin with the trees—and work up to human beings.
6. Starhawk. *The Spiral Dance: A Rebirth of the Ancient Religion of the Great Goddess.* San Francisco: Harper and Row, 1979. (The Tree of Life is described on p. 44; the Salt Water Purification on pp. 59-60.)

Other resources include.
Griffin, Susan. *Pornography and Silence: Culture's Revenge Against Nature* New York: Harper and Row. 1981

Griffin, Susan. *Rape: The Power of Consciousness.* San Francisco: Harper and Row, 1979.

Marcuse, Herbert. *Eros and Civilization: A Philosophical Inquiry Into Freud.* New York: Vintage, 1955.

Mitchell, Larry. *The Faggots and Their Friends Between Revolutions.* New York: Calamus Books, 1977. This is available from Calamus Books, P.O. Box 689, Cooper Station, New York, NY 10003.

Walker, Mitch, and Friends. *Visionary Love: A Spirit Book of Gay Mythology and Trans-Mutational Faerie.* San Francisco: Treeroots Press, 1980. This is available from Treeroots Press, 835 Folger Street, Berkeley, CA 96710.

Wittig, Monique. *Les Guerrilleres.* New York: Avon, 1969.

Chapter Nine

1. This vision came to me at a New Year's Day celebration for Alegba, God of the crossroads in the Afro-Carribbean tradition which is derived from the Yoruba people. Luisah Teish, who introduced me to the tradition, has been an influence on me and an inspiration to me.

2. For more material on all aspects of ritual, including the salt-water purification, see Starhawk. *The Spiral Dance: A Rebirth of the Ancient Religion of the Great Goddess.* San Francisco: Harper and Row, 1979.

3. For more information on the traditional festivals of the Craft, see: Starhawk *The Spiral Dance,* pp. 169–184. `

4. Imagine, for example, the local curate or rabbi deciding to rewrite the prayerbook because the service wasn't holding people's interest.

5. Made by Kimberly Breese, the banner later hung at the entrance to camp during the Diablo Canyon Nuclear Power Plant blockade.

6. When, during the heyday of the student-power movement, we complained that our high school was like a prison, we were more right than we knew.

7. Mitchell, Larry. *The Faggots and Their Friends Between Revolutions.* New York: Calamus Books, 1977, p. 34. This is available from Calamus Books, P.O. Box 689, Cooper Station, New York, NY 10003.

8. This chant, by Deena Metzger, can be found in the song "The Burning Times," recorded by Charley Murphy in 1980, on an album entitled *Catch the Fire.* This record may be obtained from Good Fairy Productions, P.O. Box 12188, Seattle, WA 98102.

Other resources on ritual include:

Budapest, Z. *The Holy Book of Women's Mysteries,* Vols. I & II. Oakland, Calif.: Susan B. Anthony Coven No. 1, 1979. This is available from Susan B. Anthony Coven No. 1, P.O. Box 11363, Oakland, CA 94611.

Starhawk. *The Spiral Dance.*

Several articles in Spretnak, *The Politics of Women's Spirituality,* are good resources:

Foglia, Gina, and Wolffberg, Dorit. "Spiritual Dimensions of Feminist Anti-Nuclear Activism," pp. 446–462.

Podos, Batya. "Feeding the Feminist Psyche Through Ritual Theater,' pp. 305–311.

Shaffer, Carolyn R. "Spiritual Techniques for Re-Powering Survivors of Sexual Assault," pp. 462–469.

Todd, Judith. "On Common Ground: Native American and Feminist Spirituality —Approaches in the Struggle to Save Mother Earth," pp. 430–445.

Appendix A

1. Bateson, Gregory. *Mind and Nature: A Necessary Unity.* New York: Bantam, 1979, p. 77.

2. We cannot understand the Witch persecutions if we view them simply as a male conspiracy against women or see them removed from the recurring patterns of persecution throughout the Middle Ages. Mary Daly's account of the Witch-hunts while in other respects excellent, manages to erase the Jews from history as thoroughly as patriarchal historians erase women. *See* Daly, Mary. *Gyn/Ecology: The Metaethics of Radical Feminism.* Boston: Beacon Press, 1978.

3. Ruether, Rosemary. *New Woman, New Earth: Sexist Ideologies and Human Liberation.* New York: The Seabury Press, 1975, pp. 100–106.

4. Quoted from Kramer and Sprenger, *Malleus Maleficarum,* in Daly, Mary. *Gyn/Ecology,* p. 199

5. This account of the Witch persecutions is based on Daly, *Gyn/Ecology;* Ehrenreich, Barbara, and English, Deirdre. *Witches, Midwives, and Nurses: A History of Women Healers.* Old Westbury, N.Y.: The Feminist Press, 1973; Murray, Margaret. *The God of the Witches.* London: Oxford University Press, 1970; Notestein, Wallace. *A History of Witchcraft in England.* New York: Crowell, 1968; Ruether. *New Woman, New Earth.*

6. Ruether. *New Woman, New Earth,* p. 11.

7. Daly. *Gyn/Ecology,* p. 197.

8. Quoted from Henry Charles Lea in Daly. *Gyn/Ecology,* p. 200.

9. Daly. *Gyn/Ecology,* p. 200.

10. *See* Daly. *Gyn/Ecology,* p. 185; Ruether. *New Woman, New Earth,* pp. 104–105; Hill, Christopher. *Reformation to Industrial Revolution: The Making of Modern English Society,* Vol. 1: 1530–1780. New York: Pantheon, 1967, pp. 89–90.

11. Ruether. *New Woman, New Earth*, p. 105.

12. I use the terms *peasant-laboring class* and *monied-professional class* instead of the more traditional terms *working-class* and *bourgeoisie* because during this period, before industrialization, class divisions had not yet assumed the characteristics associated with Marxist terminology.

13. Bateson, Gregory. *Steps to an Ecology of Mind.* New York: Ballantine, 1972, p. 338.

14. Merchant, Carolyn. *The Death of Nature: Women, Ecology and the Scientific Revolution.* San Francisco: Harper and Row, 1980, pp. 70-75.

15. Merchant. *The Death of Nature*, pp. 71-73.

16. The following discussion of feudal economy is based on: Birnie, Arthur. *An Economic History of the British Isles.* London: Methuen, 1953, pp. 39-59; Clark, Sir George. *Early Modern Europe from about 1450 to about 1720.* London: Oxford University Press, 1968; Conner, E.C.K. *Common Land and Enclosure.* New York: A.M. Kelley, 1966; Finberg, H.P.R., ed. *The Agrarian History of England and Wales*, Vol. I: Part II, A.D. 43-1042. Cambridge: Cambridge University Press, 1972; Heath, Richard. *The English Peasant.* London: Unwin, 1983, pp. 1-57; Merchant. *The Death of Nature*, pp. 43-50; White, Lynn, Jr. *Medieval Technology and Social Change.* New York: Oxford University Press, 1966, pp. 39-76; Zacour, Norman. *An Introduction to Medieval Institutions.* New York: St. Martin's Press, 1969, pp. 35-51.

17. Conner. *Common Land and Enclosure*, p. 7.

18. The following discussion of rights of common is based on Conner, *Common Land and Enclosure*, pp. 5-7, and Birnie. *An Economic History of the British Isles*, pp. 47-70.

19. Rodgers, John. *The English Woodland.* New York: Scribner's, 1946, pp. 17-29.

20. Hill, Christopher. *Reformation to Industrial Revolution*, p. 14.

21. Birnie. *An Economic History of the British Isles*, p. 72.

22. Merchant. *The Death of Nature*, p. 48.

23. Understanding the economic importance of manure might throw new light on Norman O. Brown's discussion of Martin Luther's identification of money, anality, the world, and the devil. Literally, if money is based on the fertility of land, money *is* shit. So is life. While the Protestant position could be irreverently summed up as "Life is shit—decay and death, therefore life is inherently evil," the Pagan takes the position "Shit, death, and decay are part of life and, therefore, imbued with sacredness." The ramifications this view might have on childhood toilet training and the subsequent formation of character are interesting to consider. *See* Brown, Norman O. *Life Against Death: The Psychoanalytical Meaning of History.* Middletown, Conn.: Wesleyan University Press, 1959, pp. 200-304.

24. The following discussion of market factors and enclosure is based on Birnie, *An Economic History of The British Isles*, pp. 71–97; Conner, *Common Land and Enclosure*; Hill, *Reformation to Industrial Revolution*, pp. 45–62, 115–122; Mantoux, Paul, "The Destruction of the Peasant Village," in Philip A. Taylor, ed., *The Industrial Revolution in Britain: Triumph or Disaster?* Boston: D.C. Heath, 1958, pp. 64–73; Merchant, *The Death of Nature*, pp. 42–68.

25. Conner. *Common Land and Enclosure*, p. 44.

26. Conner, pp. 137–38.

27. Mantoux. "The Destruction of the Peasant Village," p. 65.

28. Birnie. *An Economic History of the British Isles*, p. 77.

29. Clark, Alice. *Working Life of Women in the Seventeenth Century*. New York: E.P. Dutton, 1919, pp. 42–92.

30. Clark. *Working Life of Women*, p. 60.

31. Clark, p. 88.

32. Clark, pp. 88–89.

33. Clark, pp. 58–92, and Hill, Christopher. *Reformation to Industrial Revolution*, pp. 135–143.

34. The following discussion of peasant resistance is based on Conner, p. 134; Birnie, p. 79; and Merchant, pp. 42–68.

35. Although in England torture was not allowed technically, evidence exists that it was practiced, and methods such as enforced sleeplessness produced the same results. Notestein. *A History of Witchcraft in England*, pp. 202–205.

36. The classic work on folk customs is Frazer, Sir James. *The Golden Bough*, abrid. ed. New York: New American Library, 1964.

37. Ruether. *New Woman, New Earth*, p. 100.

38. Illich, Ivan. *Toward a History of Needs*. New York: Bantam, 1977, p. 89.

39. Illich, Ivan. "Vernacular Values," *Co-Evolution Quarterly*, no. 26 (1980), p. 48.

40. Illich. *Toward a History of Needs*, p. 88.

41. Clark. *Working Life of Women*, pp. 253–65.

42. Miller, Jean Baker. *Toward a New Psychology of Women*. Boston: Beacon Press, 1976, p. 6.

43. There are 12 pence (D) to a shilling (S). 1 S per day was a high wage for a male agricultural worker during harvest; women often earned less than a third as much. *See* Clark, p. 60.

44. Hill, Christopher. *Change and Continuity in Seventeenth Century England*. Cambridge, Mass.: Harvard University Press, 1975, p. 157.

45. Hill. *Change and Continuity*, p. 158.

46. Hill, p. 158.

47. Hill, p. 166.

48. Ehrenrich and English. *Witches, Midwives and Nurses*, p. 12

49. Rich, Adrienne. *Of Woman Born: Motherhood as Experience and Institution.* New York: Bantam, 1976, p. 127.

50. Daly. *Gyn/Ecology*, pp. 223–292; Ehrenrich and English. *Witches, Midwives and Nurses*; Rich. *Of Woman Born*, pp. 117–182

51. Notestein, pp. 23, 213.

52. Ehrenrich and English. *Witches, Midwives and Nurses*, p. 17.

53. Ehrenrich and English, p. 17.

54. Huston, Perdita. *Third World Women Speak Out.* New York: Praeger, 1979, p. 69.

55. Quoted from a speech by John Bourke at the Smithsonian Institution in 1892, in Altman, Marcia; Kubrin, David; Kwasnick, John; and Logan, Tina. "The People's Healers: Healthcare and Class Struggle in the United States in the 19th Century." (Unpublished ms.)

56. Altman, Kubrin, Kwasnick, and Logan. "The People's Healers."

57. Hill, Christopher. *The World Turned Upside Down*, p. 14.

58. Weber, Max. *The Protestant Ethic and the Spirit of Capitalism.* New York: Scribner's, 1958.

59. Hill. *The World Turned Upside Down*, p. 14.

60. Hill, p. 37.

61. Hill, p. 61.

62. Hill, p. 38, quoting Aubrey.

63. Gardner, Gerald B. *Witchcraft Today.* Secaucus, N.J.: Citadel, 1974.

64. Hill. *The World Turned Upside Down*, p. 38.

65. Notestein. *A History of Witchcraft in England*, p. 184.

66. Notestein, p. 185.

67. Murray, Margaret A. *The Witch-Cult in Western Europe.* Oxford: Clarendon Press, 1921, p. 238.

68. Murray, pp. 267–68.

69. Hill. *Reformation to Industrial Revolution*, p. 90.

70. Hill. *The World Turned Upside Down*, p. 22.

71. Hill, p. 23.

72. Hill, p. 165.

73. Hill, p. 165, quoting Bauthamly.

74. Hill, p. 165.

75. For evidences of the radical tradition's continuity, see Hill. *The World Turned Upside Down*, p. 89. The Witchcraft tradition has old associations in the

area: "In Windsor Great Park there used to be a withered oak under which Herne the Hunter, a forest warden in the time of Henry VIII, is said to have practiced black magic, and upon which he was eventually found hanged. While the tree stood no grass would grow around it. The ghost of Herne the Hunter with horns on his head appears when any calamity threatens the royal family or the nation. . ." (*See* Rogers. *England Woodlands*, p. 31.) Herne the Hunter is an ancient name of the God in Witchcraft who was hanged upon an oak as an enactment of the sacrifice of self that allows life to continue. The God is termed *The Horned God* in certain of His aspects, and was also associated with sacred kingship. *See* Murray, Margaret. *The God of the Witches*. London: Oxford University Press, 1970.

76. Hill. *The World Turned Upside Down*, p. 90

77. Hill, p. 104.

78. Hill, p. 105.

79. Hill, p. 111.

80. Hill, p. 112.

81. Hill, p. 114.

82. Hill, p. 173.

83 Hill, p. 172.

84. Hill, p. 259.

85. Weber, Max. *The Protestant Ethic*, p. 166.

86. Hill. *Reformation to Industrial Revolution*, pp. 119–120. Hill. *World Turned Upside Down*, pp. 262–263.

87. Hill. *Reformation to Industrial Revolution*, p. 140, quoting Petty.

88. Weber. *The Protestant Ethic*, p. 60.

89. For an overview of occupations in which women played important roles throughout late medieval and early modern times, *see* Clark. *The Working Lives of Women*.

90. Ruether, pp. 97–98, quoting *Malleus Maleficarum*.

91. Ruether, p. 98.

92. For a full analytic interpretation of the implications of mothering, *see* Chodorow, Nancy. *The Reproduction of Mothering*. Berkeley, Calif.: University of California Press, 1978; Dinnerstein, Dorothy. *The Mermaid and the Minotaur*. New York: Harper and Row, 1976.

93. Brown. *Life Against Death*.

94. Rubin, Gayle. "The Traffic in Women: Notes on the 'Political Economy' of Sex" in Reiter, Rena, ed., *Toward an Anthropology of Women*. New York: Monthly Review Press, 1975, p. 162.

95. De Beauvoir, Simone. *The Second Sex*. New York: Bantam, 1952.

96. Evans, Arthur. *Witchcraft and the Gay Counterculture*. Boston: Fag Rag Books, 1978, pp. 76–77.

97. From oral tradition.

98. Kubrin, David. "Newton's Inside Out: Magic, Class Struggle, and the Rise of Mechanism in the West" in Woolf, Harry, ed. *The Analytic Spirit*. Ithaca, N.Y.: Cornell University Press, 1981, p. 108.

99. For background on the new physics, *see* Capra, Fritjof. *The Tao of Physics*. New York: Bantam, 1977; Zukav, Gary. *The Dancing Wu Li Masters: An Overview of the New Physics*. New York: William Morrow, 1979.

100. Merchant, p. 12.

101. Kubrin. "Newton's Inside Out," p. 107.

102. Kubrin, pp. 110–121.

103. Kubrin, p. 120.

A writer, teacher, counselor, political activist, nonviolence trainer, and witch, Starhawk is a founding member of Reclaiming: A Center for Feminist Spirituality and Counseling in San Francisco, California. She is also the author of *The Spiral Dance: A Rebirth of the Ancient Religion of the Great Goddess.*